AFRICA:
A MARKET PROFILE

INDEPENDENT

DEPENDENT

AFRICA AND ITS
ISLANDS

EUROPE

MIDDLE EAST

MEDITERRANEAN SEA

Madeira

Canary Islands

MOROCCO

TUNISIA

ALGERIA

LIBYA

UNITED
ARAB
REPULIC

SPANISH
WEST
AFRICA

MAURITANIA

Cape
Verde

MALI

NIGER

CHAD

SUDAN

Red Sea

Dahlach

FRENCH
SOMALILAND

GAMBIA

SENEGAL

Bijagos

PORTUGUESE
GUINEA

GUINEA

Los

UPPER
VOLTA

IVORY
COAST

GHANA

TOGO

DAHOMEY

NIGERIA

CAMEROON

CENTRAL
AFRICAN REPUBLIC

ETHIOPIA

Gulf of Aden

Socotra

SIERRA
LEONE

Sherbro

LIBERIA

Fernando Po

SPANISH GUINEA

Principe

Sao Tome

Annobon

CABINDA

GABON

REPUBLIC OF CONGO

CONGO
REPUBLIC

RUANDA

UGANDA

KENYA

SOMALIA

BURUNDI

TANGANYIKA

Pemba

Zanzibar

Mafia

Seychelles

Amirante

Ascension

ANGOLA

ZAMBIA

MALAWI

Archipel Des Comores

St. Helena

SOUTH WEST
AFRICA

BECHUANALAND

SOUTHERN
RHODESIA

MOZAMBIQUE

Bassas Da
India

MALAGASY

Mauritius

De La
Reunion

Rodriguez

ATLANTIC

OCEAN

N

Europa

SOUTH AFRICA

SWAZILAND

BASUTOLAND

INDIAN OCEAN

Tristan da Cunha

Gough

Prince Edward

Marion

For explanatory note to this map, see contents, p. vi

AFRICA:
A MARKET PROFILE

T. L. V. BLAIR

FREDERICK A. PRAEGER, *Publishers*
NEW YORK · WASHINGTON

BOOKS THAT MATTER

Published in the United States of America in 1965
by Frederick A. Praeger, Inc., Publishers
111 Fourth Avenue, New York 3, N.Y.

© Thomas Lucien Vincent Blair, 1965

Library of Congress Catalog Card Number: 65-25486

Made and printed in Great Britain

CONTENTS

PROFILES

MAPS

EXPLANATORY NOTE TO FRONTISPIECE MAP "AFRICA AND ITS ISLANDS"

STATUS OF THE ISLANDS AND DEPENDENT AREAS:

INDEPENDENT ISLANDS:

Ethiopia: Dahalach Chebir; *Republic of Guinea*: Los; *South Africa*: Marion, Prince Edward; *Malagasy*; *Sierra Leone*: Sherbro; *Zanzibar and Pemba*: (merged with Tanganyika into the United Republic of Tanzania)

DEPENDENT ISLANDS:

England: Amirante, Ascension, Gough, Mafia, Mauritius, Rodriguez, Seychelles, St. Helena, Socotra, Tristan da Cunha; *France*: Archipel des Comores, Bassa da India, Europa, De la Reunion; *Portugal*: Arquipelago dos Bijagos, Cape Verde, Madeira, Principe, Sao Tome; *Spain*: Annobon, Canaries, Fernando Po

DEPENDENT CONTINENTAL AREAS:

England: Gambia (scheduled for independence in 1965), the High Commission Territories of Basutoland, Bechuanaland and Swaziland, Rhodesia (Southern); *France*: Somaliland; *Portugal*: Angola, Cabinda, Portuguese Guinea, Mozambique; *Spain*: Spanish West Africa; Spanish Guinea; *United Nations Organization International Mandate*: Territory of South West Africa.

LIST OF ILLUSTRATIONS*

* The photographs are arranged into four photographic essays; unless otherwise cited they are by the author.

Wherever social problems oppose African development they retard the formation of a healthy economy. It is no easy task to transform society, harness skills and erase the harsh edge of reality. Yet, the test of development lies ultimately in its net social benefit.

In modern Africa, women with their sense of thrift and beauty cast off the veil of past years and clasp the hands of change in the traditional market place and the modern salon. At work their smile greets the shopper, their mercy comforts the sick, their patience is the school child's reward. As youth, they go courting by motor scooter under moon-like neon-lit skies, and as mothers they mould the tastes of a new generation.

PREFACE

Africa: A Market Profile is a guide to understanding the ways of life, attitudes and aspirations of emergent Africans that affect marketing. It is a view of a social process involving industry and the new consumer-citizens of independent Africa.

The book begins with the African emergence and the creation of the continent's unique goal, a Century of Development. There follows a brief review of the ways in which African nations get capital and use it to sustain the rapid growth of national economies and markets. The greater part of the text is devoted to describing major consumers, charting the entry and diffusion of products and information, and indicating the social factors which affect marketing.

African markets get their dynamism not only from the growth of industry, wage earners and rising national productivity but also from the resolution of social problems, such as housing, which follow in the wake of urbanization and industrialization. In one of the concluding chapters I discuss the contributions that industries and governments in Africa can make to employee housing and urban development. In the final chapter I outline the structure of market research in Africa and explore the trends toward a consumer-orientated, development-centred and socially responsible science of market research.

Africa: A Market Profile is one of the first sociological explorations of marketing in Africa. It is not a definitive work — it is too early for that. But in these crucial initial stages of African development some general appraisal of the marketing process is needed. I have attempted to gather together some threads of knowledge, research and observation which will help guide private initiative and public action, now. Throughout the book I have tried to look at the data as social correlates of decision-making, i.e. those facts that European and African industry and government need to take into account about people and culture in order to make marketing decisions.

The book is based on three major sources, current social science research, informal interviews, and my own field studies in Africa. I have drawn heavily upon current literature in sociology, market research, economic development and the works of African writers and statesmen. I have also benefited from data collected in 150 informal interviews with African and European government officials and with directors of industrial and trading companies, development corporations, market research, advertising and media agencies completed during the year ending February 1964. This enquiry is an independent study and I alone am responsible for the views and interpretations expressed herein. Later studies will, no doubt, refine, clarify or possibly negate many of the points tentatively set down here. Further research is needed, recognizing that the ultimate test of all hypotheses about marketing in Africa lies among its people and the realities of the African presence on the world scene.

Readers may find the book useful as a basic reference. There are chapter bibliographies, three maps and more than 20 statistical tables and diagrammatic theoretical formulations relating to trade, population, education, income and expenditure, and mass communication. Appendixes I and II record the Charter and Resolutions of the Organization of African Unity; they represent the collective expression by African statesmen of present problems, future goals and the role they see for exterior forces of development. Appendix III briefly surveys resource materials on Africa available in London and indicates some of the literature produced by African writers and political leaders. Appendix IV contains a glossary of useful African words gathered from the text. Finally, four written profiles and four photographic essays have been introduced to increase the readers' awareness and interest in the changing panorama of African life.

In preparing this book I have drawn upon the assistance of many individuals and organizations; I should like to especially acknowledge some of them here.

In the field of marketing I am particularly indebted to Mr. Bernard Taylor, formerly assistant director College of Marketing, Institute of Marketing and Sales Management. In addition, the book has been enriched by my discussions with Dr. John Treasure, J. Walter Thompson, Mr. John Bittleston, S. H. Benson International, Mr. Howard Biggs, Research Services Limited, Mr. John Downham, formerly of British Market Research Bureau, Dr. Mark Abrams, Research Services Limited, Dr. W. A. Belson, Survey Research Unit, Mr. Henry Deschampsneufs, author and consultant, Miss Naomi Buhai, Odhams Press Limited and Mr. Philip Short, research director, British-American Tobacco Company. Thanks are due to specialists in the field of mass media: Mr. Robert Silvey, head, BBC Audience Research, Mr. P. J.

Saynor, head, BBC Overseas Audience Research, the BBC African Service and Mr. Asher Lee, research information officer, BBC External Broadcasting. I would like to record my thanks to Mr. E. J. Harding, Director, Drum Publications (UK) Limited, for his help in obtaining some of the illustrative material for me. Mr. David Williams, editor of *West Africa*, has been a constant source of encouragement and I am grateful for his permission to include here material from a series of articles on Kano, Northern Nigeria which I wrote for *West Africa* from June 8 to June 29, 1963.

In the fields of architecture, house-building and urban planning I wish to give special acknowledgment to Mr. William Allen, principal, Architectural Association School of Architecture and Dr. Otto Koenigsberger, head, and both Mr. Alan Mayhew and Mr. Jerry Ingersoll, of the Department of Tropical Studies. In addition I have gained many new insights from discussions with Douglas Jones, professor and head, Faculty of Architecture, University of Bristol, Mr. Alfredo Turin, chief, Housing, Building and Planning Section, United Nations Economic Commission for Africa and Mme. Tatiana Charlier, Secretariat des Missions d'Urbanisme et d'Habitat, Paris.

I am greatly indebted to the directors of companies and development corporations dealing with Africa for allowing me the opportunity to interview them. I should like to mention in particular Sir Jock Campbell, chairman, Booker Brothers, Sir Duncan Oppenheim, director, British-American Tobacco Company, Mr. T. E. Peppercorn, director, Dunlop Rubber Company Limited, Mr. Arthur Gaitskell, board member, Commonwealth Development Corporation and Mr. William Clark, director, Overseas Development Institute.

In addition, I wish to thank Miss Jeanne Pynor, Miss B. Bantu and the staff and research personnel of the various banks, embassies, trading companies, research bureaux and libraries which assisted me in this work. Finally, I wish to express my gratitude to my wife, Myrtle Desmond Blair, for her inspiration and kind forbearance during the writing of the manuscript.

T. L. V. BLAIR, M.A., PH.D.

January 1965

CHAPTER ONE

AFRICA'S CENTURY
OF DEVELOPMENT

THE EMERGENCE of Africa is an unprecedented event in mankind's progress. Ten years ago we thought of Africa as merely tinted colours on the vast canvas of Western life. Today, we realize that Africa's emancipation is a new creation in its own right and that this first century of modern African development is the opening of a dynamic and prosperous stage in human history.

INDEPENDENCE

Africa's century of development begins with the "Decade of Freedom". It spans 10 crucial years from 1954, when there were only three independent states governed by Africans, to 1964 when the flags of sovereignty waved over more than 30 new nations. The Decade of African Freedom was the last sequence in an historical process enacted on an international stage. It was a response brought forward by the ebb and flow of slavery and colonization and the quick currents of contemporary events.

Africa entered the vortex of recent world affairs with the mobilization of the Allied armies against Nazi Germany. In June 1941, amidst the bomb craters and wailing sirens of wartime London, 12 beleaguered governments met at St. James's Palace to declare "the only true basis of enduring peace is a world in which all may enjoy economic and social security". Later, during the desperate Battle of the Atlantic, Britain's Prime Minister Winston Churchill and America's President Franklin Delano Roosevelt, met "somewhere at sea" and signed the Atlantic Charter which affirmed "the right of every people to choose their own form of government".

With these words colonial peoples and the independent European nations were mobilized in the war against fascism and racism. Nigerians, Senegalese, Kenyans and Algerians joined Frenchmen, Poles, Britons and Belgians in the rejuvenated Allied defence. Victory, for the captive European peoples, meant liberation from alien Nazi rule and the triumph of the principle of self-determination. The implications of this victory trembled on the edge of every African township and village: "If it is wrong for the Germans to rule the world, then it is also wrong for Europeans to rule Africa."

Self-determination in Africa occupied a prominent place in the formation of the United Nations Organization. At San Francisco, the founder members envisaged "the creation of a world in which all people could live decently as free peoples". The u.n.o. Charter created a forum for the dependent colonies and the administering nations to ensure the progressive development of free political institutions and self-government.

Common historical experiences and common aspirations for development brought the first African and Asian statesmen together during the post-war period. Their political conferences established a third force, called the *tiers monde*, in the midst of the contending great power blocs. The emblem of the *tiers monde* was fashioned in Bandung, Indonesia, 1955, at the first Afro–Asian conference. The message reads: "Freedom, sovereignty, world peace, racial equality, non-aggression, development, positive neutralism and economic and social co-operation."

During the same period, three nations without colonial dependencies in Africa emerged and straddled the globe. As America, the Soviet Union and the People's Republic of China eyed each other warily, new symbols, ideologies and tensions were introduced into Africa. At the same time, the awesome development of the hydrogen bomb shook the political foundations of colonial affairs and formed an umbrella under which many African nations strode to freedom. For, as the eyes of the rival power blocs were riveted on those deadly cloud formations and pondered the consequences of all-out nuclear warfare, a political vacuum was created and rapidly filled by emerging African independence movements.

In Africa the rhythm of the colonial social order was upset by political and economic changes. Peasants trekked to centres of employment and the focus of African life shifted to urban areas. There, in the sprawling townships, these rough-hewn tribesmen took a proletarian stance as their traditional skills were forged in the crucible of industrial culture. Peasant migrants became urban workers and, armed with their labour and some money in their hands, they ventured to express their political opinions.

In the changing context of African and world affairs, educated *élites* emerged with new aspirations and established a broad basis of unity and co-operation with workers, traders and chiefs. Tribe and class lost their potency as criteria for participation in political affairs. New alliances and allegiances drew individuals together in vibrant nascent nationhood. The stage was set for the conversion of African colonial dependencies into independent nations participating in the international state system on the basis of equality and mutual respect.

As momentous events took place in every region of the *tiers monde*, Sudan, Ghana and Guinea burst through the cocoon of colonial status. In 1960, the "Year of Africa", a score of nations laid their credentials before the world and by 1964 few territories were left which were not independent or bestirred by the "winds of change". Symbolically, one era ended. The *"fleur-de-lis"* and the "Union Jack" gave way to the "Black Star". The *"Marseillaise"* and "God Save The Queen" faded before the anthems "Al-Djazair" (Algeria) and "Nkosi Sikelele I Africa" (God Bless Africa). Overjoyed millions in three-quarters of the Continent snaked their way in an "Independence High-life" through streets strewn with confetti and the husks of times gone by. And a new era began.

DEVELOPMENT AND CHANGE

Political independence created a surging desire for its corollary — economic independence. "Sovereignty is not real unless it is justified technically and economically," says the Senegalese statesman-poet, President Léopold Senghor, "not until its achievements ramify among all the segments of the population." At the inaugural meeting of the Organization of African Unity in 1963, Emperor Hailé Selassié of Ethiopia, Africa's oldest independent state, said dramatically: "Unless political liberty, for which Africans have so long struggled, is bolstered by economic and social growth, the breath of life which sustains our freedom may flicker out."

African statesmen wish quickly to resolve present problems with the instruments of the future, not the past. They seek to draw people out of isolation into the modern sector, to create skilled "human capital" and a viable commercial network providing a wide range of goods and services to consumers. "Independence means development; nothing must stop rapid industrialization," says President Sekou Touré of Guinea. "We must initiate a jet-propelled rate of economic growth," is a phrase often used by President Kwame Nkrumah of Ghana.

Development is seen as a legacy passed on to future generations, as the Olympic torch is carried forward from one runner to another. "Our duty is to look to the future," counsels President W. V. S. Tubman of Liberia, "and to make sure that our children do not ask: 'Why did you miss the opportunity to build a better society than the one which you inherited?'"

The "promise of tomorrow" welds African societies and the twenty-first century into a close and intimate embrace. "It arouses us with a new vitality," says President Julius Nyerere of Tanzania, "like the first touch of the strong sun's rays which catch the new-born animal lying on our Serengeti plains and sends it straightaway bounding in to life." Thus, the Decade of African Freedom is the dawn of the Century of African Development and each hour its meaning unfolds across the horizon of African affairs.

Development in Africa is a vast and evolving process moving across plateaus, savannahs, mountains and deserts, encompassing rural peasants, nomads and sophisticated urbanites, men of many creeds and colours. Development is as big as Sudan's Gezira cotton-growing scheme, the gigantic dams and hydro-electric stations at Aswan and along the Volta, Niger and Zambesi rivers. It's as tall as the factory chimneys towering over the highest palm tree. It is as deep as the pleasure of the newly-literate countryman who shouts to his neighbour: "I can read!" It is as broad as the programme of economic viability envisaged by the continental Organization of African Unity and the African Development Bank.

African development means the transformation of society and harnessing of human skills and material resources to abolish the stark realities of life. Development is a house where there was a hovel, a clinic where there was dirt and disease, a school where there was ignorance. It is the proposition that "a nation who cannot take care of the many who are poor will not have the strength to take care of the few who are rich". It embraces the desire to reconstruct healthy communities and nations in a peaceful world.

With development, new sights and sounds crowd "Main Street" Africa; highways draw peasants to the city, and horns, whistles and sirens entice them into the lightning and thunder of mill work. Development means "pay-day", cement, fertilizer, bicycles, books, canned foods, bank accounts and store-bought clothes. It is a drink of beer on Saturday night and some coins in the collection plate on Sunday. The excitement of social change crackles in the air and throbs in the market-place, the cabaret and meeting hall. Have you ever heard the shrill ululating "you-you's" of Muslim women, the syncopation of a Freetown Holiness church choir, the big beat "ba-tuc-tuc" of a Congolese jazz band, or danced the West African high-life?

THE COSTS AND BENEFITS OF CHANGE

Nation-building also involves tremendous social costs: rural depopulation, urban congestion, moral malaise, conflict and tensions. Development can be calculated in terms of conflicts within changing family structures, ethnic and language groups, in the decline of the village economy and rural poverty, and in the rise of juvenile delinquency and psycho-neuroses. Development can mean more people in prison cells and mental hospitals as well as more tons of produce and large imposing buildings.

Yet, change in Africa offers many opportunities for the creative resolution of its attendant problems. African administrators and social scientists, like Dr. K. O. Dike of Nigeria, and the young Oxford-trained philosopher Professor W. E. Abraham, are convinced that Africa need not incur the same difficulties as did the older industrial societies. They believe it is possible to foresee many problems in the laboratory of human affairs and to plan for development and change in orderly regulated ways.

Change in Africa inspires new experiments in social, economic and political institutions compatible with the emerging African image and contributing to the nation-building process. At Dakar, the first African conference on world co-operation at the town-to-town level brought together representatives of Africa's urban populations to deal with municipal problems. Auto-gestion in Algeria thrust a bold new concept of worker management into the breach left by the exodus of European populations, and established a training ground for a whole new generation of technicians and factory directors. The United Nations Conference on African education declared as its prime objective "the organization and promotion of a form of education solidly rooted in African soil drawing sustenance from African life and tradition".

SCIENCE AND DEVELOPMENT

Scientific progress and African independence are two of the most decisive movements of our time. The progress of science and technology has changed the course of man's life and African independence has altered the structure and shape of the international family.

To meet the challenges of development, everywhere in Africa the needs of nations and communities are linked with science, technology and administration. Political leaders have already sensed the enormous possibilities of the peaceful uses of the atom, the de-salinization of water and the fructification of deserts. Some have begun to survey their resources and ask the question, "What are the ways in which we can adapt science to our concrete problems?"

Food production and agricultural progress are two of the main targets. In the industrializing regions the rapid growth of urban populations in relation to food resources heralds a race against disaster. At present the yield of an average African farm family can only feed one other family. Furthermore, the production of traditional staple foods, rice, bananas, maize, yams and cassava, is inadequate to meet the needs and changing tastes of exploding metropolitan centres.

The application of scientific technology and work habits enriches the "good earth". The improvement of village life and the decentralization of industry affect favourably the conditions unemployed rural people. New forms of packaged and processed of foods, locally produced, offer quick, healthy meals.

African nations, prisoners of perishable crops, are determined to break the hold of climatic and market factors on their economies. They are planning air-conditioned silos and processing factories to warehouse crops, and control their placement on the world market.

New possibilities for economic self-sufficiency emerge with the discovery and utilization of local resources. Coastal African states ponder Japan's experience with the cultivation of marine algae for food and as a "green manure" for crops. New industries grow with the utilization of little-known but abundant tropical woods whose short fibres are ideal for paper making. Ghana and Nigeria experiment with local fibrous plants to make bags for their cash crops, cocoa and groundnuts. Tree farming and the collection of wild plants, such as papyrus in Uganda, esparto and eucalyptus in Algeria, offer untapped industrial possibilities.

Public health technicians armed with new knowledge and modern chemo-therapeutic techniques are freeing Africa from disease. They are opening up 5 million square miles in the heart of the Continent held in fief to the dreaded simulium and tsetse flies — the sentries of Africa — whose bite cripples untold numbers and bars the cultivation of nutritious meat and dairy products.

In the process of development, new products and modern innovations will revolutionize all aspects of African life from infant nutrition to harnessing the sun. A new disposable infant feeder can relieve the strain of prolonged breast-feeding and free able-bodied women for participation in industrial and commercial sectors. A new process called Accelerated Freeze Drying can freeze and dehydrate meat, fish and poultry so that they retain the freshness of frozen foods but dispense with the need for a refrigerator. New techniques in mass-produced house units can speed up the construction of low-cost housing for the workers.

The creation of artisan enterprises, maize grinding, water hauling and tool making, will be rapidly accelerated by means of the rechargeable nickel-cadmium cell battery. Rechargeable batteries can operate small machines or lathes for half an hour and be fully recharged in 15 minutes. They can satisfy reasonable power requirements anywhere and thus free artisans from the umbilical cord of wire which presently binds them to wall points.

Even the blazing African sun can now be harnessed to the Century of Development. Solar-operated power stations can produce new sources of energy in Africa; the sun is abundant, and there are large open spaces for solar collection. Solar energy can be used to grow food, dry crops, heat homes, evaporate water from salt, concentrate natural juices, ripen plants, cook and air-condition, or refrigerate food, make ice, dry air, chill or heat water and to create electric power.

THE DIALOGUE OF PROGRESS

Many a businessman has hovered on the edge of African life, bought trinkets from a Hausa trader, snapped the Chief's palace for the "folks back home", washed away the heat with a cool glass of stout and turned in at night between two clean sheets, wondering: "Who are these people, really, and what are Africans like?"

Africa is new nations emerging from the hot-house of colonial status. Africa is millions of peasants entering the cash wage economy. Africa is, in microcosm, man's will to conquer the triple burden of poverty, disease and illiteracy; it is hope riveted to a twenty-first century spaceship of economic development. Africa is one-tenth of mankind in search of trade, aid and co-operation with all the world on the basis of mutual respect.

In Western industrial nations, curiosity about the expanding African market is thrusting aside decades of indifference. "Our clients want to know what are the habits and attitudes of urban Africans," one market research manager said to me. "What are their homes like, where do they come from, what do they think about our products? And, above all, why in hell are they buying the other bloke's products and not ours?"

Thus, in the first decade of the Century of African Development, business concerns and African governments seek to co-operate in the distribution of manufactured products and the elevation of living standards. To attain their mutual goals both seek more market information and research knowledge.

The search for expanding markets and the satisfaction of consumer needs in modern Africa are not isolated random incidents in history. They are tied by the threads of history to an encounter five centuries old. They surge anew as the old political and economic relationships which undergirded sales and marketing practices in pre-independence Africa are fast disappearing.

Businessmen and consumers in independent Africa meet today — across the counter, in public places — in a new, rapidly changing situation that neither has ever faced before. Cities bursting with vitality, wage-workers and businessmen in search of expanding markets, are the main arenas of contact, communication, and co-operation. Products from all the world compete for the attention of Mr. and Mrs. Africa. Traditional consumer markets, preserves of yesteryear, disappear overnight and hundreds of new products enter shops and households. The pace of change is so swift that today's modern housewife in Dakar, Accra or Lagos knows more about the merits of tinned tuna fish, West German cutlery, French wine and perfume, Russian cars,

Indian transistors, Japanese textiles and Polish art than her counterpart in Merseyside or Kansas City.

One of the most important marketing requirements in industrial societies is the development of mutual confidence between businessmen and their consumers. In Europe, they are linked by a host of shared cultural values. In Africa, however, the businessmen are Europeans and the consumers are urban African families in the process of change. Today's marketing decisions concerning Africa require, therefore, research knowledge, understanding and sociological answers to fundamental questions about the changing African context.

What is the meaning of the African emergence and what are the economic trends for the future? Who is the African consumer; what are his needs and tastes? How dependable are Western techniques of sales and marketing? What cultural factors affect the selling situation? What is the role of the mass media and how is it affected by language and culture? In what ways can commerce and industry be socially useful in nations which have set their sights on "the best life for the greatest number of people"?

The answers to these questions are of crucial importance. New and informed sales and marketing practices can provide a common ground for a dialogue of progress between business and society in Africa. The Western businessman who understands the process of the African emergence, the expanding dimensions of her markets and needs, will be better equipped to meet the challenges of Africa's future.

CHAPTER TWO

THE SEARCH FOR CAPITAL

AFRICA, in the Century of Development, must conquer low standards of living by increasing net income. Vast amounts of capital are needed to produce the necessary industries, products, employment and wage structure. There are five major techniques of raising capital: (1) loans and grants from foreign sources, (2) trade, (3) utilizing scarce reserves, (4) domestic borrowing through national central banks, and (5) using budget surpluses. Loans and grants are the most significant source of capital; they comprise more than half of all monetary sources for the development plans of African nations. Trade is the second most important source of development capital.

To face the challenges of progress, African nations seek finance, technical assistance and improved trade relations. This is being accomplished through bi-lateral agreements with industrial nations, through multi-national European groups, international monetary organizations and the United Nations Organization. This chapter forms a brief survey of these major sources of development capital.

BI-LATERAL AID AND TRADE

The interest of all the nations of the world is focused on the new African markets. Companies and governments, competing to secure raw materials and extend the distribution of their products, are busily engaged in exploring new dimensions of trade and aid. International participation in the African market produces an exciting pot-pourri of products and equipment. It is quite possible, today, in the turbulence of modern life, for a African to be knocked down by an English bus, rushed in an East

German ambulance driven by a Japanese-trained driver, along an American-built highway, to a hospital constructed by Israelis using Swiss equipment, where late at night he can listen to a programme in an African language on an American radio set, from a station which was a gift from China's Chou En-Lai.

Britain

Britain is one of the top European producers for the African market and contributes more than a third of East and West African imports. Trade and aid relations are maintained through direct bi-lateral aid, the Export Credits Guarantees Department, the Commonwealth Development Corporation and the new Ministry of Overseas Development. Expansion has also occurred in direct private investment, multi-national aid and contributions to U.N.O. aid programmes.

Direct private investment is concentrated in the Republic of South Africa, the stronghold of British trade on the Continent. British companies have £1,000m. staked in the Republic and provide nearly 30 per cent of its imports of textiles, motorcars and machinery.

The Board of Trade's recent brochure on opportunities for British investment in Ivory Coast, Niger and Upper Volta has stimulated some interest in expanding trade with French-speaking Africa. At present the United Kingdom is a new-comer in *Afrique francophone*, but a 50 per cent rise in exports to the Ivory Coast in 1961 prompted further consideration of this market. Today, as a result of an Anglo-Algerian pact, methane gas drawn from 7,000 feet below the scorched Saharan wastelands supplies homes in British cities a thousand miles away.

France

French trade relations centre around bi-lateral agreements with her former dependencies, particularly Algeria. Recently she has begun to broaden her trade and investment to include English-

TABLE 1. BRITAIN'S TRADE WITH COMMONWEALTH-
WEST AFRICA, 1963*

Country	Imports from in £m.	Exports to in £m.
Federation of Nigeria	77·7	65·3
Ghana	21·9	38·6
Sierra Leone	4·7	11·08
Gambia	0·76	1·66

* Source: West Africa, 1 February, 1964, p. 133.

TABLE 2. BRITAIN'S TRADE WITH NON-COMMON-
WEALTH AFRICA, 1963*

Country	Imports from in £m.	Exports to in £m.
Angola	0·42	4·49
Mauritania	0·84	0·06
Republic of Mali	0·033	0·166
Republic of Senegal	0·63	1·28
Republic of Guinea	0·52	1·56
Liberia	5·42	6·62
Libya	42·6	15·2
Ivory Coast	1·67	1·39
Upper Volta	0·014	0·014
Niger	0·048	0·131
Togo	0·195	0·947
Dahomey	0·052	0·483
Cameroon Republic	6·35	2·09
Gabon	1·17	0·536
Congo (Brazzaville)	0·142	0·587
Congo (Leopoldville)	3·3	3·18
Central African Republic	0·028	0·335
Chad	0·431	0·132
Spanish West Africa	0·086	0·509
Portuguese Territories	0·002	0·394
Republic of South Africa	114·7	195·8
Zanzibar	0·709	0·237

* Source: West Africa, 1 February, 1964, p. 133.

speaking African nations. As Nigeria, Kenya and other nations seek admission to European economic organizations, France's key membership in these organizations will assist French industry to penetrate these new markets.

Independence has modified British, Belgian and French relations with Africa, and new governments have asserted their right to trade with all nations. In the changing political and economic situation other industrial countries have increased their share in markets which were traditionally the preserves of the imperial powers. America, West Germany, Japan, the Socialist states and Italy provide examples of Africa's changing trade and aid relations.

U.S.A.

America's economic relationship with tropical Africa is based on direct investment and aid coupled with a steadily-rising volume of trade. Money and technicians are channelled through two major agencies — the Agency for International Development, and the Export-Import Bank — and a variety of special projects; additional contributions are made through the World Bank group and other international organizations. More than 2·25 billion dollars of American aid has gone to new nations. The major African recipients of loans, grants and surplus food are Ghana, Tunisia, Algeria, Congo (Leopoldville), Morocco, Liberia and Nigeria. American aid has helped to build highways in Ethiopia, reservoirs in Kenya, a hydro-electric project in Liberia, educational institutions in Mali, a sewerage system in Sudan, an agricultural college in Tanganyika and secondary schools in Uganda.

West Germany

The rate of West German investment in tropical Africa is currently higher than that of Britain. The Deutsche Bank is a business partner in a hundred companies in South, Central and East Africa. In one year, 1961–62, the African share of German privately-financed investments overseas increased from 6 to 29 per cent. Africa's portion of West-German-financed credit to foreign countries increased from 4 per cent in 1961 to 20 per cent a year later. German export–import trade with African countries is increasing rapidly. In South Africa, despite heavy competition from Great Britain, West Germany has enlarged her portion of import trade. Historically, German colonial administration in Cameroons, Togoland, Tanganyika and South-West Africa was short-lived. Today West Germany capitalizes on her status as a non-colonial power to enter energetically into competition for African trade. West Germany has impressed African governments with her desire to invest in their Continent. Direct contact is accomplished through special events, "Friendship Weeks", mobile exhibitions and touring sports groups. The German post-war image is projected to African *élites* through the activities of Afrika Verein Committee and the Deutsche Afrika Society. The mutual interests of Germany and Africa were clearly expressed in 1962 when German ambassadors in Africa met at Entebbe, Uganda, and President Lübke visited Liberia, Guinea and Mali. In the same year the heads of Sudan, Mali, Madagascar, Somalia and Northern Nigeria made State visits to Germany.

U.S.S.R.

All the European socialist nations have some form of trade–aid relations with Africa. Poland, Yugoslavia, Czechoslovakia and Bulgaria have provided expertise in industrial technology and economic planning. The Soviet Union, like other industrial nations, has established diplomatic, trade, cultural and military relations with Morocco, Tunisia, Algeria, Somalia, Dahomey, Togo, Ghana, Sierra Leone and Senegal. She has financed cement and shoe factories, saw-mills, canneries and refrigeration plants, an oil refinery in Ethiopia and an atomic reactor station in Ghana.

Soviet trading relations with Africa have increased but it is only in Egypt that they constitute a significant proportion of the national economy. Russia and her fellow socialist nations purchase more than half of Egypt's cotton output. Russia contributed substantially to the building of the Aswan Dam in co-operation with the Egyptian Government and international financial groups.

China

In the winter of 1963, the changing position of the People's Republic of China in world affairs stimulated her interest in Africa. China's recognition by France and the African visit of Prime Minister Mr. Chou en-Lai enlarged the Chinese sphere of influence, particularly in the French-speaking nations. During the course of his visit to Ethiopia, Somalia, and Algeria, the Prime Minister established diplomatic representation and promised more than £10m. in aid and technical assistance.

China's aid to African nations since 1960 was reported by *West Africa*, 27 June, 1964, and other leading publications, as follows:

Guinea, 100m. rouble loan without interest (1960)
Ghana, £7m. repayable in 10 years (1961)
Mali, an economic and commercial agreement (1961)
Algeria, gift of 9,000 tons of corn, 3,000 tons of steel and 21,000 tons of medical supplies (1962)
Somalia, an unspecified amount (1963)
Zanzibar, £175,000 aid promised, and interest-free loan
Kenya, loan of £6·5m. over 10 years, without interest, and a gift of $3m.
Tanganyika, interest-free loan of £10m., and a free grant of more than £1m. to the United Republic of Tanzania (Tanganyika and Zanzibar)

Japan

Japan is a significant new-comer to African trade; her interests are in mineral ores, textiles, industrial cash crops and shipping. Traditionally Japanese trade was with the southern and central African mining areas which supply her mills with raw materials. Trade with these regions has grown in 10 years from £153,000 to £7m., according to the journal, *Africa-Japan 1963*, and plans are under way for a large capital investment in a 1,000-ton blast furnace in Central Africa.

Nigeria and Ghana are Japan's most important customers in tropical Africa. The Japan–Nigeria trading company will buy $13·5m. worth of raw cotton, cocoa and groundnuts; a £7m. credit arrangement is being negotiated for Nigeria to buy ships and capital goods. In Ghana, Japanese technicians staff training centres for textile workers. Across the Continent in Ethiopia $4m. is invested in the Dire Dawa textile factory.

Japanese skills in shipbuilding and maritime trade are highly valued in Africa and are winning customers for her. Japan's shipping lines, Mitsui-OSK and Nippon Yusen Kaisha, are adding new ports of call; the Nippon line has inaugurated a fast three-week service from Kobe to Mombasa. Japan's Cinderella rise from centuries of isolation and the débris of World War II is often cited as an example of an under-developed nation that has successfully achieved a high stage of industrialization.

Japanese businessmen have quickly moved to formalize their relations with Africa. The Africa–Japan Society created in 1961 seeks to further good-will, and a journal is printed for African readers. Business interests support an institute of African studies and current research on the market structure of African nations. The Japanese Ministry of Foreign Affairs has created an Africa Division and recently several foreign trade missions negotiated trade agreements with African nations. As part of her contribution to development Japan sends experts to Africa and conducts mass training programmes in dam construction, industrial planning and seismology at Japanese training centres.

Italy

Italy, shorn of her colonial responsibilities, has made rapid gains not only in areas of former influence, like Somalia, but in several major regions of Africa. Her economic penetration is spear-headed by three State-owned industrial and petroleum corporations, *Istituto per la Ricostruzione Industriale* (I.R.I.), *Agente Generale Italiana Petrole* (A.G.I.P.) and *Ente Nazionale Idro-carburi* (E.N.I.). Companies associated with I.R.I. have expanded their business with Africa; they include the Italian Shipping Line, Alitalia airlines, Alfa-Romeo motorcars and Italy's largest commercial banks, construction companies and steel plants. E.N.I. has won exclusive rights to build oil refineries in Morocco, Tunisia, Ghana, Congo and Tanzania. By offering attractive terms to governments (for example, options to buy up to 50 per cent of the shares) E.N.I. has consistently won contracts from the major international oil companies.

MULTI-LATERAL TRADE AND AID

Of the foreign exchange earnings of African nations, 90 per cent come from the export of agricultural primary products; almost one-third is traded with European nations through multi-lateral agreements. Three examples of multi-national trade–aid organizations are The Common Market, The Council of Europe, and the General Agreement on Tariffs and Trade (G.A.T.T.).

The European Economic Community (The Common Market)

The Common Market is the single most important nexus of European trade and multi-national aid to Africa. The E.E.C. was established by the Rome Treaty of 1958 and includes six members, France, Germany, Belgium, Netherlands, Italy and Luxembourg. Originally restricted to "The Six" and African countries in "special relations", the E.E.C. has broadened to include associates from all parts of independent Africa. In the course of its growth the E.E.C. has abolished customs duties, quotas and tariffs on certain produce and trade. Africans maintain the right, however, to keep any restrictions necessary for their own development and industry.

African associates are entitled to receive aid from the European Investment Bank and the European Development Fund for the modernization of economic resources. Under the Convention of Associations signed with 18 African states in 1957 the Fund has made available $500m. for a variety of projects: digging wells in Chad, land improvement in Burundi, railways in Congo and the resolution of cattle plagues in Niger.

The Council of Europe

The Council of Europe is another multi-national trade and aid organization linked with Africa. The Council was established in 1949 to promote European unity and it includes most European nations in its membership. Like E.E.C., the Council was initially interested in developing economic relations only with the African dependencies of its members. In recent years, however, it has broadened its scope to include all interested independent African nations. The Council has recommended a guarantee fund against political risks incurred by private investment in Africa, and more liberal terms of trade between European and African partners.

The General Agreement on Tariffs and Trade

G.A.T.T. is an international trade group created in 1948. It was originally composed of European nations but expanded to 61 full members, half of whom are developing countries. In response to demands from African countries for new international trade policies, G.A.T.T., nations participated in a U.N. trade and development conference U.N.T.A.D. in 1964. The U.N. conference at Geneva brought together 2,000 delegates and observers from 123 nations to consider ways of stimulating more effective collaboration between the industrialized and developing countries.

The United Nations Organization

A brief consideration of patterns of aid through U.N.O., the Organization of Economic Co-operation and Development (O.E.C.D.) and the World Bank will complete our survey of multi-national aid to Africa.

United Nations resources are channelled through two major aid and development programmes. The Technical Assistance programme sends experts to African nations and grants fellowships for study abroad. The Special Fund supports natural resources surveys and aids research institutions. The establishment of the U.N. Economic Commission for Africa has encouraged African and European specialists to come together and formulate plans for development. E.C.A. is financed directly from the U.N. budget and contributions from African States; it has a staff of 250 experts employed at its Addis Ababa headquarters and regional agencies at Niamey, Niger and Tangier, Morocco.

The Organization for Economic Co-operation and Development

This organization was founded in 1960 and includes the United States and the United Kingdom and 18 European countries. O.E.C.D. member countries expend more than three-quarters of the world's public and private aid to developing countries. In 1960, when the total world financial resources directed towards developing countries was $8,234m., it was estimated that the United States, France and the United Kingdom contributed $6,000m. while the Soviet Union and China contributed $183m.

The World Bank Group

This is the most important international financial agency providing aid funds for Africa. The Group includes three units, the International Bank for Reconstruction and Development, the International Finance Corporation and the International Development Association. By the beginning of 1964, the World Bank Group had extended $1,000m. in loans, investments and credits to develop transport, power and agriculture in 20 African countries.

Once capital assistance has been received the next obvious problem is how to use it, how to put it to work in raising the standard of living and the purchasing power of the African market. The next chapter briefly explores the main features of modern African economies.

CHAPTER THREE

AFRICAN ECONOMIES

THE CHANGING ROLE OF INVESTMENT

THE PURCHASING power, health and well-being of African consumers and the size of markets are rapidly increasing as productive capital pours into the private and public economic sectors of new African nations. Dynamic growth is achieved by directing capital through three principal arteries: (1) investment by governments (African and foreign), (2) mixed capital or multi-national investment by both foreign or African private and governmental agencies, and (3) direct investment by business in the private sector.

New techniques are being devised to direct and regulate economic growth; they include investment banks, produce marketing boards, co-operatives and development agencies. In addition, governments are stimulating the mobilization of the collective efforts of citizens to create what President Touré of Guinea calls a "human investment" in the developmental process. How does the distribution of capital affect the growth of the African market? How is the role of investment capital changing and what trends lie in the future?

Trading Companies

In the process of change many colonial trading companies have radically reorganized their patterns of investment and participation in the African market. In the past they were mainly engaged in buying African produce and selling Western manufactured goods. Today, they are gradually moving towards direct investment in industrial development and selling mass consumer goods in large modern urban shops. Some companies involved in

c 21

this process in West Africa are *Compagnie Française de l'Afrique Occidentale* (C.F.A.O.), *Société Commerciale de l'Ouest Africain* (S.C.O.A.), A. G. Leventis, Mandelas and Karaberis, Paterson and Zochonis, Union Trading Company and the United Africa Company. The Kingsway Stores of U.A.C. are already known throughout West Africa as *the* place to buy everything from the latest fashions to "bangers" and chutney. In Nigeria, according to an article in *West Africa*[1], U.A.C. Companies are redirecting their capital into more than a dozen industrial projects ranging from yarn-spinning, textile mills and breweries to transport and soap factories.

Investment Corporations

New investment and banking institutions have also stimulated the growth of African industries and markets. An example is the Investment Corporation of Nigeria (I.C.O.N.) now the Nigerian Industrial Development Bank (N.I.D.B.), headed by the self-made millionaire, Chief Mathias Ogochukwu. I.C.O.N. was created in 1959 under the sponsorship of the Commonwealth Development Finance Company. There were 96 non-Nigerian shareholders including Barclays Bank D.C.O., United Africa Company, Bank of West Africa, British American Tobacco Company and Imperial Chemical Industries. Most of the capital was invested in private enterprise development and handled through West Africa's first financial stock exchange at Lagos.

In 1963, I.C.O.N. was reconstituted into the Nigerian Industrial Development Bank (N.I.D.B.). The earlier sponsors joined with the Nigerian Government (which gave a £2m. interest-free loan), the International Finance Corporation and eight banking and investment institutions in Europe, America and Japan. The main functions of N.I.D.B. are to encourage and finance growth in the industrial and mining sectors and to sell investments on the Lagos Stock Exchange. Of the Bank's voting capital, 51 per cent, estimated at £1m., is in Class A shares reserved for Nigerian subscribers. At present the majority of Class A shares is held by the I.F.C. and the Central Bank of Nigeria. The number of private

Nigerian investors is increasing and they now hold more than £20,000 worth of shares.

African Development Bank

One of the most significant events in contemporary African economic affairs is the creation of the African Development Bank, conceived as the nucleus of finance capital for continental development. The Bank was organized with an initial capital of £250m. under the auspices of the U.N. Economic Commission for Africa; it is directed by African governors and financed by contributions from the African states.

Mixed capital

Mixed capital ventures play a great part in large-scale industrial projects, for example, dams, industrial estates, power plants and hydro-electric stations. President Nkrumah, while presenting the new seven-year development plan to the Ghanaian Parliament, called Ghana's Volta river dam an example of "fruitful collaboration with American enterprise in the shape of the Kaiser group of industries". He went on to say, according to the London Times,[2] "I regard this scheme as an example of the way in which careful and proper planning together with foreign investment, public control and participation and the devoted labours of the people, can revolutionize the economic base of society."

Two areas of African economies in which specific investment is encouraged are the local processing of all exported primary raw materials and the production of consumer goods from local resources. African based industries are desired because they are the training ground for Africa's new industrial labour force and create wage-earning consumers. In addition, the local production of clothing, shoes, packaged foods, aluminium, cement, furniture and household wares makes definite contribution to raising the standard of living, and conserves scarce financial resources now spent on imported manufactured products.

Produce marketing Boards

The activities of produce marketing boards and development agencies also affect the rate of growth of industry and consumer markets. The boards are public corporations which buy from local producers and sell on the world market. Marketing boards are among the most prosperous institutions in newly-developing areas and their budget surpluses are employed to promote development in vast rural regions.

Development agencies

Development agencies are public corporations or statutory bodies established to attract foreign capital, to oversee land resource surveys, manpower studies and transport improvement. In addition they have the responsibility for managing the operation of large enterprises.

TWO DEVELOPING ECONOMIES

Nigeria

Nigeria with its 60 million people is the Colossus of Africa and the biggest potential market in the whole Continent. One out of every four Africans is a Nigerian. One-third of all the people in tropical Africa and more than half of the population of West Africa are Nigerians. Northern Nigeria alone, with its 30 million, has a larger population than any African nation.

Nigeria's abundant material resources and cultivable land make her one of the brightest economic prospects of all the newly-emerging nations. Her national income, growing at the rate of 2 per cent per annum, has surpassed £500m. As a result millions of pounds, dollars, deutsche-marks, francs, yen, guilders and lira pour into Nigeria annually. In every region of the Federation, factories, homes and schools are being built at an astounding rate.

Nigeria's relatively stable political structure, diversity of resources and the enthusiastic measures taken by Regional Governments to encourage investments are attractive to investors. The Federal Government has shown constraint in both internal and external investment dealings. As a result, the bulk of foreign investment enters through Regional Government and their regional development corporations, planning agencies, local authorities and enterprises.

Shell and B.P. Limited has sunk an estimated £60m. in the search for oil in the Niger Delta; Dunlop Nigeria Industries Limited, in co-operation with the Western Region Government, produces tyres utilizing 80 per cent of Nigeria's rubber and meeting half of her needs. The Northern Nigeria Government announced a six-year development plan for a £5m. sugar industry at Bacita managed by Booker Brothers with investment participation by Tate and Lyle. It also plans a £1·5m. cotton mill at Gusau, a cube sugar mill and match factory at Ilorin and a complex of pharmaceutical, leather goods and canning factories in Kano. The Federal Government's plans to harness the Niger river and to extend the Bornu railway, will develop new markets in the interior of the nation and the Continent.

Nigeria maintains the bulk of her trade with Great Britain. However, 35 per cent of her exports are with the European Common Market countries and she is seeking to create closer links with this important export market. New links are also being sought with Nigeria's African neighbours. For example, a joint customs post on the Dahomey border provides the basis for a common customs union between the two countries and a link within the future African Common Market.

Ghana

Ghana has one of the most viable and diversified economies in Africa; her *per capita* income of £200 is more than twice that of any other tropical African state. Capitalizing on her large sterling balance and the enterprise of peasant cocoa farmers and urban workers, Ghana has made rapid strides in the modernization of the agricultural and industrial sectors of her economy. In announcing the new seven-year programme President Kwame Nkrumah declared that by the end of 1970 the foundations will be laid for transformation of Ghana's economy to an industrial basis.

In the process of development Ghana has called upon the assistance of all the nations of the world. The Volta river project has attracted £100m. of financial aid from the United States and European nations. The Black Star shipping line, begun with the assistance of Israel, has developed with the participation of British and Dutch shipyards. The new port installation at Tema, a major contribution to the economy, was completed with the cooperation of international finance.

Tema, like Kumasi, her sister city in the interior, is a centre of new secondary industries. In early 1964 a £2m. Lever Brothers soap factory was opened by Dr. Nkrumah. In his speech he congratulated the Company on its ability to adapt itself to the fast-changing economic pattern in Ghana. On that occasion he also announced the creation of the Workers' Order of the Black Star, an official award of merit for productive community-minded workers.

Planning, and government participation in the private and public sector, have set the pace for Ghana's development. As in other West African states the government regulates the activities of agricultural cash crop production; in addition, Ghana has recently created 14 public corporations related to industrial development.

TOWARDS NEW THEORIES AND DEVELOPMENT PRACTICES

The trade, financial aid and investment and marketing practices of Western governments and companies in Africa are many-faceted expressions of the cultural and economic intentions and impulses which grow out of their Western experience. Inevitably in changing Africa, the intentions and actions of foreign enterprise are adjusting to the goals and priorities of African nations. As the resolution of differing points of view proceeds there will be a quickening period of growth in the African market. Where are some of the main areas of economic tension between Europe and Africa in the economic sphere? What are some of the suggestions offered by Africans and Europeans for their resolution? And, how will this affect the future growth of the African market?

Aid: step-child of European budgets

Aid to Africa is the step-child of the budgets of European nations and international organizations. Africa receives the smallest share of the United States' foreign-aid budget, little more from the United Kingdom than is allocated for British Railways, and less than half the subsidy given to u.k. farmers. Only 12 per cent of the u.n. assistance funds go to Africa and the Special Fund contributes only one-tenth of the total monetary assistance received by African nations.

These revealing facts have come to light through the research activities of many organizations, the Board of Trade, Barclays Bank Overseas Economic Surveys and the Overseas Development Institute. Mr. William Clark, director of o.d.i., has published a number of pamphlets and articles outlining the necessity for a new approach to the African market. In *After Independence in East Africa*[3] and *Strategy for Development*,[4] Mr. Clark suggests a programme for reorganizing assistance and calls for a special study of European aid to Africa.

Aid and trade are often used as instruments of economic and political policy, as "means to ends" unrelated to Africa's developments needs. In America, where there are several well-organized associations of scholars dealing with Africa, a call has been made for a new American policy. A document[5] by the Africa League directed to the United States Government said:

" . . . . our policy for Africa must be examined in terms of the problems of Africa and not as a mere by-product of our relations with the Soviet Union or Western Europe . . ."

The quest for economic independence places the African states in the midst of a great dilemma : each must search for capital for development, each seeks to ward off forms of economic dependence which may negate sovereignty. President Julius Nyerere of Tanganyika has put the case succinctly :

> "African states have to tread cautiously in their economic and trading relations with outside countries. Their leaders have to justify in the eyes of their own people the way they have governed the country since independence. So they have to find capital for development, skilled personnel, and also markets in the outside world. But all the same they have to ask themselves how far certain economic and trade agreements are likely to have political strings hidden in them, and how far these new influences might undermine the country's independence."

Loans : new costs and problems

One of the main difficulties associated with financial aid is the cost of servicing loans. Many nations find that they are often poorer after getting several loans and grants, and must borrow in order to meet their payments. Furthermore, given the terms of these loans, it is difficult to channel them into productive sectors, to cut down administrative expenditures, to support basic resource research and to meet rising costs of electricity and transport.

Needs and cost estimates are rapidly overtaken, even before the ink on the contract is dry, by the extraordinary growth in the rate of population. Nigeria, for example, sky-rocketed from 35 million people to 56 million in 10 years. The expansion of African consumer markets depends on governments determining a predictable relationship between four primary factors : population, capital, estimated rate of economic growth, and resulting net income increase.

The over-riding significance of these factors was pointed out in an editorial in *West Africa*:[6]

> "Whereas the u.k., with an annual population increase of 0·5 per cent, needs only a 4 per cent rate of economic growth to ensure a 3 per cent rise in income, Ghana, with a 2½ per cent population

growth, needs to maintain the rate of growth in the economy at 7 per cent to achieve the same 3 per cent rise in living standards."

Nigeria, given the same 2½ per cent population increase, is hoping, less ambitiously, for a 4 per cent growth in the economy with a 1·5 per cent rise in national income.

Trade: the $100 vs. the $1,000 nations

Trade between Africa and the industrial nations cannot be viewed separately from the complex relationships which exist between the rich and the poor nations. The hard fact is that the gap between what Professor P. M. S. Blackett of Imperial College has called the "$1,000 and the $100 countries" is growing, even with increased aid and trade. Professor T. Balogh of Balliol College, Oxford, describes the present situation in his article "Notes on the United Nations Conference on Trade and Development".[7]

> "There is general agreement on the need to reduce the crass inequality in the international distribution of income and, I take it, also about the undeniable fact that this inequality has been increasing, despite a growing volume of aid in terms of technical assistance and resources, not the least because of the worsening of the terms of trade between primary goods and manufactures."

International trade organizations appear to African leaders as "rich men's clubs" whose structures are unable really to tackle the problems of three-quarters of the world. Part of the reason for this, as Tom Mboya remarks in his book *Freedom and After*[8], is that ". . . . Africa is moving on to the international scene at a time when most of the international agencies have been established, and no attempt is being made to reorganize them to take account of the emergence of Africa . . . they will presumably continue to function on the basis of what their original sponsors wanted them to achieve, without considering what is in the best interests of the newer nations".

Some of the defects of the present situation have been under continuous study by governments, the United Nations and independent scholars. "Trade, and especially an induced improvement in terms of trade, is no alternative to a well-conceived programme of aid combined with internal reform," says Professor Balogh in his article.[2] He suggests that the present client relationship between rich and poor nations is a "fiction of equal partnership" and outlines a new approach which includes the reorganization of the international agencies dealing with aid, the establishment of effective regional planning to channel aid and ensure, through reforms, its effective use.

The Oxford economist, Professor I. M. D. Little, is engaged in a three-year survey of trade and aid and has published his preliminary findings in the o.d.i. pamphlet, *Aid to Africa.*[9] In it he suggests the creation of a career service for technical assistance, more research, cheaper loans and an expansion of multilateral participation in African development.

The first u.n.o. trade conference (1964) succeeded in establishing a permanent body to review these matters. Dr. Raoul Prebisch, the Argentinian Secretary-General of the conference, has summarized the tasks yet to be accomplished:

1 increase the representation of the developing nations;
2 deal with trade as a part of the general problems of development;
3 solve trading problems between the developed countries and Africa, and between African nations themselves;
4 accord a place for the centrally planned economies of Africa in the international tariff system. These tasks, he says, require careful evaluation and possibly the creation of a new world trade organization.

Investment and social utility

Investment and marketing relations with Africa are often marred by simplistic theories and practices which are inapplicable and incompatible with the realities of African development. In the laboratory of development four assumptions common in European countries are being challenged:

1 that the role of government is limited to "non-economic" functions;
2 that the good use of capital depends on the prior existence of a viable economic infra-structure;
3 that the profitability of an investment is a measure of its social usefulness;
4 that an investment's prospective receipts reflect the real worth of the product to consumers.

Classical economists confined the sphere of governmental activities to "non-economic" functions such as defence, education and the maintenance of a police force. But today in Africa government plays a large role in the operation of the national economy. Governments are the largest employers of wage-workers and conveyor belts of capital.

What, then, should be the economic role of government in undertakings which, according to traditional theory, are needed for the functioning of the economy, but are too expensive and/or not profitable enough to be provided by private incentive and profit-motivated business?

Direct investment of productive capital may be withheld because, it is said, an underdeveloped nation does not have the pre-requisite institutions to make good use of the capital. Yet, it is fairly clear that no African nation can create these institutions — literate skilled manpower, etc. — without capital and widespread investment. Without capital to get ready, so to speak, many nations are doomed to poverty, disease and perpetual under-development.

The profitability of an investment is not always a good measure of its social usefulness, nor does an investment's prospective receipts always reflect the real worth of the product to consumers. This point of view has been expressed by the American economist Sayre P. Schatz[10] in "The American Approach to Foreign Aid and the Thesis of Low Absorptive Capacity".

Professor Schatz contends that investment in the production of goods of high utility for low-income consumers continually lags behind other investment sectors. Large numbers of people, therefore, never taste the fruits of independence. The reason, he says, is that enterprises of undoubted national merit may seem insufficiently profitable and uneconomic to investors. As a result, the criterion of profitability leads to high money receipts but low real social benefit. One example is the diversion of land from food production to more remunerative cash crop export production. Valuable external economies are created thereby, but without a corresponding rapid growth in the internal economy and the consumer market.

Professor Schatz suggests that more experiments are necessary to test the degree to which "uneconomic" short-term projects have long-term real benefits. He cites their potential contribution to the development of labour experience, managerial and *entrepreneurial* skills, and to the acclimatization of workers to modern productive processes. "Uneconomic" projects may prove profitable in the long run and provide real social benefits, new markets and the stimulation of growth in other segments of the economy.

Planning

Many pathways to development traverse Africa, a Continent three times the size of the United States of America, and composed of many new nations. All African governments have chosen, however, to initiate planned control over the growth of the private and public sectors of their economies. Planning provides a way of organizing development programmes, allocating priorities, measuring progress and utilizing resultant benefits. Planning is also a method of organizing and mobilizing resources to express a social and economic view, an emergent collective personality, aspiration and *élan vital*.

Alhaji Sir Ahmadu Bello, Sardauna of Sokoto and Premier of the Northern Region, Nigeria, expressed the views of many leaders when he said in his book, *My Life*:[11]

"What we want of capitalism is to get some of the capital flowing our way . . . we welcome foreign capital, provided we have the say in how it is to be employed and also an eventual option to buy it out in due course. The days have passed when foreigners can come into the country and take out great profits, leaving behind nothing more valuable than a few rotting tin sheds."

A member of a Congolese political party, speaking at the Ibadan Seminar on Representative Government and National Progress in 1959, concluded that ". . . countries newly arrived at independence cannot avoid planning. The bitter struggle for independence is based not only on the desire for freedom, but above all on the misery into which the African people have been plunged by the colonial powers".

Economic planning for long-lasting development involves the co-operation and equal participation of governments, industry and people. ". . . careful and proper planning together with foreign investment, public control and participation and the devoted labours of the people, can revolutionize the economic base of society," declared President Nkrumah in his speech to the Ghana Parliament during the introduction in 1964 of the seven-year budget.

Planning involves critical choices of far-reaching implications for industry and African governments. What is the effect of imported consumer goods on the balance of trade and the domestic economy; and at what point should the local production of goods be encouraged? What shall be the degree of co-operation; and where shall the power of decision-making lie?

Sir Jock Campbell: one man's view

In developing Africa, the industrialist and businessman in search of markets will be inexorably drawn out of the *laissez-faire* attitudes of the past into the evolving structure of future-orientated societies. Europe's "Bible of Free Enterprise" in Africa's Century of Development may well be based on a set of principles expressed by Sir Jock Campbell, chairman of the Booker Brothers Group, and a man of much experience in investment activities.

Sir Jock's forward-looking views were recorded in an article by William Clark[12] in the Unilever quarterly; the text of his remarks on this subject are as follows:

"The daunting weight of their economic problems makes it inevitable that many of the new régimes will be *dirigiste*: there will be much state control, planning and participation in industrial enterprise. Nevertheless there remains plenty of work to be done, and plenty of room for profitable investment, by private enterprise in underdeveloped countries. But this requires the directors of private investment to understand the problems and realities of the countries in which they are operating, and to adapt themselves to their societies and economies as they evolve, not as they would expect them to be in London and the Home Counties. For the new government, it demands that, in making new rules, they recognize the problems of investors and their need for a sufficient return; and having made the rules, they must fairly and squarely explain them and stick to them. Uncertainty about the intentions of governments is the worst deterrent to investment.

I think that companies who do invest and operate in the new nations must, *inter alia*, concentrate on the following:

(*a*) running the business efficiently, productively and profitably, but always remembering, and being seen to be remembering:

(i) that they owe responsibility not only to shareholders — without whose investment the business cannot exist . . . but also to employees, without whose management and skills it cannot operate; and to the community in which it is rooted, and whose acceptance it must gain to survive;

(ii) and that the values and standards of any business concern cannot on the one hand be too out of tune with the standards and values of the society in which it operates, nor on the other hand too out of tune with the realities of industrial discipline and the facts of industrial life; thus, evolving compromise and synthesis are always needed.

(*b*) To the above ends, training nationals to do all the jobs in the business from top to bottom. And this really means from the top to the bottom. In many educational and training schemes and concepts, there is a danger that they will produce nothing but imitation expatriate technicians, interpreters and thirds-in-command; and no leaders in the national idiom.

(c) Encouraging nationals to buy shares in the business. A great deal of thought needs to be given as to how best to facilitate this — in terms of the mechanics of sale and purchase, of security, of the size of the unit, and of intelligibility.

(d) I should have added the need to re-invest, and to be seen to re-invest, a fair share of profits in the under-developed country concerned. And I think that exchange control measures should be instituted sooner rather than later — so that they can be worked out empirically and efficiently before people take fright; rather than at the last moment when they always break down and prevent new investment without successfully preventing the flight of capital."

In modernising Africa there are five basic and inescapable principles of foreign corporate behaviour:

1 *Understanding.* Western enterprise must understand the problems and adapt to the realities of the countries in which they are operating;

2 *Social utility.* Companies have a responsibility to the African community to become means to the end of producing wealth, distributing goods and services;

3 *Training.* They must train nationals to do *all* the jobs in business from top to bottom;

4 *Sharing.* They should encourage nationals to buy shares in the business;

5 *Re-investment.* They should re-invest a fair share of profits in the under-developed country concerned.

It is highly probable that in future the test of a "profitable investment" in the African market will be not only its monetary return but its net social benefit. That is, its contribution to economic independence, planned progress, a diversified economy, the development of skilled cadres and the diffusion of worthwhile products.

REFERENCES

1 *West Africa,* 11 April, 1964.

2 *The Times,* 12 March, 1964.

3 CLARK, W., *After Independence in East Africa,*War onWant, London, undated.

4 CLARK, W., *Strategy for Development,* Overseas Development Institute, London, 1962.

5 *A New American Policy Toward Africa,* The Africa League, New York, February, 1960.

6 *West Africa,* 18 April, 1964, editorial.

7 BALOGH, PROFESSOR, T., "Notes on the United Nations Conference on Trade and Development", *Bulletin of the Oxford University Institute of Economics and Statistics,* **26,** Basil Blackwell, Oxford, February, 1964.

8 MBOYA, T., *Freedom and After,* André Deutsch, London, 1963.

9 LITTLE, I. M. D., *Aid to Africa,* Overseas Development Institute, London, 1964.

10 SCHATZ, SAYRE P., "The American Approach to Foreign Aid and the Thesis of Low Absorptive Capacity", *Quarterly Review of Economics and Business,* **1,** 4, University of Illinois, November, 1961.

11 BELLO, ALHAJI SIR AHMADU, Sardauna of Sokoto, *My Life,* Cambridge University Press, London, 1962.

12 CLARK, W., "Governments are not Enough". *Progress,* The Unilever Quarterly, **50,** No. 279, London, January, 1964.

1. New times, new trends

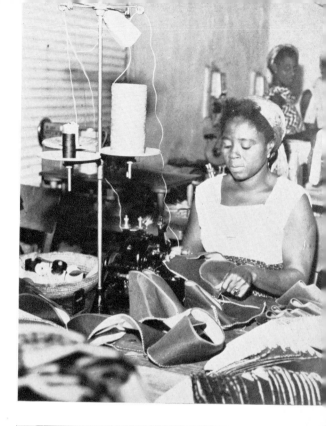

CHAPTER FOUR

MARKETS IN THE ARENAS OF CHANGE

MARKETS IN Africa do not coincide with tidy geographical boundaries. They burst forth from the arenas of change where work, men and money hold a fateful rendezvous. They emerge from the expanding cities, the heat of agro-industrial mills and mines and the cocoa and coffee seedlings of peasant farmers. They rise with the rhythmic chorus of plantation workers hunched to the *panga* and the hoe, and pulsate with urgency like the steady gait of the migrant, homeward bound, head bent to the wind.

Today new Africans are born on the periphery of traditional life. Markets grow with African development and take their shape according to a man's occupation, his place of work, where he lives, his aspirations and the place he sees for himself in his nation's future.

A BRIEF OVER-VIEW OF AFRICAN MARKETS

Africa is the second largest land area in the world and represents 22 per cent of the world's land area. Its population, nearing 300 million people, is made up of men of many races, creeds and colours; the majority of them are Africans indigenous to the Continent from time immemorial. There are 5 million Europeans, and 1 million Indians, most of whom live in southern, east and central Africa.

There are 36 independent African states* which comprise 80 per cent of the Continent's land population and they are listed below:

* At December, 1964.

Algeria	Mali
Burundi	Mauritania
Cameroon	Morocco
Central African Republic	Niger
Chad	Nigeria
Congo (Brazzaville)	Ruanda
Congo (Leopoldville)	Senegal
Dahomey	Sierra Leone
Ethiopia	Somalia
Gabon	South Africa
Ghana	Sudan
Guinea	Tanzania (Tanganyika and Zanzibar)
Ivory Coast	Togo
Kenya	Tunisia
Liberia	Uganda
Libya	United Arab Republic
Malagasy	Upper Volta
Malawi (Nyasaland)	Zambia (Northern Rhodesia)

Within these nations there are 10 major characteristics of change:

1 People are living longer; there is a rapid expansion of population due to a startling decline of deaths among infants and the aged due to better medical care.

2 A youthful population structure; an increasing segment of the populations consists of the able-bodied age group, 15–44.

3 More children are entering and remaining in school; 34 per cent of the school-age population is in school and more than 10,000 students are pursuing higher education.

4 More people are entering the cash wage economy; the bulk of cash wage employment comprises unskilled labour and petty trade but ranges into the higher levels of modern life.

5 More goods and services are being produced more efficiently for export and domestic use.

6 Incomes are rising; 70 per cent of the people earn up to £50 per annum, 25 per cent £50-£75, and 5 per cent of the incomes range upwards from £75 to many thousands of pounds per annum.

7 Literacy is rising at an accelerating rate; in Ghana, Uganda, Kenya and Congo 20-30 per cent of the population is literate.

8 More people are entering urban areas; from 10-20 per cent of the Continent's population live in urban areas of 20,000 or more people; there is also a high density of population in cash-crop growing regions.

9 More persons are entering non-agricultural occupations.

10 More workers are engaged in organized incorporated enterprises, factories, co-operatives and public works.

CITIES

Cities, with their industries and wage-earning workers, are the focal points of development and change in modern Africa. They are points of contact between people and products. Industrial estates and homes blossom, in the wake of bulldozers, on land reclaimed from forests, swamps and shanty towns. Strident factory whistles accentuate the cadence of work and play. Petrol stations dot the city-scape and traders in traditional flowing robes make their rounds by car and motor scooter. Life vibrates with action and stimulates the growth of incomes, consumer markets, new tastes and preferences.

Cities are not new in Africa. In ancient times, city-states and feudal kingdoms enclosed large, densely-populated permanent settlements within their barricades. Urban-centred mining civilizations prospered from Katanga to Cairo and from Ethiopia to Senegal. Eighteenth-century cities in West Africa ranged in size from 10,000 to 40,000 inhabitants, according to the observations of more than 20 European and Muslim travellers.

Nigeria, for example, was one of the most highly urbanized regions in all Africa. City-dwelling among the Hausa of the

Northern Region is 1,000 years old. Six modern Nigerian cities with populations over 100,000 grew from ancient Yoruba communities. Lagos is an old Yoruba settlement, and Ibadan, the "Queen of Yoruba land" with her 700,000 people, is the largest indigenous city in Middle Africa. The ratio of town-dwellers to rural peasants among the Yoruba was higher in 1931 than in Canada and four European nations, and was exceeded only by Great Britain and America.

What is new is the rapid rate of urban growth and wage-labour which has followed the establishment of Western enterprises. Cities everywhere flourished in response to new crops, factories, mines, administration, transport and commerce. Western enterprise and administration pushed old cities into oblivion and created new towns or, failing this, enveloped ancient ones with slag-heaps, irrigated fields and rings of iron tracks. The old walled city of Zeila in Somalia, once a thriving market centre, declined into "an empty shell, a desolate place of ruined mosques and tombs". Ebolowa'a and Sangmelima in southern Cameroons grew up with the cocoa crop and became modern towns with paved roads, electricity and canalized water.

Wage-earners in old capitals like Kumasi, Ghana and Ségou, Mali, have doubled their numbers. Khartoum, once the site of a nomad camp at the junction of the Blue and White Nile rivers, became capital of the Sudan and grew into a triple-city metropolitan complex. Within a radius of 20 miles a population of 300,000 developed around a nucleus of transport facilities, industries, universities and religious shrines.

Millions of workers flocked into centres of employment in the wake of industrial penetration; and new cities grew up around them. Coal mining transformed Enugu, Nigeria, from a sleepy hamlet into a sprawling cosmopolitan centre of 100,000 people. In 30 years the iron-mining town of Lunsar, Sierra Leone, sky-rocketed from a few work gangs to 20,000 wage-earners. Railways and cotton mills made Bouaké the second largest metropolis in the Ivory Coast and a cross-roads of West African migrant labourers. This traditional capital city of the Baoulé kingdom grew from 3,500 in 1921 to a half million today.

In Central Africa, 300,000 workers settled in Rhodesian copper belt towns; Luluabourg, Congo and Lusaka, Zambia became centres of administration, commerce and industry. Usumbura, Burundi, on the shore of Lake Tanganyika, doubled its population in five years. Jinja, Uganda, the new cotton-growing and hydro-electric centre in the heart of the ancient Busoga kingdom, tripled its inhabitants in three years.

Are African cities really cities? The answer is yes. Sociologists have defined the city as an urban area with a principal grouping of 50,000 people or more, in an area of 100,000 people, of whom 65 per cent are engaged in non-agricultural pursuits. According to this definition formulated by the demographer Professor Kingsley Davis, there were 48 African cities in the early 1950's, 17 in Tropical Africa and seven of them in Nigeria.

In general, cities and densely-populated areas grew most rapidly where men transformed crops and minerals in processing mills and at trans-shipment centres where products moved from a man's back to power-driven machines. Today Central African cities are typically mining and manufacturing centres with an embryonic industrial proletariat. East African urban areas are centred in cash crop and farming regions or dominated by trans-shipment industries. West Africa is urbanized to a greater degree and has more than 15 industrial and seaport cities along the Atlantic Coast.

√ The major urban centres of wage-earning populations in tropical Africa may be listed as follows:

1 West African seaports, processing and manufacturing and capital cities: Dakar, Bathurst, Conakry, Freetown, Monrovia, Abidjan, Takoradi, Accra, Tema, Lome, Cotonou, Lagos-Apapa, Port Harcourt, Douala, Libreville, Port Gentil, Pointe-Noire.
2 West African interior cities: for example, Bouaké, Ivory Coast, Kumasi, Ghana, Ibadan and Kano, Nigeria.
3 The Brazzaville–Leopoldville complex on the Congo river.
4 Stanleyville, Congo.
5 Jadotville and Elisabethville, Congo, and the Copper Belt,

Zambia, and 10 mining–commercial–administrative centres in Southern Rhodesia.

6 Kampala, Entebbe and Jinja, Uganda, near Lake Victoria.
7 Nairobi and environs in Kenya.
8 Blantyre, Zomba and Limbe, Malawi.
9 East African seaports and trans-shipment centres: Mtwara, Tanga and Dar es Salaam in Tanganyika; Mombasa and Chisimaio in Kenya; Berbera and Djibouti in Somalia, the major outlets for Ethiopia; Massawa in Eritrea and Port Sudan in the Sudan.
10 Khartoum, Wad Medani and the Gezira-Managil cotton-growing area in central Sudan.

The African city and its rural periphery is the centre of the modern cash economy and the most significant market for consumer goods. In cities, men, work, and cash wages meet and generate new needs and the possibility of their attainment. Urban life is moulded by the rapid expansion of the economy. The focal points of interaction are warehouses, docks, railway stations and public works. On the job, the primary ties of kinship and village give away to new group memberships based on occupation, education, skill and income. The aspiring worker learns to adjust and to manipulate the instruments of the new urban industrial culture: "Shall I save to buy a bicycle? Is it better to work day shift or night shift? If there are two of us who might get promoted, how can I make sure that it's me?"

Urbanization and industrialization create new definitions of man's relation to his fellows; they introduce a new occupational hierarchy and distribution of income ranging from the highest officials who get more than £5,000 a year down to the humblest labourer.

The city takes on a new shape as immigrant Africans, Europeans, Asians and Levantines take their places in the economy. Cities are intricate mosaics of ethnic, religious and occupational groups. Five typical neighbourhoods emerge:

1 The modern commercial and administrative centre.

2 The well-kept residential areas of Europeans and African senior officials.

3 The old city with its narrow streets, markets and densely-occupied buildings.

4 The "stranger's quarters": the *sabon gari* or *zongo* of non-indigenous Africans and "Syrian quarter" of Arab, Asian or Levantine traders who live above their shops.

5 The sprawling areas of squatters, the "trespassers of desperation", on the edge of the city.

Each of these enclaves is a cubicle of culture; yet, though cut off from one another, the walls of former times are pierced by the spear-tips of employment and economic dependency. African wage-workers are agents of change, links between the modern world outside and the inward-looking traditional community. Each wage-worker, factory hand or houseboy is part of a chain of distribution of products and ideas reaching from the industrial capitals of the globe into the darkest room in a mud house. And, as more successful Africans with greater prestige mass across the horizon of national and international affairs and interact with Europeans in all aspects of social life, they shape the tastes and habits of the common man.

AGRO-INDUSTRIAL TOWNS

Processing plants, the most typical form of industrial manufacture, lie on the edge of African cities and in the agro-industrial towns of the interior. There, in the heat of soap and groundnut factories, the smell of tanneries, the dust of cement, tobacco and fertilizer plants, and the subdued roar of timber and textile mills, African workers "shuck off" age-old cultural patterns and take on the skills of industrial society.

Typically, the work force in processing plants varies in size from 50 to 3,000 workers. The occupational groups form a job hierarchy: general labourers, skilled workers and foremen, clerks and supervisors; African wages range from 20s.–60s. or more a week, depending on skill and education. The plants operate three 8-hour shifts around the clock, six days a week with time-and-a-half on Sundays and double time for public holidays.

Industrialism, the culture of industry, draws men into new factory disciplines. Young illiterate workers from widely differing backgrounds learn to co-operate in collective labour. Absenteeism, where it existed, dwindles; and when examined scientifically is not as abnormally high as "guessed at" by supervisory personnel. Wells and Warmington in a study of industrialization in Nigeria suggest that employers pay too much attention to unsubstantiated "high rates of absenteeism" and too little attention to the pressing problems of workers, such as malnutrition and job conditions.

Mill work is no longer cheap labour; workers support large families and must buy supplies in the money economy. For every worker there may be 10 dependants and factory payrolls support communities many times their size. Where modern concepts of worker–management relations are introduced, stability is encouraged, the social horizons of labourers broaden and incomes are spent on items which contribute to their well-being and uplift.

MINING TOWNS

Africa's consumer-citizens grow in number as the mining centres of independent nations rapidly become huge urban complexes with stable wage-earning populations. More and more, mining activities are being integrated with local processing plants and expanded trans-shipment and export facilities. In every region, as secondary industrial and manufacturing factories develop, more workers have a chance to shop in the supermarket of world products.

In the Republic of Guinea, for example, the mining-processing-evacuation activities of the *Société Bauxites du Midi*, a subsidiary of Aluminium Limited (Canada) has modified the life patterns of the entire western region. New towns at Landgaredji, Boké, Port Kakande and Kaleyre along the Rio Nunes provide workers with an opportunity to live in healthy communities with a wide range of shopping facilities.

The rich mineral areas of Central Africa are among the Continent's most important growing urban industrial centres. They have attracted more than 200,000 Europeans and a million Africans to the mines and prosperous farming regions which surround them. The independent state of Malawi (Nyasaland), for example, has its main centres at Zomba and Blantyre/Limbe with a total population of 78,000; one out of every eight persons is gainfully employed in industry or farming. In Southern Rhodesia, eight mining and commercial centres together with Salisbury and Bulawayo, have a working population of 328,000 out of a total of 661,000 persons.

TABLE 3. POPULATION TOTALS IN THE COPPER BELT, ZAMBIA*

(with additional information on Lusaka and Broken Hill)

Town	Total population	Africans	Europeans and others	Total in employment
1 Bancroft	20,300	18,000	2,300	8,000
2 Chingola	43,600	38,000	5,600	15,000
3 Kitwe	89,500	77,000	12,500	31,000
4 Luanshya	56,900	51,000	5,900	17,000
5 Mufulira	67,900	61,000	6,900	20,000
6 Ndola	84,500	73,000	11,500	20,000
TOTAL	362,700	318,000	44,700	111,000
7 Lusaka (capital)	85,800	72,000	13,800	30,000
8 Broken Hill	35,300	30,000	5,300	11,000
TOTAL	483,800	420,000	63,800	152,000

* Source: *Industrial Guide to Towns*, Federal Chamber of Commerce, Federation of Rhodesia and Nyasaland, 1963.

TABLE 4. MINING, MANUFACTURING AND FARMING URBAN AREAS, SOUTHERN RHODESIA*

Town	Total population	Africans	Europeans and others	Total persons employed
Fort Victoria	12,300	10,000	2,300	5,000
Bulawayo	195,000	140,000	55,500	93,000
Gatooma	13,500	10,500	3,000	7,000
Gwelo	35,100	26,000	9,100	15,000
Qvingstone	28,600	24,000	4,600	11,000
Liue Que	22,800	18,000	4,800	10,000
Salisbury	299,200	205,000	94,200	155,000
Shabani	10,800	9,000	1,800	6,000
Umtali	36,200	27,000	9,200	16,000
Wankie	18,200	16,000	2,200	10,000
TOTAL	661,700	485,500	186,700	328,000

* Source: *Industrial Guide to Towns,* Federal Ministry of Commerce, Federation of Rhodesia and Nyasaland, 1963.

TABLE 5. POPULATION TOTALS OF MINING, MANUFACTURING AND FARMING URBAN AREAS, MALAWI*

Town	Total population	Africans	Europeans and others	Total persons employed
Zomba	15,500	14,000	1,500	6,800
Blantyre/Limbe	62,400	54,000	8,400	25,000
TOTAL	77,900	68,000	9,900	31,800

* Source: *Industrial Guide to Towns,* Federal Ministry of Commerce, Federation of Rhodesia and Nyasaland, 1963.

The Copper Belt towns of Zambia (Northern Rhodesia) are a unique phenomenon: seven sprawling communities along a billion-dollar mineral vein stretching from Congo to the borders of the Zambesi river. These modern town centres have developed in relation to mining activities; briefly they are:

1 Bancroft — one of the newer mining towns.
2 Chingola — Nchanga copper mine.
3 Kitwe — centre of the Copper Belt/Nkana mine.
4 Luanshya — Roan Antelope Copper mine.
5 Mufulira — Mufulira copper mine.
6 Ndola — headquarters of the Western Province, is an industrial commercial and distribution centre for the Copper Belt and is on the main railway line to Southern Rhodesia, Congo and Angola.
7 Broken Hill — headquarters of the Central Province, the Rhodesian Railways and site of the large Broken Hill mine.

Lusaka, capital of Zambia, lies at the tail end of the chain; it is an administrative, manufacturing and marketing centre at the junction of a road network leading to all areas of East and Central Africa.

The typical African community is a company town on the outskirts of a European residential town centre. For example, in Ndola there are three African townships, Main, Kabushi and Chifubu. Mine workers on the Copper Belt are recruited from peasants and fishermen from many neighbouring and distant regions. They receive an annual wage varying from £50 to £137 with subsidized housing food rations. With independence achieved, rapid increases in wages, purchasing power and standard of living are on the horizon. As governments, industries, mining companies, and trade unions resolve existing wage and salary differentials, Central African workers will become a significant consumer group.

CASH-CROP FARMERS

Growing and selling industrial cash crops is the main source of cash income among Africa's money-earning population. By

TABLE 6. AVERAGE ANNUAL EARNINGS IN MANU-
FACTURING INDUSTRIES 1958–1961

| | Zambia | | Southern Rhodesia | | Malawi | |
	African employees	Other races†	African employees	Other races†	African employees	Other races†
1958	£101	£1,324	£108	£1,156	£58	£1,067
1959	£112	£1,382	£115	£1,181	£61	£1,139
1960	£118	£1,449	£125	£1,216	£64	£1,173
1961	£137	£1,493	£135	£1,253	£66	£1,153

* Source: *Industrial Guide to Towns,* Federal Ministry of Commerce, Federation of Rhodesia and Nyasaland, 1963.

† Mainly European.

contrast, the selling of labour forms only a small part of annual incomes. In many African countries, money derived from the sale of farm products accounts for more than half of the total domestic product and wages amount to only one-sixth.

Industrial cash crops are the key money-makers for the growing numbers of money-earning rural peasant farmers. Coffee, cocoa, cotton, tea, black wattle and pyrethrum have brought prosperity to thousands of village communities and their first contact with Western manufactured products.

Farmers have moved swiftly to seize new opportunities offered by industrial cash crops. In Ruanda and Burundi after the first coffee trees began to bear fruit there was a great demand for free seedlings; new farming techniques spread to the production of staple food crops. Coffee was introduced in the Ivory Coast in the early 1920's and today there are more than 300,000 hectares of coffee grown exclusively by Africans. The Guisi of Kenya's Kisii Highlands grow black wattle, pyrethrum, coffee and tea and have a co-operative union of 28 societies. The 10,626 members average £10 per year per crop.

Cameroons

Cocoa production is the main source of cash among the Bulu farmers of Cameroons. In 40 years, since its introduction by the

Germans, millions of cocoa trees have been planted; today farmers have an average holding of 2,000 trees. Individual incomes have rapidly increased and the lure of cocoa has touched the roots of the society. "Only fools do not grow cocoa" is a common saying and most urban workers dream of retiring to their little village cocoa garden. Cash incomes are used for house construction and bride-wealth, to purchase bicycles, sewing machines and to pay debts and taxes.

Ghana

In Ghana, the Tetteh Quarsie Hospital at Mampong commemorates the name of the "man who first brought cocoa to Ghana". Peasant farmers in Ghana are among the top cocoa producers in the world; they are Ghana's richest rural cash-earning group and the mainstay of the economy.

Senegal

A similar role is played by the groundnut farmers of Senegal. Groundnuts represent 75 per cent of the value of Senegal's exports. Kaolack and Diourbel regions, which have half the rural population, are the nation's largest groundnut producers. In these regions the average annual income for a 5-member family is £184 as compared with £30 for the nation as a whole.

Tanganyika

Tanganyika's rural development has progressed with the extension of industrial farming and the co-operative movement among Africans. The Chagga, for example, modified their traditional system and now operate the Kilimanjaro National Co-operative Union, the nation's most successful coffee co-operative. In 1961, 45,000 Chagga people raised a £2½m. coffee crop. Their fellow citizens the Nyakusa, Bukoba and Sukuma, have successfully produced cotton and tea as well as coffee. The enterprising Iraqw farmers have mastered the production of European-introduced crops, white potatoes, onions, and wheat, and sell them to Indian traders. In one recent year, prosperous Iraqw livestock owners sold 27,000 cattle, goats and sheep for an estimated $400,000.

The Tanganyika co-operative movement, strengthened by the guidance of the Tanganyika African National Union, is the largest in Africa. There are 800 registered co-operative societies, 40 co-operative unions, a bank and a nation-wide consumer co-operative movement. One-quarter of the total value of Tanganyika's exports, worth £13m., is marketed through co-operatives, a higher proportion than any African state and equalled only by Denmark and Israel in the world.

Northern Nigeria

Traditional knowledge of local soils enhanced by scientific agronomy pays high dividends for peasant farmers. The Hausa of Northern Nigeria responded quickly to the profitable production of groundnuts and tobacco. In Zaria incomes from industrial cash crops constituted one-third of all cash incomes in rural households studied by Mr. Fred J. Pedler in 1948. Today, farmers in this land of variable soils have begun to master scientific farming; incomes have increased and prosperity has spread to other segments of the community.

Kenya

In Kenya, Kikuyu farmers with good land "are producing crops equal to those on European-owned farms", observes Barbara Ward; this indicates, she says, that with opportunity and an appropriate economic framework African farmers and workers can not only do well, but better than their tutors. Melville Herskovits, dean of American anthropologists, once remarked that agriculture was an ancient art created in the tropics and scientifically developed in temperate climates facing relatively simple problems. Today, when Western science and African folk wisdom come together the results are often astounding.

In some nations, as development progresses, key sectors of the rural agricultural community are touched by new opportunities. The rural landed peasant is slowly freed from inefficient agriculture and his indebtedness to money-lenders through the assistance of marketing agencies. He is transformed into a prosperous modern farmer equipped with a broad economic outlook and the equipment to modify his environment. The modern farmer takes part in a variety of regular business activities. As a business partner or member of a collective enterprise he applies the rudiments of accountancy and is able to assess the rational conduct of agricultural production. He can walk into a bank or import–export firm, state his needs and meet his financial responsibilities. In short, the modern farmer is an innovator, the main rural consumer of new products and ideas, a productive and enlightened participant in the life of his country.

PLANTATIONS

Modern plantations are an extension of the industrial world into the backlands of Africa; and for many rural peasants they are stepping-stones to the city. Plantation workers are a significant segment of the wage-earning population; in some West and East African countries they are a third of all employed workers. Plantation work is gang labour, doing "tasks": picking up a cubic yard of stones or "weed-chopping" a line of 75 coffee plants. The tasks get done from sun-up to sundown to the sound of the *panga*, the holler of the gang boss and the deep-throated voices in response.

Plantations have, in the past, operated on the principle of low-paid, inefficient gang labour. However, wages and productivity have increased considerably in the last 10 years; workers make 3s. a day now compared with 6d. a day in the 1930's.

In many East African plantations, workers are given wages plus free housing and food rations. Wages are paid by the *kipande*, a unit of 30 days' labour. An average labourer gets from 40s.–80s.; houseboys £4–5 a month, foremen £7; masons, bricklayers and carpenters £7–10.

Few men are permanent workers; most are migrants on their way to and from home, or seasonal agricultural migrants. They are "target workers", peasants who enter paid employment for a brief period to obtain a sum of money for a specific purpose. This pattern of circular migration is quite common among the large mass of African wage-earners and is an important avenue for the introduction of new ideas and products into their home communities. Professor Elliott P. Skinner of Columbia University observed that the satchel of a Mossi migrant returning to Upper Volta from work in Ghana's cocoa fields contained two kerosene lamps, bottles of kerosene, blue shirts, khaki shorts, hand mirrors, tubes of Thermogene, jars of Vaseline jelly, pairs of sandals and a bottle of perfume. Others return with bicycles and sewing machines. Customs duties on goods imported by migrant workers makes a considerable contribution to national treasuries. Along the Ivory Coast border it is estimated that customs duties on goods imported by migrants earn the National Treasury more than 150m. c.f.a. annually.

MIGRANT LABOURERS

Africa's migrant labourers are an important link in the distribution of manufactured goods and the diffusion of cash incomes. For example, many of the Lugbara of Uganda go south to work the cotton fields and return with £50 cash after several years' work. The Somalis who sail as ship stokers and have immigrant communities in Marseilles, Cardiff and London are an extreme instance of labour migration. They and their kinsmen, traders in Kenya, Aden and Tanzania and miners in South Africa, return home intermittently to invest their savings in camel herds, goats, and business.

The Zambara migrants from the French-speaking nations north of Ghana, who comprise a third of the wage-earners in Ghana's rural and urban areas, provide another example. When they have saved enough to buy a few necessities and presents they return home. Upon arrival they distribute the presents among relatives,

2.
Kano
an
ancient
city
in
change

KANO CITY
WALL
MATA GATE
KOFAR MATA

(ANGINA 1415)

**NEED STRONG HEALTHY BLOOD
FOR AN ACTIVE FAMILY LIFE**

body builders. So take Hommel's regularly. Start
al body in perfect health you need
d. To keep your blood strong and
today ! MEN : with a champion's physique you
will excel at work and play. MOTHERS : you
need iron, proteins and vitamins. In
will enjoy life with a happy family.
need HOMMEL'S HAEMATOGEN
CHILDREN will grow straight and strong, a
gives your family the real
oxygen, iron, and other valuable
credit to their parents.

START STRENGTHENING YOUR BODY TODAY WITH

HOMMEL'S HAEMATOGEN

pay their taxes and settle down to work their land before starting
out on another work tour.

MARKETS AND CHANGE

Markets in Africa emerge from the interaction of internal and
exterior forces of development. The general framework for
market expansion is established, as we have already discussed,
by the ways in which policies and capital shape the structure of
emerging African economies. In such a vast continent, of course,
the pre-conditions for market development vary considerably.
However, in each domestic economy a modern and a traditional
subsistence sector exist side by side. Modernization in either sector
generates work, money and markets. In rural areas the generative
force is the transformation of peasants from a subsistence livelihood
to the production of cash crops for export. In urban centres of
employment, highly-capitalized mines and industry place money
value on labour.

In sum, development expands the sale of crops, labour and
services in a money economy. New dynamic situations generate
needs, create savings and disposable incomes and the means of
spending earned wages. The expansion of urban shops and internal networks of trade introduces more manufactured goods
and increases the incentive to work to obtain them. Thus, in
the rapidly developing arenas of change, from cities to the
remotest coffee *shambas*, Africans are induced to become cash-
earners and consumers and markets are generated by their
efforts.

The markets of tomorrow, and the day after tomorrow, are
fashioned from these six crucibles of economic change, the city,
agro-industrial towns, mining centres, the cash-crop farmers,
plantation and migrant workers. A rational assessment of future
markets and consumer needs, whether undertaken by businesses
or governments, begins with the question: "Who are the clientèle
for new products and the potential audiences for product information in Africa? Is it the 5s.-a-day worker who shops in the

market-place, the field hand at the cross-roads canteen, an urban mass market 'still-a-borning', the growing expatriate community or the clerks and administrators who stock their homes from the shelves of an urban store?" The answer is, it is no *one* of them, it is *all* of them.

PROFILE: THE CITY AS
A MARKET AREA

THREE CITIES, Kano and Lagos, Nigeria, and Wad Medani, Sudan, illustrate the crucial aspects of the urban environment which affect the tastes, attitudes and consumption habits of urban Africans. Kano is an ancient city that has adapted to Western economic influence and become a large urban nucleus. Lagos, capital of Nigeria, is a thriving seaport and industrial complex. Wad Medani, in the rich Gezira cotton-growing region of the Sudan, has grown up along with a prosperous cash-crop tenant farming class.

Kano, "Giant of the North"

Kano City, "Giant of the North", capital of the ancient Hausa kingdom, is a teeming commercial *entrepôt* on the cross-roads of Middle Africa. Kano's rich commerce and trade in groundnuts, hides and skins, her expanding industries and fertile land, attract workers from all over Nigeria. Today there are more than 200,000 urban residents. In addition, 1½ million people live within a 30-mile radius of the city, making Kano one of the most densely-populated urban regions in Africa. The importance of Kano takes on additional meaning because it is the largest and most industrialized city in the northern region which as we noted before, is larger than any African nation.

In the Central city called Birnin Kano, where the Muslim Hausa-Fulani people live, the tower of the mosque casts its shadow on an organic mosaic of mud houses enclosed by a great rambling wall. To the south lies the Emir's palace, noble and imperial, the native authority offices and the well-kept compounds of courtiers and salaried employees. To the east, amidst the turbulence of the

55

old camel caravanserai, the new textile mill and railway, are the compounds of the blind and the vast residences of the Dantata trading family under the shadow of which lie the cattle yards and the teeming workers' quarters. To the north and west, lying green and fallow, are the semi-rural districts whose fertile soil comprises half the area within the city.

Blessedness, fame, riches and prestige are the traditional goals, and their attainment orders a man's life in relation to other men. A complex tapestry of social classes from rich to poor, *saraki* to *talauci* has developed. The Emir emerges from his palace on a white-tasselled mule, to the booming sounds of Dane guns and gongs, flanked by courtiers, musicians, praise-singers and archers; and as he passes, the praises drop before him: "*Ranke Y Dade!*" ("Long live the Chief!") "*Allah ya kara maka imani!*" ("May Allah increase faith in you!")

Down the scale of respect and deference each social status may be identified: the *attajirai* or wealthy, richly-attired traders, contractors, *alkalis* and Native Authority officials; the "middle-class" *matsakai:* shop owners, lorry drivers, barber-doctors and *malams*; the *musu-karamin karfu* or "those who have little strength": urban peasants, labourers, house servants, musicians and dyers; and finally the *fakirai*, the indigent and poverty-stricken who beg "alms for the love of Allah".

Economic growth has brought new systems of work and morality, streets teem with labourers, immigrants and transients, the streets echo to the hooves of cattle. Family land tenure gives way to individual tenure, rooms are let, property values and rents rise, houses are bought and sold for investment and speculation. From Kano's dense working-class quarters come the tenacious traders known throughout Africa and the modern Hausa proletariat.

New classes emerge: salaried employees, factory workers, contractors and middle-men, domestics in European homes, and shop boys in the large firms. A hierarchy of social mobility develops around incomes, social status and education. Incomes expand, ranging from the Emir's £14,000 to the officials' and traders' £600-£300 and downwards to the 4s.-a-day labourers.

New enclaves grow up outside the walls of the Muslim Hausa

city: Europeans living in the Government residential area, Levantine traders living above their shops in the "Syrian" quarter; and Ibo and Yoruba workers in the *Sabon Gari*. The *Sabon Gari*, or "new town," is the largest of these localities; the residents are southern Nigerian labourers, artisans, clerks and professionals who followed Lugard and the railway north to new opportunities. In the course of 50 years, these Christian-educated wage-workers have occupied strategic positions in the modern economy. Today, 40,000 southerners, a quarter of the city's population, are the focal point of Westernization in the African community.

Southern Nigerians in Kano are mediators between two worlds. They are bound to the Hausa community, lying across an open field, by a web of footpaths of trade and social intercourse. And at the same time they are innovators of change. Like Pa Barlatt Hughes, venerable "Mayor of Sabon Gari" and the first local African to ride a bicycle, these southerners are promoters of new styles of life: hotels, cinemas, Western-type schools and churches; they are the major African market for manufactured goods.

The Hausa community reflects all these external forces. The meaning of independence and development trickles down every narrow footpath into every mud house. In the market stalls battered copies of foreign books appear: Kennedy's *Profiles in Courage, Islam or Marxism* from the English Working Mission and President Nasser's *Philosophy of the Revolution*. Hausa women shop for canned goods in the European, Syrian and Indian stores and go to work in factories without veils. Their girl-children go to school and families of marriageable daughters seek more valuable presents from prospective bridegrooms. *Malamin tsibbu*, who practise traditional medicine, give injections and sell powdered aspirin and "pep-pills", purchased at Kingsway Stores, along with ancient curatives, *rawaya* root for yellow fever, *bahin* incense for chills and *shabbai yammal* for "bad breath". And in the fields the peasant farmer and his wife pause in wonder at the jet plane rising from Kano's International Airport and turn back to work muttering: "*Allah ya sani*" (Allah knows all).

Metropolitan Lagos

Lagos, capital of Africa's most populous nation, is one of the fastest-growing cities in Africa. It has changed from a small Yoruba town with walled houses and small farm plots to a metropolitan industrializing giant. Today 400,000 people crowd Lagos Island and 300,000 spill over on to the mainland. Each day new migrants enter the city from all over West Africa; three migrants take up residence for every child born.

Lagos is a city on the move; 100,000 wage-workers stream daily into the industries, shops and markets of the city to perform the new rituals of urban life. Every morning and evening thousands of cars and cycles cross Carter Bridge, the sole vehicular connection between Lagos, Apapa and the suburbs.

Most of the workers are employed by the Federal Government, municipal agencies and private commercial establishments. Monthly incomes range from £7 for unskilled labourers to £15 for skilled manual workers and £18 for clerks.

Central Lagos on the island has half the city's population. Most of the householders are Muslim Yoruba or migrants from northern Sudanic areas. Home for many workers and their families is a 54s per-month room in a six-roomed cement block structure with a corrugated-iron roof.

Trading in textiles, provisions, cigarettes and foodstuffs is a key source of income for city dwellers. The types of traders range from the large importer and middleman with an annual turnover of £100,000 to the side-street hawker of pencils and combs. Trading is a more lucrative, though less predictable, occupation for men; many of them have a monthly income higher than office clerks. Trading is also the main source of cash income for working women; three-quarters of the working women in Central Lagos engage in some form of trading activities.

Lagosians spend their money on a wide range of consumer items — cars, jewellery, processed foods, home improvements and household items, radios, gramphones, dining sets, cutlery and refrigerators. An increasing amount of family budgets is spent on newspapers, books and children's education.

In the next quarter-century a new Metropolitan Lagos will arise with industries and residential areas stretching 20 miles into the interior. Already, an efficient rail line carrying 200,000 passengers a year and roads accommodating 7,000 vehicles a day link the thriving business of Lagos Island, the port and industrial estates of Apapa, and the mainland as far as Agege and the Ikeja industrial area. Agege is a fast-growing town of 55,000, 20 miles from Lagos; by 1984 its population will reach 200,000. To provide new work opportunities the present commercial farming of citrus fruits, meat and dairy products will be augmented by canning, packing and refrigeration industries. The near-by Ikeja industrial area and technical institutes when expanded will provide the nucleus of a new Nigerian skilled working class.

Wad Medani, Sudan

Man's civilization began in fertile river valleys and plains like those of the Sudan's Gezira region and many differing peoples have left their imprint on contemporary life: Libyans, Greeks, Romans, Orientals, Arabs and Africans. Today, the Gezira region is the scene of one of Africa's largest and most profitable cotton-growing areas. By 1964, some 40 years after its inception, the net income of individual tenant farmers has risen to $250 per year and the Sudan Government has been able to balance its budget, to increase social welfare services and finance new undertakings. Cotton has placed the Sudan in the world market and brought new farming skills to Gezira peasants.

With the development of the Gezira scheme, social patterns in the rural agricultural area changed and life began to focus on a near-by city, Wad Medani. Wad Medani lies along the Blue Nile and is a major marketing, administrative, transport, hydro-electric and light industrial centre. It is linked with Khartoum, the nation's capital, by rail, air, water and telephone communications. But, more important, it lies on the great east/west route from Ghana and Nigeria to Ethiopia and the Middle East; and along the great north/south route from Alexandria to Capetown.

Wad Medani has grown from a small settlement founded by

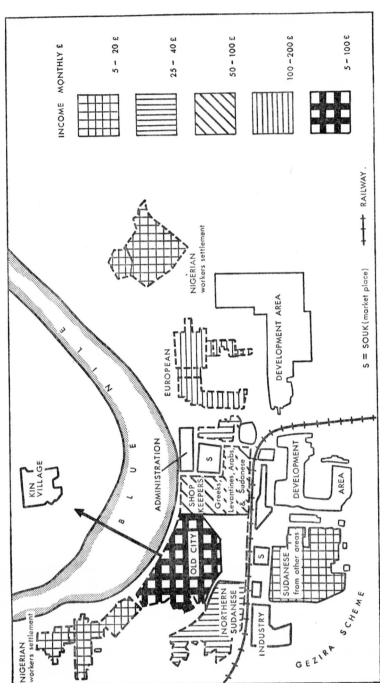

Townsmen and Strangers: Income, Culture and Residence in Wad Medani, Sudan

the followers of a religious leader to a town of 60,000, the nation's fourth largest city. Its population is expected to reach 100,000 by 1985. The major factors causing this rapid population expansion have been the economic development of the Gezira scheme. The cash economy attracted migrant labourers from southern Sudan and northern Nigeria and many of their migrants settled in the town. As factories developed there was a decrease in the population gainfully employed in farming and an increase in urban industrial labourers and shopkeepers.

The urban area of the city with its ginning mills and railway and cinema is the new centre of social contact between the river tradesmen, farmers of the Nile banks, the new industrial working-class, the immigrant African population of Nubians, Bejas, Dinka and Hausa and the various foreign populations of Greeks, Armenians and Indian traders. In the new labouring quarters like Medani El Gadeeda, mud and wattle houses give way before cement, the mosques compete with the modern entertainment areas and the donkey is overtaken by the motorcar. Mass housing and improved residential stability, civic allegiance and improved health and education draw more people into the consumer market.

CHAPTER FIVE

THE CHAIN OF DISTRIBUTION

EVERY DAY millions of pounds' worth of food, clothing and capital equipment move along the chain of distribution which binds European factories to the consumer in the remotest African village. The links in this chain are the large merchant houses and shops, the *dukkas* of Asian, Levantine, Arab and Indian wholesale and retail traders and the African market-place with its teeming masses of buyers, traders and middlemen. The sale of consumer goods takes place in widely differing settings: the modern shop, the African market-place, the cross-roads *dukka* or under a shady tree. The sale of a single item often involves differing ethnic groups, "mother-tongues" and cultural habits. This chapter explores the ways in which modern products reach the African consumer and the relevance of patterns of distribution for the satisfaction of consumer needs.

THE EUROPEAN LINK

All African countries depend on Western industrial nations for the satisfaction of basic needs, food, clothing or shelter. The degree of dependence ranges from 75–90 per cent in Senegal or Tanganyika to 40–50 per cent in Egypt and Ghana. The introduction of manufactured products rests almost entirely in the hands of locally-based expatriates or their designated representatives. There are five basic agencies through which this is accomplished: export–import merchant houses, sole indent agents, stockist-distributors, subsidiary companies and large urban shops.

Export merchants perform two main functions: buying manufactured goods from Europe to sell in Africa and buying African raw materials to sell on the European market. They have a well-developed organization which provides personnel, transport and distribution, and warehousing facilities. They often give credit to traders and finance the production of primary raw materials. Export merchants have the advantage of knowing local dealers well but are often too large to deal adequately with all local distribution outlets. The trend today is towards selling imported products through a chain of subsidiary shops.

The British exporter can also supply African consumers through the order of the sole agent. The sole indent agent works on a commission basis and is useful when the market for a product is scattered over a large area. One of the disadvantages of this system is that the agent handles many items and his facilities may be too limited really to "sell" each manufacturer's product efficiently and effectively.

The stockist-distributor buys goods from overseas on his own account and sells to both wholesalers and the retail trade. He deals mainly in capital goods, equipment, consumer durables, chemicals, pharmaceuticals and branded products. His services are attractive to businessmen and consumers because he deals more directly with customers and provides repairs and servicing.

In addition subsidiary and branch companies are recent developments and tend to develop as the demand for products increases. Another recent development is the large department store chain; some, like Kingsway shops, are directly associated with large export merchants, others like Chellaram's are independent expatriate firms.

THE DUKKA

The next step in the distributive process is controlled by the "middle group": Lebanese, Syrians and Indians in West Africa and Indians and Arabs in East Africa. After the European export-import houses and shops, the "middle group" controls the largest outlets for consumer products they have a greater degree of daily contact with Africans. The members of this group perform a variety of functions; they act as middlemen for foreign concerns, and as proprietors of urban shops and chains of department stores.

More typically, in many parts of rural Africa it is the small shop and its "middle group" owner which the African knows best. Once we leave the urban shops, the next modern selling situation for Western products takes place inside a small wooden shack in a rural area. The name for this type of shop varies throughout the Continent but I have chosen to use the East African *dukka* as an illustration.

The *dukka* is a general shop found largely in rural areas; it is a cross between the African market-place and the modern urban shop. Selling takes place indoors and it is the rural African's first contact with the Western buying situation. The typical owner, or *dukkawala*, is an Asian or Levantine; in recent years, however, many Africans have become *dukkawalas*.

Inside the drab windowless wooden building, modern display counters, Coca-Cola machines, fridges and colourful posters stand out against the wooden racks and shelves filled with goods from all over the world. Every member of the family takes a part in selling and the ever-present clerk or porter is there to pack and load supplies. You can buy almost anything you want, at any time of day, and at night the *dukka*'s paraffin lamp is the sole stab of light in the rural darkness.

There are two types of *dukkas* in terms of goods sold: the European-orientated *dukka* which deals in perishables and luxury items, and the dry-goods *dukka*.

In towns with a large European population or demand for Western products the *dukka* sells such items as canned goods, staples, cheese, butter and margarine (though not usually eggs and milk), beer, liquor and soft drinks, tobacco and cigarettes, cosmetics, cooking utensils, brooms, dishes, paint, radios, lamps, torches, batteries, pharmaceuticals, shirts, children's clothes, cameras and stationery.

The dry-goods *dukka* carries staple foods and a wide range of household equipment such as basins, buckets, towels, blankets, paraffin, hardware, cheap clothing and shoes, cloth and sewing equipment. The owner's trademark is the ever-present sewing machine in operation outside the door.

Normally, if a community is large enough to support two *dukkas* they will divide according to these two types. If there is only one *dukka* it will tend to be of the dry-goods type and lay on beer, cigarettes, sweets, biscuits and soft drinks which appeal to travellers.

The *dukka* is, above all, a centre of communication. It is the local post office, travel agency, bus stop, petrol station and transport centre. The *dukkawala* serves as middleman in various business negotiations; he transports passengers and goods to remote areas. His shop is a community centre and a stopping place for mobile banks, health units and cinemas.

Dukkas owned by Africans tend to develop near large farms, cross-roads and labour camps. They do a thriving business with resident labourers especially on week-ends and paydays. In East and Central Africa, where certain areas were set aside as "African reserves", African-owned *dukkas* became profitable enterprises. In Kenya's Kericho district, in 1962, 600 shops were owned and operated by Kipsigis *entrepreneurs*; 15 per cent of them were individually operated, the remainder were owned by groups of partners. In Uganda, trading shops called *hoteli* are located at cross-roads to cater for travellers. In the evening the *hoteli* becomes a pub where the locals can sip a pint of beer and listen to the radio.

THE AFRICAN MARKET-PLACE

Most Western products pass from hand to hand in the African market-place, not in the smart European-owned shops or the *dukkas* of Asians and Levantines. Few African governments or Western companies have analysed the economic importance of indigenous market-places. Only recently have anthropologists themselves brought together many disparate observations into a monumental volume entitled *Markets in Africa*.[1]

The market-place is the site where buyers and sellers meet. African market-places are commonly located at cross-roads, lorry parks, railway stations and centres of transport and labour concentration. The economic activities of the market-place are regulated by a market principle; it involves the operation of price-mechanisms by the forces of supply and demand. This market principle regulates the production and distribution of goods for local consumption as well as the export and import of commodities which form a part of the world network of trade. The African market economy includes, therefore, sellers, products, a transaction site, a range of occupations associated with production and distribution, buyers and a "price-mechanism".

There are three ways in which the needs of people are satisfied through the exchange of goods and services in the African market-place: the age-old practice of barter, the modern money economy and the more common combination of both the money and barter systems. Each has a particular constellation of market factors.

The traditional barter economy is associated with an earlier stage of Africa's history. It grows naturally out of the African past and expresses what Adam Smith called "man's natural propensity to truck, barter, traffic and exchange". In the more remote areas and among semi-nomadic groups, there are few specific market-place sites and casual inter-personal transactions form the basis of the market principle.

The money-barter economy represents a mid-point along the continuum between the old barter system and the modern money economy. In this case rudimentary market-places exist and the market principle operates peripherally. Peasants are not dependent, however, on the market for the acquisition of the basic necessities of life.

The market-place and market principle as we understand them today assume full importance in large cities and towns. In the urban area people sell their labour, land or crops to get cash, food, clothing and shelter. The market-place is the primary source of daily needs and cash income of both buyers and sellers. The growth and adaptation of the money economy to the needs of Africans within the market-place has proceeded rapidly in West African cities.

What is the African market-place like and what types of products are sold there? Market-places differ in size and variety of goods and services supplied to meet consumer needs. Most people shop at the daily market and at the big "Saturday" market once a week. In many regions there is a system of rotating marketing days which assures that every town will have a market day where a greater variety of products are offered. Fringe markets and night markets along highways and at road intersections assure the housewife that she can buy a few last-minute items without travelling too far.

The local trading centre is a main point of entry of manufactured products into African life. In an Ethiopian market town, Arab traders sell Egyptian tennis shoes, Czechoslovak razor blades, English Lux soap cakes and American sun-glasses. In southern Dahomey, market traders sell canned foods, perfume, cosmetics, drugs, talcum powder, quinine, and laxatives alongside antimony (used as an eye-shadow) and chalk for pregnant women. Even in the smallest market enamelled basins have taken the place of earthenware pots, and jerry cans filled with pebbles are used as musical instruments. In larger markets workers can buy bicycles, pressure lamps, iron beds and transistors.

The circulation of goods and services is only one function of the market-place; it is also the focal point of many social activities and ways of life. It is a common ground, a meeting-place for people and authorities, and a forum of "public opinion" where many differing points of view are expressed. When market-places are under the jurisdiction of traditional authorities they also serve as judicial and religious centres.

Market-places are centres for news from home, official announcements, political rallies and the starting point for mass literacy, health and community development programmes. For many persons the market-place is the sole contact zone for the handling of Western products and discussion of their merits.

"Going to market" provides an opportunity to buy a drink, flirt with the girls, meet friends and contract alliances. In Upper Volta, a Mossi man talking to the anthropologist Elliott P. Skinner[2] expressed this point succinctly: "I must go to the market, and when I get there I look for three persons — my girl-friend, my debtor and my enemy; if I do not know whether any of them are at the market I am ill at ease. And when I go to the market and do not see them all, the market is not good."

The market-place is a lunch-room and meeting-place for school-children, a haven for migrants, and a bargain centre for the clerk and his family. It is a "Hyde Park" for politicians and hallowed ground for traditional custom: infant-naming ceremonies, funerals and communal rites.

Beneath the hustle-bustle of market life there are rational forms of organization and division of labour. Custom regulates participation in trading; for example, women may be restricted to dealing in foodstuffs, imported cloths and all local trade while men deal in livestock, new instruments of production and long-distance trading.

Age may also be a factor in determining who sells certain commodities. Traffic in medical plants in southern Dahomey is reserved for old women and forbidden to the young. Often women in mourning are traditionally forbidden to trade in food, to prepare food containing salt or to make *akasa*, a staple food. And when you ask, "Tell me, Mother, why aren't you trading today?", she replies "Death has taken *akasa* away from me and filled my hands with wood."

Social custom also regulates the relationships between buyers and sellers. Preserving one's honour is always an important aspect of trading among the Hausa. If the buyer's status is unknown to the trader he must guess how high to set the price without running the risk of being mocked. Both, then, "play a game". The trader makes veiled threats to the hesitant buyer to cover his own discomfort. The customer may reply "Come on now, give me a good chicken; I am not expecting a hyena for dinner" (i.e., "this bird is so old and tough it is only fit for a hyena") and so on until the deal is concluded with appropriate salutations. If, on the other hand, the customer is a "stranger", a European for example, the problem is very simple, customarily the seller charges double the ordinary price and the deal is concluded promptly!

The market-place is a main source of income for many groups in the socio-economic structure: sellers and producers, market managers, and subsidiary occupational groups, e.g., porters and policemen. Its revenue also supports the exchequer of local governments, for example, in Kenya's Kipsigis district, where cash sales in markets average more than £21,000 a year, the council took in an estimated £3,000 worth of fees in 1962.

Astrid Nypan has presented some interesting data on the daily sales turnover in Accra markets in her study on *Market Trade*, for the Economics Research Division, University of Ghana.[3] In Accra, Miss Nypan found 11,000 market-stallholders in 11 markets and an estimated 25,000 traders. She calculated a mean daily turnover of 76s. on goods ranging from 2s. for inexpensive green wrapping leaves, to 1100s. for such costly items as barrels of oil. The estimated daily turnover in 4 markets was 346,144s., among a total of 4,746 traders.

For all these complex reasons the African market-place will remain a common feature of African life for some time to come. As Fred J. Pedler points out in his book, *Economic Geography of West Africa*:[4]

"Although the number of shops in West Africa has increased, the markets are likely to remain comparatively more important than in Europe, for the climate of West Africa is suitable for open-air trading all the year round. The market-stall, with its low capital cost, is a low-cost distributor compared with shops. Furthermore, the market is a valuable social institution . . . It provides many of the amenities of the department store and self-service which are regarded as advanced retailing techniques in New York and London."

THE TRADER

Traders are the human links between Western products and the African consumer. They buy their goods from distributors and sell at a profit along a complex continuum of trading relationships to the peasant in the remotest village. There is a wide variety of traders from the itinerant hawker to the highly-successful businessman using modern accounting techniques. Alhasin dan Tata of Kano, for example, has used bookkeeping and "big-business" methods to build a huge trading empire from Leopoldville to the Mediterranean coast.

Traders can be classified in a number of ways. Perhaps it is easiest to think of them as ranging in degree from prosperous bulk wholesalers, who buy direct from European or "middle-group" importing firms, to small retailers. Starting with the bulk whole-saler, goods travel to his regular trader-customers, who buy smaller lots and then sell them on to their trader-customers, and so on, in an ever-widening chain. Larger traders may buy cases and sell tins; the smallest trader in the chain may buy a pound packet of sugar and sell single cubes.

Traders in the first degree are "credit" customers of importing firms; they have a passbook which entitles them to buy a specified amount of goods. These wholesale customers receive a monetary commission on each sale; it is not uncommon for a successful woman trader to accumulate £6,000 worth of commission with one firm over 30 years.

As a petty trader becomes more skilled and successful in the sale of Western items he may progress from one level in the trading hierarchy to another. For example, a youth might start with 3s., and purchase a box of matches, a pack of cigarettes and a bar of laundry soap. With 15s. he could buy a 4-gallon tin of kerosene and sell it by the beer-bottleful for a tidy profit. With £10 he could get a stock of singlets, towels, scarves, buttons and thread, inexpensive costume jewellery, 3d. exercise books and 1s. ball-point pens, and so on.

Traders perform many important economic functions within national economies; where they trade across national boundaries they bind several economies together. The *fatauci* Hausa move cattle, groundnuts, cotton, locust beans and cloth down to Lagos and return with Western products, kola nuts, ginger and Yoruba cloth. The *dillali* Hausa traders act as middlemen between the cattle-owning Bororo Fulani of Niger and their markets in Kano. Prosperous traders have their fingers in many pies; some are part-owners of tractors and earth-moving equipment, others are *rentiers*, builders, landowners and maintain huge fleets of lorries to transport goods and passengers.

Traders are their own best consumers of Western goods and hence a powerful stimulus for imitation by lesser folk in the community. Most have radios and bicycles, many have cars and use Western tableware, sleep in beds with springs and mattresses, wear the latest-style shoes and carry umbrellas. Their houses are larger than average with permanent metal roofs, elaborate doors, and walls of cement.

How does a shipment of manufactured goods start its way through the African trading system? Typically, the process begins when a large importing firm lands a shipment of, let us say, underwear on the docks. The shipment may be earmarked for an export-import merchant house or bought-up by large wholesalers who are able to acquire large stocks on credit. They get in touch with a trader who takes £1,000-worth of goods against a deposit of £200; he then sells the goods to smaller dealers, each taking £50–£100-worth. Some of them sell retail; others sell to village and petty traders. In this way manufactured goods are bought in bulk at the dockside, then sold in increasingly smaller units.

This chain of distribution, which has many flaws, nevertheless provides trading opportunities for African *entrepreneurs* who do not have large amounts of capital but do have access to short-term credit. Since goods must be disposed of quickly, an elaborate organization of middlemen is devised. Modifications in the distributive process take place as more traders or combines of traders can afford to build warehouses and to keep capital tied up in unsold stock for long periods of time.

Village and petty traders are by far the most numerous type of traders in Africa. The village trader has many functions. He buys local produce to sell to European companies for a commission. He is a pawnbroker and moneylender. He is a conveyor belt by which goods are distributed through vast territories where transport facilities are inadequate. He stimulates innovation and ensures that nothing of value — packing cases, old tins, bottles and paper — goes to waste.

Petty traders serve many useful purposes in cities and rural villages. By "breaking bulk" a trader brings goods to the consumer in a quantity and at a price that he can afford. He also saves his customer much time and trouble. For example, a village housewife near Ibadan may want some cloth to wear to a special family celebration; if it is not available locally, the trader carries her order to Ibadan; one of his contacts goes to Lagos and buys it from an intermediary who has got it from a textile importer. Despite this complex process of supplying consumers, the petty trader can often bring goods to the housewife more efficiently than she could get them herself. She is saved a long journey and loss of her own working time; and in the end she might not have been able to find exactly what she wanted on such favourable terms.

Eventually, as the ever-widening circle of trade pierces the hinterlands, Western products reach the rural peasant and nomad. In North Somalia, for example, a small trader draws a loan from his kinsman and ventures out to buy skins from nomadic herdsmen. The skins are sent to a wholesaler-exporter in a regional commercial centre. He then sends back razor blades, cigarettes, cloth and foodstuffs which the trader retails at a profit.

In the future many changes will come to the African market. Already Ghana has made a number of important modifications. The Ghana National Trading Corporation has plans to operate mobile shops in inaccessible rural areas. In urban areas where the place of work is far from the central market area "People's shops" are being opened to enable workers to shop during their off-work hours.

Africa's chain of distribution, a zigzag patchwork over the Continent, binds different cultures and economies together. Tenuous and involved as it is, it has many predictable elements and can be subjected to quantification and analysis. What is the input of goods? What is the direction and intensity of product flow? What is the volume of sales at given selling points and related price changes? All these questions lend themselves to distribution research and can lead to relevant answers about the varying situations in which African consumers come into contact with modern products.

REFERENCES

1 BOHANNAN, PAUL, and DALTON, GEORGE (eds.) *Markets in Africa,* Northwestern University Press, 1962.

2 I am grateful to DR. E. P. SKINNER, author of *The Mossi of Upper Volta,* Stanford University Press, 1964, for this·information.

3 NYPAN, ASTRID, *Market Trade,* Economics Research Division, University of Ghana, African Business Series, **2.** 1960. Cf Peter Garlick. *African Traders in Kumasi,* University College of Ghana. Economics Research Division, Accra, 1959, and "African and Levantine Trading Firms in Ghana", Nigerian Institute of Social and Economic Research Conference Proceedings, Ibadan, December, 1960.

4 PEDLER, FRED J., *Economic Geography of West Africa,* Longmans Green and Company Limited, London, 1955.

CHAPTER SIX

THE CHANGING
AFRICAN CONSUMER

TODAY, AFRICA's four most affluent consumers are governments, social institutions, *élites* and Europeans. They buy 60–80 per cent of the imported consumer goods and durables. The mass market for many items, however, is composed of urban workers. In the next 10 years, if only 10 per cent of Africa's population attain an annual wage of £300, they will have a purchasing power of close to £10,000m. And the trend is in that direction.

Standards of living are rising at an accelerating speed. They will increase more rapidly still as the output of goods and services rise with the advance of technology, investment and manpower skills. By 1984 Africa's standard of living will have risen as much, in 20 years, as it did in the first 60 years of this century. Furthermore, cultural tastes and habits will change as more people become better off. They will want new things out of life and be prepared to work to get them.

Thus, in a complex but inter-related way, increasing opportunities for well-paid jobs and education have their consequent effects on buying habits. In this chapter I shall deal with the crucial determinants of the changing behaviour of African consumers and look at the trends that appear on the horizon of Africa's Century of Development.

OCCUPATION AND INCOME

Occupation, income and education are the three most important variables associated with consumer behaviour in Africa. And, they are the three factors which are changing most rapidly.

As the modern economy encroaches on the traditional subsistence sector, new jobs fashion a new occupational status structure and, as a result, men are ranked among their fellows. In general, the emerging rank order of jobs and social status can be roughly schematized as follows:

Cash income	Occupation-status
£3,000 plus	1 The highest officials, administrators and parliamentarians, chiefs of large areas.
£1,000–3,000	2 Professionals: lawyers, doctors, university teachers; and rich wholesale traders.
£700–1,000	3 Civil servants, teachers, office workers, and administrative personnel.
£600–2,000	4 The self-employed: landlords, builders and contractors, lorry-owners, shop-owners, big cash-crop farmers, artisans who own cottage industries, lesser chiefs and clan officials, elders, religious ministers and large retail traders.
£240–600	5 Skilled technicians and workers in modern industries, seamstresses and trade unionists, small cash-crop farmers.
£60–120	6 Unskilled labourers, petty traders.
£20–60	7 Casual migrants.
£5–20	8 Peasants with some share in the land.
Less than £5	9 The unemployed and landless.

In the next decade the relative position of these occupation-income groups will undergo many more changes. Already the proportion of hard, unskilled jobs is declining and the number of skilled machine operators is increasing. More women are entering the labour force, more skilled workers are young educated persons. The gap in wage levels and standards of living will decrease, especially between unskilled and skilled workers and between factory technicians and civil servants. In many parts of Africa today, some traders have higher monthly incomes than clerks, and some cash-crop farmers make more than city workers.

As more people enter into organized economic activities, wage

TABLE 7. EDUCATIONAL SITUATION IN AFRICA TODAY*

Country	Enrolment by level		Ratio of enrolment to school-age population by level			
	First level (primary school)	Second level (secondary school)	First level		Second level	
	No. of students	No. of students	Estimated pop. 5–14 years (000)	Ratio of enrolment adjusted to pop. 5–14 for duration of school	Estimated pop. 15–19 years (000)	Ratio of enrolment adjusted to pop. 15–19 for duration of school
Bastutoland	119,478	3,042	165	90·5	67	4·5
Bechuanaland	31,193	485	84	46·4	34	1·4
Cameroons (U.K.)	54,844	1,404	391	20·0	164	0·8
Cameroon	371,421	13,808	795	77·8	332	3·0
Central African Republic	45,774	1,480	280	27·2	117	0·9
Chad	53,973	1,473	647	13·8	271	0·4
Congo (Brazzaville)	78,962	3,259	187	70·3	78	3·0
Congo (Leopoldville)	1,460,753	51,671	3,405	71·5	1,426	3·0
Dahomey	81,107	3,618	431	31·3	180	1·4
Ethiopia	158,005	8,144	5,338	3·8	2,235	0·5
Gabon	39,763	1,156	101	65·7	41	2·0
Gambia	4,595	794	72	10·7	30	2·2
Ghana	483,425	178,581	1,208	66·7	506	29·4
Guinea	79,373	4,563	671	19·7	281	1·1

Liberia			22·4	127	
Malagasy Republic	364,217	25,290	1,299	46·7	544	1·4
Mali	42,053	2,749	918	7·7	384	0·5
Mauritania	6,493	291	155	7·0	65	0·3
Mauritius	109,370	16,243	153	100·0	64	18·1
Niger	11,811	395	603	3·3	252	0·1
Nigeria	2,545,336	117,414	8,129	42·9	3,403	2·9
Lagos	56,688	6,376	83	85·4	35	15·2
N. Region	230,000	8,098	4,439	7·4	1,858	0·3
W. Region	1,037,377	73,282	1,657	100·0	694	8·8
E. Region	1,221,271	29,658	1,950	78·3	816	3·0
Rhodesia & Nyasaland						
N. Rhodesia	243,926	4,948	566	53·9	237	2·6
Nyasaland	269,693	3,042	667	50·5	279	1·4
S. Rhodesia	433,459	6,485	649	83·5	272	3·0
Ruanda-Urundi	246,149	5,480	1,156	35·5	484	0·9
Senegal	80,473	6,102	561	23·8	235	1·9
Sierra Leone	74,481	8,277	590	21·0	247	2·8
Somalia	16,485	1,828	325	10·2	136	0·8
Sudan	288,395	60,941	2,819	12·8	1,180	6·5
Swaziland	29,934	1,066	67	55·9	27	4·5
Tanganyika	422,832	15,315	2,193	24·1	918	2·1
Togo	78,689	2,373	411	31·8	172	1·0
Uganda	501,699	41,633	1,603	52·2	671	4·4
Upper Volta	40,543	2,447	991	6·8	415	0·4
Zanzibar	14,982	1,232	75	25·0	31	5·0

Source : Statistics of population and pupils taken by the Unesco Statistics Division from official publications and country replies to the questionnaires, 1957–1960.

*Source: Final report: *Conference of African States on the Development of Education in Africa, Addis Ababa, 15–25 May, 1961.* UNESCO.

differentials tend to be reduced, particularly between the lower and semi-skilled levels. The gaps which hitherto separated the largest segment of the communities — peasant-workers — from a small skilled minority are being rapidly bridged. Trade unions, co-operatives, and job-training programmes are major operative forces in this trend. By the end of this decade workers who climb the job ladder will make twice as much money as they do now and the consequences will be felt in all areas of life.

PATTERNS OF EDUCATION

Education is the key to occupational mobility and higher income. Education in its fullest sense, training for service as well as reward, and the revitalization of communities through fundamental education and community development, is a stepping stone for a better life.

All families want their children to attain higher levels of education. When a village has "educational fever" it can put up a school in a fortnight and clear a path five feet wide to the main road for the teacher's jeep. More African mothers, like their counterparts in England, are going through that once-in-a-lifetime *rite de passage*, seeing their children through the 11-plus exams! A generation of children born in the first year of the Decade of Freedom will be teenagers shortly and educated adults in another 10 years.

In an expanding job market, education tends to lead to a better job and higher wages. Being a clerk in an office is the goal most often cited by school-children. A clerk's status is associated with a white collar, modern surroundings and a secure annual income. Wages in fact rise considerably with a few grades of education. In Ethiopia a graduate with eight grades of elementary school can become a teacher or clerk earning $125 (Ethiopian) per month. This is as much in one month as the average land-owning peasant gets in one year. The Lugbara of Uganda call the successful educated mobile persons the "new people" because they do new things, consume modern products, and live in, or close to, cities.

THE NEW ÉLITES

In emergent Africa a premium is placed on acquiring new skills. Development means the creation of skilled human capital in administration, the professions, artisan crafts, commerce and agriculture. As more people attain these skills they make more money and occupy highly-valued places in the nation and local community. "New Africans" appear at all levels of society. In their daily work they handle modern tools, products, concepts and ideologies.

At the pinnacle of modern society, some people develop a collective character by working and associating together, and living in the same residential areas. They hold a pre-eminent position over others; many of their members are popular heroes whose tastes and preferences are widely imitated.

What are the occupations and status characteristics of Africa's top-most *élites*? In general, people rank four groups at the top of the status hierarchy: public officials, traditional rulers of vast domains, professionals in medicine, law, university teaching and the senior civil service, and wealthy traders and businessmen.

One of the few studies of African *élites* is *The New Nigerian Elite* by the American sociologists, Hugh and Mabel Smythe.[1] Their findings, based on an exhaustive study of almost 1,000 persons, represent an estimated 20,000 Nigerian *élites* and corroborate the more general characteristics suggested by observers in other parts of the Continent.

Ten characteristics distinguish Nigeria's top-most *élites*; they are:

1 *well-educated professionals:* almost half of them hold university degrees from Europe, England and America and 45 per cent completed secondary school;
2 *young:* half of them are less than 40 years of age;
3 *civic-minded, top-level administrators:* three-quarters of them are holders of public offices in Federal and Regional governments;
4 *well paid:* their salaries, £3,000–£14,000, place them in the top 0·01 per cent of society;

5 *new élites*: two-thirds of them have risen from the common ranks;

6 *internationally recognized*: 20 per cent have received titles and honours;

7 *urbanized with Western styles of life*: they live in Western-style homes and surroundings;

8 *well travelled*: 60 per cent have travelled abroad;

9 *family-centred*: their lives are centred on home and children; families take meals together;

10 *social leaders*: most of them belong to societies and social clubs.

African *élites* are national leaders and a most important segment of the consumer market. They are more exposed to new ideas and products, have large sums of disposable income, a high level of aspiration, and a confident self-image.

New *élites* are not the sole arbiters of life in the traditional or modernizing community, however. Power in African society is widely diffused and controlled by many social *mores* which link the rich and poor in a bond of kinsmanship.

Élites often hold valued, and hence regulated, status in the customary hierarchy. An *élite* may be a chief, an eldest son, or a *malam* (a Muslim religious teacher). Modern *élites* have responsibilities and obligations in both the new secular and the traditional sacred culture. For example, Nigeria's first Prime Minister, Alhaji Sir Abubakar Tafawa Balewa, started his career as a *malam*, is an *alhaji* — a devout Muslim who has made the pilgrimage to Mecca, a knight in the hierarchy of British Commonwealth titles, and Prime Minister in a secular state.

It is also necessary to understand that class and culture do not operate in the same way yet in Africa as in the West. In Western industrial nations the well-to-do social classes can be distinguished from others by their choice of marriage partners, the number of children they have, their residence in the "right neighbourhood", their accent, dress and social behaviour. These factors do not differentiate Africans to the same degree.

Rigid class barriers have not as yet arisen. Fertility is not associated with income; the rich man may have as many children as the poor man, or more. *Elites* maintain a cultural preference in their homes for *kenke, gari, fu-fu,* groundnut stew and other traditional African foods. By and large, successful men maintain their residences in the older African community and their attachment to valued cultural habits.

In traditional urban areas the rich and poor live side by side and class distinctions in housing types are not obvious. In a neighbourhood of ordinary houses a wealthy man rubs shoulders with an artisan who works in the railway shop. Housing types may range from dilapidated "swish" buildings worth no more than £30 to imposing edifices of brick and cement valued at £5,000. The woman next door, who lives in two small rooms with her daughter and grand-children, may be a "penny-penny" trader or the proprietor of a lucrative textile export business. Slum areas around market-places are often the residence of the most prosperous self-employed segments of the urban population, namely the traders.

The highest public officials are, however, a notable exception to this pattern of egalitarian residence; this exception is explained in terms of their ascension to the symbols and seats of power formerly held by Europeans. In the past, certain "government areas" were reserved for European personnel and their families. With the dawn of independence and Africanization of the upper ranks of administration, African officials qualified for accommodation in government areas. Today the proportion of African residents to expatriates in these enclaves has increased; and it is probable that they will become *élite* residential communities.

It is important to note here, however, that as the numbers of educated persons grow, there is a tendency for advertisers to direct product messages to them as *élites*, unwittingly augmenting a sense of separation from their fellows. This approach may in the long run have a boomerang effect since, in many states, political and trade-union officials deplore the development of a "leisure class" separated by income, residence and standard of living from the rest of the people. As President Sekou Touré of Guinea has said: "The African *élite* is not to be recognized by its diplomas, by its theoretical or practical knowledge, or by its wealth, but only by its devotion to the evolution of Africa."

Here we have another example of how political philosophy intersects with, and moulds, the marketing process in new African nations. Consumer behaviour, normally considered by business-men as the proper sphere of individual choice, is viewed by many African leaders as a social question with national implications.

FAMILIES, HOUSEHOLDS AND HOMES

Urban families are changing in size and their type of residence. They are responding to the new cultural and economic forces regulating their environment, land tenure, housing and living costs. Most urban families rent rooms in a one-storey mud or cement house, roofed with corrugated-iron sheets. This dwelling-place, the backyard compound and side streets, establish the perimeters of household life. Within them, urban families are changing from the traditional extended family to the conjugal family type of Western industrial society. A brief review of homes and households in Lagos will help us to understand the relationship of changing families to the structures that enclose their lives. Recent studies on this subject include Peter Marris's book, *Family and Social Change in an African City*,[2] publications by the Nigerian Government Bureau of Statistics,[3] and housing surveys by architects and town planners.

In the traditional setting, the Yoruba lived in walled houses with farming land in the countryside surrounding. Each of the family compounds housed a lineage tracing its descent from the same ancestors. Rooms were arranged round four sides of a courtyard with a single gateway and a private room and parlour for the most senior member of the family. Other adult members had their own rooms and the children slept either with their mothers or on the surrounding veranda.

Descent groups, whether in one house, clustered together or in separated compounds, "lived together", acknowledged the authority of their most senior member and were represented as a group in the affairs of the community.

A house was not merely a house; it was a haven in time of need, a beacon for a wayfaring "kinsman" and the focus for family and town meetings and celebrations, mutual help and friendly societies.

Family life today takes place in entirely different circumstances; few houses are family-owned and occupied. Of all dwellings 67 per cent consist of one room and less than 6 per cent of the population lives in three-room dwellings. Family house-building is curtailed by outmoded customs and inadequate laws, and the average density soars to 150 persons per acre on standard plots.

Today's typical Lagos house is a modification of the traditional type. It is a one-storey house with cement walls and a corrugated-iron roof and a central corridor with four to ten rooms on both sides. It is built on a 50 ft. × 100 ft. plot and has a shop in front with a kitchen block and latrines in a compound at the rear.

The conjugal family type has become a more common urban phenomenon. Peter Marris studied a neighbourhood of 29 houses, consisting of 110 households living in 151 rooms and found that 40 per cent of these were occupied by a male householder, his wife and unmarried children. He concluded that the traditional extended family group no longer shares a common home. It is true, however, that family members and relatives tend to live within a few minutes' walk of each other and are not therefore isolated from their kinsmen.

THE FAMILY AS A PARTNERSHIP

The relationships between husbands and wives are changing towards partnership in decision-making. As more workers move across the face of Africa the dependence of young couples on family and relatives is seriously disrupted. In the new situation, the couple are thrown on their own resources and tend to take a greater interest in furnishing the home. The younger, educated, working couples run their households as a partnership and make major buying decisions together.

Husbands and wives are jointly interested in improving their homes and social position. Women contribute to the achievement of family goals — education, a house or car — by going out to work or engaging in trade. Modern couples are willing to work harder to buy better products: packaged maize containing vitamins, bicycles with built-in generators and torches, and sturdy shoes for their children.

As aspirations advance beyond income many husbands engage in "moon-lighting", that is they hold several jobs. It is not uncommon for a mill worker to work the night shift and then to work for a local farmer during the day to get staple foods for his family. In Central Lagos, Marris found that 40 per cent of the wage-workers he studied traded on the side. An assistant at a Syrian textile mill also traded in Nigerian tobacco; a sanitary inspector dealt in second-hand bicycle parts; a post office clerk had a thriving poultry business.

HOUSEHOLDS AND PERSONAL CARE

The interior of homes is changing as more people spend money on home entertainment and leisure (books, radios, gramophones, television sets) and household equipment (sewing machines, linoleum floor covering and furniture).

Attitudes towards personal hygiene and cleanliness are changing; more people want better bathing and washing facilities indoors. The bathing-place is moving indoors from the rivers, streams and compound backyards. There is an increasing number of people switching from traditional soaps and washing techniques to medicated and toilet soaps for personal bathing and soap powder for washing clothes.

Younger couples spend more time and money on household and personal care, and are more "brand" conscious. Husbands in younger families are interested in the home, partly because it is a part of their social status. The possession of money is not yet the key factor in buying behaviour, although the better-educated households spend more money but prefer more expensive and refined goods. What is important, however, is that choices are no longer wholly based on communal custom but are increasingly determined by individuals.

FAMILY BUDGETS

As people become better off their patterns of spending change. This is expressed in five areas of family budgets: recurrent expenditure, food, household interior, house exterior and investment.

(a) *There is an increase in the cost of recurring expenditure and in the maintenance of the household.*

Participation in the modern sector is not without its cost in housekeeping, allowances to dependants, rent and maintenance. Many workers travel 2–3 hours a day to and from work. Families spend as much as 15 per cent of their monthly budgets on bicycle tyres and tubes, or on daily public transport.

(b) *As income increases, there is a decrease in the proportion of income spent on cheaper commodities and foodstuffs, and an increase in the purchase of more expensive commodities, particularly processed foods and meat.*

In general the diet of unskilled workers — starchy staples, stews and sauces — does not undergo a basic change in content. The traditional African diet consists of a porridge of dough dipped into a tasty sauce or thin stew. The porridge is made from a starchy staple food, such as grains, fruits, roots and tubers, which provides most of the calories. Sauces are made from a wide variety of ingredients, palm oil, groundnuts, dried fish, peppers, eggplants, okra, tomatoes, onions, etc., which provide the bulk of fats, vitamins, and mineral content.

In Ghana,[4] for example, the most common foodstuffs used in daily meals are as follows, ranked in descending order by volume of consumption in grams:

G

1 Manioc and manioc products
   Fresh roots
   Kokonte (dried roots)
   Gari (meal)
2 Plantain
3 Yams and cocoyams
4 Maize and maize products
   Kenke (fermented dough-balls)
5 Meat (fresh, red)
6 Rice
7 Dried fish and snails
8 Palm nuts
9 Vegetables
   Egg plant
   Tomatoes
   Peppers
   Onions
   Okra
10 Miscellaneous
   Milk
   Fruit
   Sugar
   Salt
11 Bananas
12 Drink
   Palm wine
   Akpateshi
   Beer

Poorer workers spend proportionately more money on food than higher-income groups but the proportion of wages spent on food decreases with rising income. Among lower-income groups a large proportion of monthly income, 30 to 80 per cent, is spent on food. In some cities, those making £10 per month spend 70 per cent on food and cooking fuel and those making £20 spend only a third of their wages on these items per month.

Today's educated workers supplement their diets with processed and more expensive types of foods. There is also a marked change among educated workers from drinking traditional African alcoholic beverages — *akpateshi*, palm wine, *pombe* and *burkutu* — towards wines and spirits, processed beer and mineral waters. A gradual shift takes place to processed tobaccos from the use of customary stimulants, such as chewing kola nut in West Africa and "smoking" *ghat* in East Africa.

It is interesting to pause for a moment and consider the question of alcohol consumption in Africa. This, like so many other aspects of human behaviour in developing societies, is considered a national question. It is believed that the taking of spirits, whether local "illicit gin" or imported types, saps meagre financial resources and physical strength, and becomes a mental health hazard. Some governments have encouraged the expansion of a beer industry to act as a buffer against increased consumption of spirits.

The offensive against the use of harmful traditional spirits has been led by Ghana. The target is *akpateshi*, a drink made from either sugar cane, palm wine or corn, which has had grievous effects among rural and urban populations. Government buying agents purchase *akpateshi*, through producers' co-operatives, purify it and then re-sell it in a number of popular forms. The new Ghana Distillery in Accra makes vodka, schnapps, rum, vermouth, whisky, Ghana gin, Queen Elizabeth gin, brandy, industrial alcohol and perfume — all from *akpateshi*.

The distillery was first started by Gilbey's and then was converted to a re-distilling and rectifying plant. The factory produces 15,000 12-bottle boxes per month and makes about £100,000 worth a year at a 10 per cent profit. Ghana gin, the best seller, markets for £5 per box. Following Ghana's success in converting *akpateshi*, other nations have become interested. Nigeria and Sierra Leone, with its *omole, akaregbe* and *ospikin* ("house piccin" or child of the house), have shown an interest in this process.

(c) *There is an increase in expenditures on home improvement and house-building, particularly in rural areas.*

Among country folk, as incomes rise there is an increasing expenditure on better clothing, durable goods, especially corrugated-iron roofs, carpenter-made doors and windows, and cement-facing, on homes. People first make general improvements to the exterior appearance, then proceed to furnish the interior. More money is spent by affluent urban workers and farmers on purchasing the services of other people: servants, water-carriers, maize-grinders and casual labourers.

Radical changes in consumption habits take place as farmers pursue the cash-crop markets offered by processing mills, marketing boards and exporters. Cash-crop farmers in Kenya and Gezira, Sudan, provide examples of how aspirations and patterns of expenditures change as people become better off.

One thousand "better farmers" among the Kipsigis of Kenya

spend an estimated £68 each annually on clothes, taxes, blankets, school fees, medicine, food, household items, boots and shoes, soap, kerosene and cooking fat.

In Wad Medani, wealthier tenant farmers are city-orientated and have changed their long-established tastes and preferences. They have vacated their windowless loam huts and built new houses with doors, window-frames, reed curtains and shutters. They purchase manufactured consumer items, bicycles, furniture and large quantities of nutritious store-bought foods. Many traditional household duties are abandoned and their wealth creates new paid occupations as they hire the services of water carriers and maize-grinders. They also support more schools and hospitals than any comparable region in the Sudan.

(d) *There is an increasing investment in capital goods to produce new income.*

The life history of a prosperous Kipsigis farmer, recorded by the anthropologist Robert Manners[5], indicates the way in which values, innovations and living habits cluster and create a rural *entrepreneur* and an incipient "middle class".

Some years ago a mission-educated youth acquired a plough and prepared a five-acre plot of maize below his hut. In a few years he had enlarged his field to 25 acres. He built a water mill and ground maize for sale to Asian traders and the tea estates. Later, he bought a wagon to transport the grain to local trading centres and helped build a road to the market. He now owns a warehouse and two general merchandise shops that are run for him by hired employees. Recently, after buying a car and a truck, he built a new brick house with windows of glass. He shops more often in Nairobi, 200 miles away, and wears Western-style suits, shoes, shirts and neckties. He educates his children and is considered an outstanding local leader. Perhaps, one day, he will seek a government post.

Uganda an example

A hierarchy of income groups is developing in rural cash-crop areas and patterns of spending vary among these groups. Valued products range from food, the immediate interest of poorer persons, on and up through household items, mass media, home improvement and capital investment, which are the interests of wealthier farmers.

In a study done in Uganda, cash-crop farmers were categorized into three groups according to average annual income. The categories were: Group A, £4,000 and above, Group B, £2,000–£3,999 and Group C, less than £2,000. These farmers had similar sources of income, coffee *shambas*, secondary crops, shops and beer, and spent money on food, clothing, blankets, and porters' wages for sand hauling. Wealthier persons, however, expend a considerable amount on consumer durables and exhibit a revolutionary expansion in aspirations and purchases in the modern market.

TABLE 8. AVERAGE INCOME OF CASH-CROP FARMERS, MASAKA, UGANDA*

(by source in shillings)

	Group A £4,000s and over	Group B £2,000s to £3,999s.	Group C Under £2,000s.
†Coffee	2,733	1,138	276
†Cotton	105	46	113
†Secondary crops	1,114	159	90
Regular employment	—	138	99
Casual employment	22	—	130
Craft	324	310	192
†Shop or business	3,622	512	110
Interest	242	—	17
Rent	3	69	2
†Beer	1,402	293	127
Sale of land or cattle	46	37	—
Other sources	335	15	12
All sources	9,949	2,718	1,168

* Source: *Market Surveys Uganda*, 1956, A Report by the Marketing Development Company Limited, Uganda. By Commission of the Protectorate Government, May, 1956.

†*Note*: Obviously multiple answers were given. The largest categories of responses were coffee, secondary crops, shop or business, and beer.

TABLE 9. AVERAGE EXPENDITURE OF CASH-CROP FARMERS, MASAKA, UGANDA*

(by source in shillings)

	Group A £4,000s and over	Group B £2,000s. to £3,999s.	Group C Under £2,000s.
Food	1,935	1,216	696
Drink and tobacco	281	285	75
Clothing and blankets	1,282	430	219
Books, stationery	37	12	2
Household consumable foods	237	128	68
Maintenance	328	86	24
†Porters' wages	1,426	384	122
Services	1,142	230	144
Total current expenditure	6,668	2,744	1,350
Durable goods	1,011	328	103
Total expenditure	7,679	3,072	1,453

* Source: *Market Surveys Uganda,* 1956. A Report by the Marketing Development Company Limited, Uganda. By Commission of the Protectorate Government, May, 1956.
† Hired by farmers to haul silt or sand from crop areas.

TABLE 10. AVERAGE INCOME AND EXPENDITURE OF CASH-CROP FARMERS, MASAKA, UGANDA*

(in shillings)

	Group A £4,000s. and over	Group B £2,000s. to £3,999s.	Group C Under £2,000s.
	(18)	(23)	(29)
Expenditure			
Current	6,668	2,744	1,350
Durable goods	1,011	328	103
Total expenditure	7,679	3,072	1,453
Income	9,949	2,718	1,168
Net saving	2,270	354	285

* Source: *Market Surveys Uganda,* 1956. A Report by the Marketing Development Company Limited, Uganda. By Commission of the Protectorate Government, May, 1956.

Individuals in Group C were basically concerned with the satisfaction of basic needs: increased consumption of meat, fish, sugar, salt, clothing, and African drink. As incomes rose they began to buy household equipment: beds, blankets, sheets, folding chairs, cooking pots, looking-glasses, lamps, fitted doors, bicycles, corrugated-iron roofs; to improve, or build new, traditional homes. They had aspirations to buy radios, gramophones, fertilizer, insecticides.

Group B members had already satisfied many of their basic needs and proceeded to improve their homes with cement. They also bought watches, clocks, motorcycles and more expensive clothing. Farmers in Group A had not only satisfied basic needs and improved their homes but had also begun to buy capital equipment to generate income. They owned taxis, lorries and rent-bearing property: houses and shops with electric lighting.

PERSONAL SAVINGS

In traditional communal African societies the fruits of collective labour were the bounty of all. No one went without the necessities of life. Harvests were set aside for hard times; even today in many regions it is the Chief's function to feed orphans and widows from his granary. Reverence for elders, many well-married children and good relations with kith and kin were adequate insurance against old age.

Change has disrupted traditional economic systems and, as the modern economy develops, peasants become aware of what wage-earning labour and money can do. Awareness brings about a complete mental revolution. More traditional folk are saving their money through guilds, trading associations, mutual aid and provident funds; many still simply place their earnings in the ground inside the house.

The meaning of money to the countryman was vividly expressed by a Southern Rhodesian peasant and recorded in Rev. Ndabaningi Sithole's[6] book, *African Nationalism*:

"Today all people do not need to have goats, cattle and sheep in order to live. They only need money. If they have money, why, they have cattle, goats and sheep right in their purses. Money is the cow that does not move, breathe, drink and eat grass. It is a very good cow. You can milk it any time; You can eat and drink it any time. It is a cow that does many things for us."

Today, millions of modernizing workers have caught the savings "bug" and place their money in formal institutions: postal savings, insurance, commercial banks and shares in businesses, co-operatives and housing loan societies. Nigeria's experience with personal savings indicates that Africans save substantial amounts of money. In 1961, Nigerians owned £21m. worth of bank savings. Postal savings reached 300,000 persons in 1962 with an average deposit of £12; and 2,200 thrift accounts were opened in the Chase Manhattan Bank in the first year of its operation.

Public thrift and investment in the domestic economy are encouraged by all governments and viable consumer markets will grow as money which is presently idle is brought into circulation. An unestimated amount of idle money or savings is kept in the home, its use takes two forms: savings for a specific purpose and hoarding. Once savings are spent people begin saving for a new specific purpose; as a result considerable amounts of money are out of circulation for lengthy periods.

INVESTMENTS

The African wage-earner is becoming more aware of new ways of investing money; there are already two stock exchanges in Africa, at Nairobi and Lagos. Traders and *élites* have been among the first to deal in the investment market. As *The Economist* points out in an article "Nigerians Take To Investment",[7] traders with large sums to invest are not a new phenomenon, but it is worth while to pause a moment and look at the new pattern of investment saving in Nigeria.

In 1961, a stock exchange was opened and managed by the

Investment Company of Nigeria (I.C.O.N.). Its turnover rose sharply from £2·3m. to £4m. in the first 10 months of 1963. Some 37 securities are quoted on the exchange, including government issues, the Nigerian Broadcasting Corporation, Alcan Aluminium, the Nigerian Sugar Company, the *Daily Times* and a number of industrial companies. Government securities account for 90 per cent of the turnover, mainly because of the income-tax law which requires pension and provident funds to invest up to one-half of their resources in government stocks.

The role of the small investor is becoming increasingly important in the activities of the exchange. The first two years of operation indicate that Nigerians are willing to invest in industry. For example, 40 per cent of the applicants for the Nigerian Sugar issue applied for amounts less than £100; half the subscriptions were for £100–£200 blocks. Three out of every 10 investors were traders and one out of 10 was a clerk; and four politicians subscribed for £6,600.

THE MARKETING CHALLENGE

Marketing in developing Africa faces the most challenging tasks in its history. In the future, rising productivity, that *cachet* of efficiency without which no nation is modern, will thrust the African market spiralling upwards. The African consumer-citizen will be employed at higher-paying jobs and will have more disposable income. People who could only buy "x" amount of goods 5 years ago buy "x plus 8 or 15 per cent" today; and, more important, will buy "x plus 20–30 per cent" 5 years from now. Consumers will have more choices from the delicatessen of world goods in their local shops. They will be able to buy as they desire, shift brands or stop buying if they desire. What are they likely to do?

How, in what directions, and in what degree will the spending habits of families be influenced by family size, occupation, income, liquid assets and future expectations?

How will consumer spending in an African nation be influenced by the rate of formation of new families, by changes in manpower distribution and by geographical and social class mobility?

How will workers spend their money, if taxes go up or if prices go down?

To answer these questions, marketing in Africa's Century of Development requires a dynamic future-orientated approach, one which will take into account the people, their restless energies, rising efficiency, cultural tastes and capacity for change, their optimism and delight in the brand-new prospects for the future.

PROFILE : THE CHANGING WOMAN CONSUMER

WOMEN HAVE been profoundly affected by the surge of events and the momentous changes that are taking place around them. And, as they make contact with the modern elements, they bring to bear their instincts of thrift, beauty, motherhood and home-making.

How has the role of women changed in African society and what is their potential as consumers?

In African traditional society, women hold highly-valued positions of status and occupation. They are revered and respected as mothers, elders, householders, wives of chiefs and nobles, guild members and *alhajiyya*, honoured female pilgrims to Mecca. Their advice is sought as specialized professionals, soothsayers, herbalists and therapists.

The modern money economy and the needs of new nations have opened up new opportunities for women to participate in family decision-making and national progress. The increasing power of women in the consumer market comes from their economic role as traders and as workers in the modern sector.

Women traders have created large personal incomes through trading in cloth, provisions, foodstuffs and imported goods. Their activities in the local market-place are crucial for the satisfaction of daily needs — selling cigarettes, matches and sweets to travellers and migrants, bowls of soup to workers, and noon-day snacks to school-children. Through their regular business trips they extend products and services to neighbouring communities. It is not unusual for a petty trader to travel 50 miles a week with a calabash of goods on her head and a child strapped on her back.

Women wholesalers in textile goods, in some capital cities, do a brisk international trade and handle accounts worth £100,000 a year.

A woman's earnings from trade are her own; therefore, her business is an important source of security and independence. Trading helps a housewife supplement the family income; and some working housewives earn £7–£20 per month. The power of the female £.s.d. is consolidated in trading associations, benevolent societies and substantial accounts with leading banks and merchant houses. In Kumasi, for example, Mr. Pedler recalls that 85 per cent of 615 trader accounts at U.A.C. were held by women.

Trading opens up a new life outside the household and a woman trader plays a varied and important role in all spheres of society. A life history of a typical successful woman trader in Lagos will illustrate this point.

Mrs. A. was born of trading parents and has been trading for 30 years. She deals directly with two or three European firms in textiles, hardware, provisions and perfumes. She has six assistants and 40 trading customers in the city and outlying villages. Her monthly turnover is £4,000 and she feeds, clothes and educates 30 dependants and provides the bulk of her household's cash income. She engages in many social and political activities, she is the president of the Market Traders Association, committee member of a national federation of women, member of the Society for the Blind, a deacon of her church and head of the local committee of her political party.

The female worker and educated woman are creations of the march towards independence and the rapid pace of social and economic development. In countries on the move, opportunities exist for women in education and jobs that they could never have contemplated in the past. It is universally recognized that "you can't industrialize with half your potential labour force enslaved by custom and tradition". Women are therefore encouraged to develop their skills and seek employment as factory-hands, clerks, telephonists, air-line hostesses, nurses, teachers and legislators.

As women are drawn into the mainstream of national life they gain self-assurance in the world of men. In Muslim Kano city, women have cast off their veils and earn 30s. a week working in shoe, textile, perfume and sweets factories. Today's African women are pioneers as headmistresses, teachers, magistrates, journalists and legislators, and set the pace for the women of tomorrow.

Women have demonstrated an intellectual and social potential equal to men. At first, the pioneers of women's education had to plead to go to school. Today, in some nations there are more girls in one class than there were at school throughout the whole country 15 years ago. Young women recognize their value as citizens, educated housewives, wage-earners and, even as status-symbols for their husbands. In Muslim areas like Northern Nigeria, where women's education has only just begun to take firm root, graduates of the Kano Women's Training College are in great demand as wives of traders and government officials.

What tastes do Africa's female consumers and housewives have? How are their tastes and buying habits changing? Modern women are familiar with Western products and brands. They have greater sense about money and a desire for goods which provide comfort and beauty and are time-saving. Women desire cleaner, healthier homes. They complain that their households are insect-infested and hard to clean; they want better insecticides, soaps and disinfectants. They want improvements in household lighting facilities, and simple, inexpensive furniture and cooking utensils. Luxury items are also beginning to attract the beauty-conscious woman. Recently a well-known cosmetics firm announced a plan to introduce a line of cosmetics especially designed for African women.

Personal grooming and hair care is a prime example of changing habits among African women. They are changing from plaiting and weaving their hair to going to hairdressers and using a hot comb "American Negro-style" in the home. They are using petroleum Vaseline jelly to soften the hair instead of the traditional shea butter and vegetable oils. Women who traditionally dyed their hair with natural henna are changing to store-bought hair colorants; and many prefer perfumed and medicated soaps.

More able-bodied mothers want to be freed from household drudgery and enabled to participate in the economic sector. Young mothers welcome innovations in infant nutrition which can relieve the strain of prolonged breast-feeding and provide nutritious milk food for their children. Pet Milk Company's disposable infant feeder is an example of a product innovation which might have great success among young modern mothers. This device is a simple tin container holding a liquid baby food formula that requires no refrigeration and no heating. The mother removes a sealed, sterilized nipple from the top, punches a hole in the container, replaces the nipple and pops it into the infant's mouth. The tin is thrown away after use.

Modern women seek household equipment which can serve two purposes: produce services for the household and also be a source of money income. With a sewing machine, for example, a housewife can clothe the family and also step into a lucrative and prestige-bearing occupation as a seamstress.

Do modern African women have tastes and requirements distinctly different from those of white women? "All our experience points to the contrary", says Mr. Pedler, speaking of the U.A.C. Kingsway stores. In an article in *Progress*,[8] Mr. Pedler says, "The experience of our department stores supports the view that women in West Africa readily adopt European attitudes — African women want the same styles and goods and respond to the same types of promotion as European women." Mr. Pedler has observed a certain "homogeneity of taste" among women of widely differing cultural backgrounds from Freetown to the Muslim women of Kaduna. Tastes do vary by education and degree of sophistication but, "subject to slight adjustment for these reasons, all these people are seeking status through the acquisition of material goods". He concludes, "Like European women, they are very subject to influence points — one type of thing associated with Paris, another with America, another with Britain."

With the rising level of female literacy and the increasing number of working women, the mass media are making a bid for women as customers. Every major journal has developed a woman's section with commentaries on the changing courting, marital, food and buying habits. In a recent issue of *Drum*, March, 1964[9] the new role of young women was clearly indicated in an exchange of letters between "Dolly" and a reader entitled "What went wrong?"

"When I got my salary of £15, I took my girl-friend with me to help me buy a shirt and a tie. We came out of the shop with a blouse and two pairs of nylons for her and neither tie nor shirt for me. I still don't know where I went wrong," *signed* A. Yaw, Kumasi.

Dolly's reply was:

"Lesson — never take your girl-friend into a shop when you have any money on you. Look the other way the minute you see anything for sale whenever she happens to be around. This is no reason why you cannot give her presents though!"

REFERENCES

1 SMYTHE, HUGH and MABEL, *The New Nigerian Élite*, Stanford University Press, California, 1960.

2 MARRIS, PETER, *Family and Social Change in an African City*, Routledge & Kegan Paul, 1961.

3 For example, *Report on Lagos Housing Enquiry, 1961*. Lagos, Federal Government, Office of Statistics, June, 1961.

4 See, for example, THOMAS T. POLEMAN, *The Food Economies of Urban Middle Africa*, Food Research Institute, Stanford University, 1961.

5 MANNERS, ROBERT, "Land Use, Trade and the Growth of Market Economy in Kipsigis Country", in P. Bohannan and G. Dalton (eds.) *Markets in Africa*, Northwestern University Press, 1962.

6 SITHOLE, REV. NDABANINGI, *African Nationalism*, Oxford University Press, Capetown branch, 1961.

7 *The Economist*, "Nigerians Take To Investment", 4 January, 1964. *Profile*.

PROFILE

8 *Progress*, The Unilever Quarterly, **48**, No. 272, February, 1962.

9 "Dear Dolly Column", *Drum*, March, 1964.

CHAPTER SEVEN

RESEARCHING THE MARKET

IN RESPONSE to the developing African market, industries sense the need for basic information and make increasing demands upon market research agencies. Market research has the responsibility of gathering the facts, monitoring the behaviour of existing products, exploring ways to better existing products and to research the possibilities for new products.

Once a research brief is agreed upon it is up to the researcher to decide what to do (define the problem), how to do it (select and develop appropriate techniques) and advise on what to do with the facts (interpret the findings). In the following discussions we shall briefly survey the main areas of market research, distribution, product development, advertising, mass media and consumer behaviour and raise some questions for further research.

DISTRIBUTION RESEARCH

Due to the major role which distribution plays in consumption in Africa, it is essential to seek information about the distributor. How many shops exist in a given area? What brands do they stock? How does a product enter a community? What percentage of a product is bought by Africans and where? What is the size of the market, the points of sale and the volume of sales at each point?

Many of these questions are as yet unanswerable due to the dearth of accounting systems and record-keeping among distributors and shops. Few shop audit reports are kept to provide data about goods that reach the consumer, and it is either very difficult or impossible to obtain invoices for "shop purchases". It is only among the larger chain stores that purchasing information can be obtained. Thus one of the challenges to the product researcher is to devise a method of locating all outlets and determining the pattern of product distribution.

There are a number of methods for the continuous observation of market behaviour which might be fruitfully explored in Africa. First there is the analysis of the imports and sales of merchant houses. Second, the Nielsen survey, a sales research technique for measuring how much comes into a shop, how much goes out, and how much is left during any observation period. The Nielsen survey is essentially a shop audit; it reveals what and how much a shop stocks, the rise and fall of stocks, and the breadth of distribution of various brands. Thirdly, there is the Attwood survey or consumer household panel. It identifies the consumer of products by social types, the stores where products are bought and the frequency of buying. Finally there is the Brand Performance Survey, a device for the continuous observation of the use of products in the home. Periodic visits are made to selected panel households and users are asked "What brands of 'x' commodity did you buy last week or month?"

No marketing research investigation in Africa is complete without a thorough investigation of the role of the trader and the market-place in the distribution of goods. A number of questions already discussed provide useful research hypotheses. What rules govern the continuous buying and selling for personal and household use? What proportion of items bought in the urban European shop are bought by employees of Europeans, are purchases for personal or household use, or are bought with the intention of re-sale?

Some relevant hypotheses for investigation are:

1 Goods are bought and sold in a progressive series of transactions extending from (a) the European wholesale shop to the African market-place and (b) from the urban area to rural areas.

2 Goods will be bought and sold until their utility for generating money or barter decreases.

H

3 In general, goods move out from the urban area along an established indigenous trading chain (getting smaller in bulk and cheaper in price but costlier in price per unit) towards the surrounding market-places and from them to the most remote places, in a systematic way.

Theoretically, if each of several investigating techniques are applied along a continuum from the arrival of goods at the local merchant house to actual use in the household, a broad picture could be obtained of the marketing distribution process. A tentative model for examining the flow of goods might be set down in the following manner.

TABLE 11. THE FLOW OF GOODS FROM WHOLESALER
TO CONSUMER: A TENTATIVE RESEARCH MODEL

Source of data	Technique	Types of questions
1 Wholesaler audit (European, Arab, Levantine, Asian, African)	Nielsen	How many boxes arrived, how many went out, how many are left? More specifically, to whom were they distributed, e.g., traders, shops, etc.?
2 Shop audit (European, Levantine, Arab, Asian, African)	Nielsen	As for 1 above.
3 Market traders	Nielsen	As for 1 above.
4 Consumer household panel	Attwood	What items have you purchased recently? Where did you buy them, e.g., shop, market-place, etc.?

CONSUMER BEHAVIOUR

Once the general flow of products is ascertained we need to know something about why the African consumer bought the product, his attitudes towards the product and the uses to which it is actually put. It is necessary to conduct consumer surveys to uncover the facts about consumer opinions and behaviour.

Various standard consumer research techniques are applicable in the African situation. Once the relevant demographic data are known it is possible to test the power of these factors — age, sex, education, etc. — in relation to buying and consumption behaviour. Extended interviews, group discussions and panels can explore underlying attitudes and predispositions.

Research is needed into a host of social and psychological factors which characterize the emergent African. New patterns of self-image emerge in the process of change. Emergent Africans have desires for new experiences, response and recognition. In a mobile society, people express their egos through acquisition of material goods, to show people "what kind of man I am". The pursuit of material goods, holidays abroad, trips to Mecca, all of which make undisputed contributions to self-development, all become status symbols. Among men it is undoubtedly true that personality traits such as sociability, neuroticism, gregarious-ness, imitation and extroversion play an important part in spend-ing habits and choices of Western products. But *what* part do they play and *how* do they affect specific choices?

As the standards of living and conditions of life improve, signifi-cant changes take place in standards of personal cleanliness and hygiene, bathing and washing of clothes. It is probably true that individuals with adaptive personalities working in the modern sector of an economy exhibit patterns of personal care similar to that of Europeans.

Throughout the world, in all types of societies, people interact and respond to each other through the things they possess. Dress, ornaments, facial marks, hair and body dyes, all become elaborated and conspicuously used, in large part, because of the impact they have on other people. Often, as in the potlatch ceremony of some North American Indians, valued possessions are burned conspicu-ously in public at social gatherings. In emerging African societies there are many social traditions which provide opportunities for social gatherings and conspicuous use of manufactured products.

They include festivals, holy days and the rites of passage: births, child-naming ceremonies, marriages and funerals. When a product is attached to a particular social act it sweeps through a community on the wings of collective approval.

FAMILY DECISION-MAKING

As families improve their incomes and standards of living, in what ways do their patterns of spending change, and why? Do the changing structure of the family and the relationship between husband and wife, parents and children, affect consumer choices? Do families become more price-conscious? What governs their attitudes towards "quality" products?

The analysis of decision-making among African families is a fundamental starting point for the study of consumer behaviour. It can specify a wide range of concepts, the diffusion of buying control, "hidden family influencers", the determinants of buying action, and "buying agents". It also has relevance for resolving many problems along the path to national development. It can tell us where food and dietary tastes begin and whether they are changing towards more nutritious products, as more workers enter the urban-industrial sector.

The simple question: "Who buys what and for what reasons?" provides a beginning for a study of decision-making in the African family. Then we may ask:

1 How is the decision to buy arrived at? How does it operate, and with what products?
2 Is there diffusion of buying control? That is, is it the husband, the wife or both who decide what to buy?
3 Who or what are the "hidden influencers": teenagers, children, new customs?
4 Who buys what products, where and for what reasons?
5 What are the determinants for buying action?
6 Is the housewife a "buying agent" for family tastes?

7 Is it the man (who works in the modern sector) who initiates innovations?

One way to research this question of "who buys what, for what reasons?" is to ask men and women "What products did you decide to buy personally, or collectively with your spouse?" It would be possible to get a scaleable frequency for "him", "her" and "both of us", as outlined below, which could be compared by products, by social classes and by time periods.

TABLE 12. HYPOTHETICAL SCALE OF FREQUENCY OF INDEPENDENT AND COLLECTIVE BUYING DECISIONS BY BOTH HUSBAND AND WIFE

1 Type of decision	Independent decision	Mixed to some degree	Collective decision	Mixed to some degree	Independent decision
2 Who makes decision	*"Him"* e.g. hoe		*"Him"* and *"Her"* e.g. refrigerator		*"Her"* e.g. cloth, perfume
3 Power over decision	*"Mainly mine"*		*"Both of us"*		*"Mainly mine"*
4 Variations in the flow of decision	e.g. from *"mine* (his)" and *"mine* (hers)" to *"Both of us"*.				

MASS MEDIA SURVEYS

Mass media surveys are among the most structured and quantified instruments in market research. Their use, however, often leads to a simplistic aura of well-being, which is disastrous when applied to Africa. "It's quite simple," one media man said to me in Nigeria, "they either have it or use it or see it, or they don't."

The first tasks of media research are, of course, to measure the audiences, to determine the most efficient vehicles for advertising expenditure, and continuously to monitor media behaviour. But counting things must be supplemented by understanding how the media articulate with buying behaviour and the fabric of society. I have listed below 66 researchable questions, the answers to which may contribute to a more comprehensive knowledge of the mass communication process in Africa:

Media distribution

1 What is the availability and distribution of mass media facilities?
2 What type of control is exercised over the media?
3 How accessible are the media to different segments of the population?
4 What are the restrictions on accessibility?
5 What is the relationship between accessibility and actual exposure?
6 What social innovations in the dissemination of information have been introduced; for example, is there collective reading and collective radio listening as a result of restricted accessibility?

The communicator and the message

7 Does the message appeal to the audience to which it is directed?
8 Is it phrased in a way that is understandable to the audience?
9 Will it attract the audience and hold its attention?
10 Does it convey the information in a clear and consistent fashion?
11 Will the audience act after receiving the message?

Audience reception and response

12 How do people use the mass media?
13 What factors affect selectivity and recall of mass-media information?
14 Does the role of mass media as disseminators of news and opinions vary for different groups within the audience?

15 What is the degree of audience exposure to media in small intimate groups?

16 What resistances to exposure exist among the population?

17 What images and attitudes do people have of mass media?

18 What factors induce negative or positive images and what are their influences upon information exposure?

19 What media preferences exist among the audience? For example, which media are regarded solely as sources of entertainment or news and which media are believed to be more trustworthy, accurate, etc., than others?

20 Who are the persons exposed to only one medium, to two, and to all the media?

21 Is exposure to a combination of two media more effective than to either alone?

22 Does use of one medium stimulate the use of another, for example, does radio-listening promote newspaper reading?

23 What correlations exist between newspaper-reading and radio-listening and cinema attendance?

24 Does the prestige of a medium vary according to its perceived credibility?

25 What is the role of social centres, for example, beer halls, and posters and transport advertising in diffusing media information?

26 Do hypotheses from Western society hold true for Africa? For example is it true that the poorer and less educated the listeners the more they tend to listen to the radio but the less they tend to listen to "serious" radio programmes?

27 Does use of mass media vary by occupation, literacy and other social and economic factors?

28 Does radio-listening increase and reading decrease among literates as one descends down the socio-economic scale?

29 Are families with young children heavier purchasers of TV sets and radios?

30 Are audiences for the cinema mainly young?

31 Is there collective newspaper-reading and radio-listening?

32 Is there a higher or lower degree of reading among literates than might normally be expected?

33 Why don't literates read more and why do they read what they do read?

34 Do more people read weekly papers than daily papers?

35 What are the distribution centres of newspapers?

36 Does the language of the newspaper or its prestige in the African community affect its readership?

37 What are the characteristics of the newspapers that people read?

38 What language of broadcast do people prefer?

39 Do people listen more to broadcasts in one language rather than another, for example, in situations where there are several African languages competing for the attention of multilingual audiences?

40 Do people listen to English-language programmes more often than those in African languages known to them?

41 Is there a relationship between radio-ownership and income and education?

42 Are housewives who have radios more affluent and more literate?

43 Are they older or younger than those who do not own radios?

44 Are they opinion leaders in the community and do they spread media information to ever-widening circles of friends, relatives and acquaintances?

45 What stations and programmes are listened to, how often and why?

46 Why do people choose to listen to foreign, i.e., non-national radio stations?

47 Where there is a choice of two stations, do people choose to listen to one station more than the other?

48 How many people own wired sets, mains-operated radios, portable radios run by batteries or transistors?

49 What is the "normal" type of advertising over radios? Do people understand it?

50 What factors are correlated with going or not going to the cinema?

51 Is lack of cinema-attendance due to distance, money, types of films shown, etc.?

52 Where are the cinemas in relation to clusters of houses?

53 What hours of the day do film-showings begin and end?

54 How much does it cost to enter a cinema and what films are shown?

55 Do more literate than illiterate people go to the cinema?

Traditional means of communications

56 Do informal face-to-face and word-of-mouth information networks play a significant part in the diffusion of product information?

57 Is oral rather than visual communication more effective with less educated audiences?

58 Is there a higher retention of simple material when it is presented orally rather than visually?

59 Is oral communication more effective than printed matter in changing opinion?

60 Is face-to-face communication, which allows for greater interaction and flexibility of appeal, more effective than radios and newspapers?

61 Is there greater learning and retention of material when the individual sets his own pace for absorbing the material and when he is participating and involved in the process of learning?

62 Is holding an opinion highly valued; and is being "in the know" socially esteemed?

63 Does the ownership or consumption of mass media affect a man's status in the community?

64 Who are the "influentials", the leaders of opinion formation and carriers of news and opinions, and what is their role and function in the community?

65 What is the relative importance of oral inter-personal communications measured against direct exposure to media as a channel of information?

66 Does the role of oral communication vary according to the degree to which mass media are accessible?

ADVERTISING EFFECTIVENESS

Advertising research in Africa can provide useful information on a range of factors from product planning to consumer-purchasing habits. The measurement of the effectiveness of advertising starts with a clear knowledge of the purposes of the advertisement and advertiser. What are the general aims? Is it to improve the overall attitude of a population towards a brand, to increase brand awareness, to highlight a specific dimension of the product or to raise the level of knowledge about it? Is it a simple reminder of the product or a detailed story?

Sound media planning helps choose the best message to be transmitted to attain the specified objectives. By pre-testing the copy, the layout and impact of the message, media research can answer the question: "Is it delivering the message efficiently and effectively to a given population at a given cost?" To complete the cycle of investigation, media research tests the effectiveness of the advertising campaign by measuring the results obtained against the original goal.

Little is known about the penetration of advertising into the consciousness of Africans or about patterns of attention, perception and comprehension. More psychological information is needed on the effect of advertising on an individual's mind while he is receiving a message and its manifest and latent effects. We assume that effects are measurable in terms of strength, potential, flow, velocity, depth and duration of retention; but what are the facts? Are the dynamics of communication, from exposure to purchasing, simply a question of seeing, perceiving, comprehending and acting? Exactly how does the advertisement of a product bring an audience from no knowledge about the product through stages of awareness to the point where individuals are stimulated to buy the product?

In associating a brand product with a media programme it is

necessary to ask: "What should be the relationship between my product and the programme?" New research may reveal that the effectiveness of product recall may be greater when associated with a radio or TV programme which is educational and socially useful than when sandwiched between the usual daily output of popular music.

PRODUCT RESEARCH

Modern business institutions are rapidly becoming aware of the role of new products in the life of the African consumer. Greater understanding is necessary, however, about the values which give meaning to the product within the fabric of African life.

Knowledge of culture and society is important because sales and marketing depend to a large extent on the skilful use of social values and symbols. But whose values should they be? Selling points are created to appeal to status aspirations, social class symbols, needs, urges and desires. But are these appeals reflected in today's — and tomorrow's — reality?

In the long run, the success of a given product will depend on an awareness, understanding and acceptance of the values of the consumer and his society. In this way consumer needs can be met in a consistent and gratifying manner within the framework of African development.

Policy decisions

In appraising the general market, prior to the planned introduction of products, a number of vital policy decisions have to be made. These may be expressed in questions under these headings; (a) product planning, (b) assessment of competition, and (c) marketing strategy, sales and manufacturing policy.

(a) What kind of products do people really want? What are the varying customer preferences and requirements? Does the pattern of social differentiation, e.g. élite, Europeans, workers, peasants, affect the development of a mass market? What image does or should the product have? Is it specially designed with the characteristics of quality, performance, shape, colour, styling and price most appropriate to the market? What areas of the market are susceptible to this kind of product — to which age groups, income brackets, etc.? Why should it be the manufacturer who alone dictates what kind of products should be sold?

(b) What are the areas of competition, either direct (one brand against another) or indirect (substitution of one product for another)? What local goods compete with foreign products (palm wine versus Coca-Cola)? What foreign products compete with other foreign products? What companies dominate various types of markets? What share of each market does each company hold? What products of the same kind are already on the market? What quantities and features? Does the population exhibit consumer loyalty or brand-switching habits?

(c) What facilities exist? What organizational set-up? What channels should be used? What is the policy to the distributive trade? Shall we have local agents and local organizations? What is the role of traditional markets and middlemen in the distribution of products? What shall be the determinants of pricing, discounting, advertising and delivery service to diffuse products to the widest number of customers? What profit margins shall be allowed for? What systems of handling, storing, and transport? What kind of salesmen will be needed, whom should they visit, and how often? What type of advertising, consumer promotion, trade promotion, direct consumer contact and public relations will be required? Where shall the product be produced? In what circumstances — local manufacture, made abroad and sold locally, or made abroad but assembled locally?

Utility and Saleability

The emergence of new African nations and consumers has relevance for every aspect of product manufacture, design, packaging, marketing and sales. At the outset, the manufacturer, advertising agent and distributor ought to avoid the proverbial problem of "selling refrigerators to Eskimos". They should question the inherent utility and saleability of each product. For example, "should we promote 'pale-face' powders or create a line of beauty aids which augment the tastes and beauty of African women?"

Ingredients, design, specifications

New African markets may require changes in the ingredients, in design sizes and specifications. Pork fat in a product precludes its sale in Muslim areas; body types and sizes for men, women and children vary from average British norms. Medicines and pills are generally sold in smaller quantities, for example, individually wrapped aspirins in strips of four sell better than a large quantity in a bottle.

Every product from pen to power cable needs to be re-examined in the light of new markets. What is its function? What does it do? Is it appropriate? If a machine can only operate efficiently with small loads over a short distance, then it is of little value where the problem is carrying heavy loads over a long distance. How does it do it? Many machines require skilled labour which is not readily available at point of use; climate and temperature also influence the saleability of a product.

Packaging, colour, and pack message

The packaging of products in useful containers may enhance sales. Petty traders use beer bottles for selling paraffin and ground-nut oil. A cup of *shaah* tea in East African backlands may be served in a Player's round 50-cigarette tin. In villages, Esso petrol tins filled with water straddle a donkey's back from stream to field and home; flattened they line the roofs of urban shanty towns and bidonvilles. A plastic toothbrush container appears at school used as a pencil case. Do these innovations suggest new products?

Colour choices affect sales and hence become an important part of design schemes. What is the effect of adapting pack messages to local national and regional languages and placing multi-lingual leaflets inside the box?

Modern products in traditional culture

The saleability of some products will depend on whether they can compete successfully with locally-produced or home-made articles of the same nature. Would a product such as beer compete successfully in areas where home-made palm wine is drunk in great quantities? Would mass-produced, machine-ground maize flour store better and taste better than home-ground maize flour, and still be economical? Most of the groundnut oil and cake consumed in Nigeria is still produced in the local community by simple hand methods. To what extent can popular tastes be shifted to a more nutritous processed groundnut product?

Research can uncover new secondary uses of natural resources. In the production of cotton seed flour in Nigeria, it was found that the by-products of refining could be used for soap making, animal-feed, plywood glue, plastics and fertilizers.

New markets emerge within rural societies when modern products are substituted for traditional objects. In Central Africa machine-made blankets have replaced traditional handwoven ones; in West Africa a plastic comb with double rows of teeth replaced the traditional comb. Slowly lipstick is replacing ochre and betelnut as an instrument of female beautification. A number of preliminary research studies indicate that there are hierarchies of customs which range from those held rigidly to those which are modified in changing situations. Although many traditional customs resist or compete with innovations, some of them may actually assist in the introduction of modern products, new tasks and civic values.

Testing new concepts and techniques

Experimental research among housewives and other family members offers a possibility of testing new product concepts in the laboratory of human behaviour *before* the product is actually manufactured. For example, a set of designs or pictures of the proposed products might be given to an African housewife. She is asked: "Which one of these looks attractive to you?" "Which one do you think you would like to use?" "How much would you be willing to pay for it?"

This simple technique has several possible functions. It is a way of inducing the expression of opinion by African consumers, of "taking them into account". It also tests a product's potential appeal before a large capital outlay is made. As a result it optimizes the benefits of the costs of product development and the utility of the product to the African consumer.

Consumers and branded products

Modern marketing in Africa also requires experimentation with a wide range of specific product research techniques. These include consumer panels, attitude and motivational research, paired product comparison tests, and blindfold and flavour discrimination tests. They have utility not only for specific product research but for establishing a body of knowledge about the general characteristics of African populations.

Ten questions which can provide new information about the relationships between consumers and branded product buying are:

1 Who and what factors establish a consumer's purchasing standards?

2 How much and what kinds of information does a consumer need to make an intelligent buying decision?

3 Is there an emerging pattern of "brand loyalty", and if so, why?

4 What role does price play; is pricing an effective influence on buying habits?

5 To what extent is there family interaction in consumption decisions?

6 How important are the "newness" of products and the symbol "just arrived from overseas"?

7 What is the relationship between "loyalty" to a brand and to the shop which sells it?

8 What causes styles to be accepted as favourable and in "good taste"?

9 Who are the "influentials" in buying?

10 How do products enter into the popular vocabulary?

The shop image

The place where products are bought and the sales force which sells them are other crucial areas for research. As we have discussed earlier there are a variety of shopping places available to the African consumer. In the urban areas the Kingsway store, Chellaram, an Indian or Syrian shop, and indeed even the marketplace, may all sell the same products. In the future, competition among these shops will increase; will the "shop image", among other factors, play an important part in determining who buys what, where?

The broad outlines for the study of the urban shop image, of shopping conditions, display and other factors, might be patterned as follows:

1 *Image:* What are the urban shops like, who are their customers, why do people like or dislike a shop? How functional is it to be thought of as the "white man's shop"?

2 *Shopping conditions:* Do shoppers have opinions about crowded conditions, queues, carrying their goods in push-baskets, prices, time spent shopping, service, courtesy, and the "atmosphere" of the shop?

3 *Social factors:* Is "going shopping" exciting, an outing from the cares of home? Is the shop a place to meet friends; do people shop together or alone?

4 *Display:* Do customers really *see* each product or merely a jumble of colours? How many people pass by a display, look at it and respond to it? What are the reactions of shoppers to a display?

5 *Transport and distance:* Does shopping depend on the distance of home from the main shopping centre, on social-

class factors, or owning a motorcar? Is it true that the higher the social class and the younger the person, the more likely an individual will travel to shop in an urban store? If the same product at the same price were available in the traditional market-place, an African-owned shop in the African residential and in the European-owned urban centre shop, what types and proportions of people would choose to shop in each place, and why?

The search for insights

Finally, there are a number of general questions which stimulate the search for answers along other lines.

1 The functional aspects of a product may be solved, but the product may not sell, why?
2 How to establish the dimension of the markets for products? For example cigarettes; who smokes, what is smoked, how much do they spend, how do they buy cigarettes, e.g., one at a time, 10 at a time, or a full pack of 20?
3 It is true that the sales of many consumer goods, luxuries and durables are increasing, but why do they sell?
4 What is the role of the sales force in selling?
5 How important is the range of differing food choices within a population? Do they affect the possibilities for mass production?
6 What are the physical factors which affect use of products, e.g., hard/soft water, heat, dirt and dust and insects?
7 On what basis should the names of new products be developed?
8 What is the relative pulling power of the same product when labelled "made in England" or "made in Nigeria"?

Basic research of this order is a long-term operation. In the short run market research is expected to "pay-off" in terms of workable selling propositions and advertising programmes.

I

When research findings are translated into products, symbols and messages they have to be communicated to people. To do this requires an elementary knowledge of the availability and accessibility of media and an awareness of the social factors which affect communications. In the next two chapters I shall discuss these points and their relevance for marketing.

CHAPTER EIGHT

THE MEANS OF
COMMUNICATION

IN THE course of African history the ways in which man speaks to man have profoundly changed. The modern media which span the Continent are marked elaborations of man's experiments in African to conquer distance, time and meaning. Modern techniques of communication are successors to the gesture and oral language, to the shouts and calls which simulate the abundant wild-life, and to the unknown artisans who carved their ideographs in the caverns of the southern tier. Mass media are heirs to the signal fire on the sloping Rhodesian hills, the drums in the moist darkened forests and the foot-runners on the sun-glistened banks of the Nile.

Oral language in all its colourful variety, poly-tones, rhythms and "clicks", remains the pillar of communication in Africa. In the past, the spoken word was the sole means of transferring the integrity of cultural units, from mouth to ear, down the ladder of generations from old to young. Troubadours, courtiers and wisemen were the stenographers of oral literature, epic and lyric poetry, stories and legends, praise-songs and the chronicles of states, kings and dynasties.

Later, written African languages like Vai, Amharic and Geez, evolved naturally. The spread of Arabic and Hebrew influenced many oral languages. Written documents appeared in Swahili, Arabic, Old Nubian, Meroitic, Hausa, Fulfulde, Kanuri, Nupe and Dagbani. During the colonial period European languages were introduced, and the sounds of many oral languages were converted to written use.

The introduction of writing, printing and reading helped to change the course of African affairs. Written languages, European and African, became vessels for Africa's resurgent culture, preserving bitter-sweet memories, formulating new ideas and passing them on to future generations. In the hands of a literate minority the written word blazed a pathway to independence.

The advance of tele-communications and mass media, in the few short years of independence, has revolutionized the purposes and methods of transmitting ideas and symbols. They have enhanced the expressiveness, permanence, adaptability, swiftness and scope of information diffusion.

Modernizing Africa is on the verge of a big leap forward in the field of mass communication. Existing facilities, limited by comparison with contemporary Europe, will be rapidly surpassed as great strides are made in science and technology and as financial and technical resources are harnessed to development and consumer needs.

A WORLD PERSPECTIVE

"It's hard to know where a man is going unless you know where he has come from", and in this sense it is necessary to locate Africa in the world media situation before entering into a specific discussion of media facilities. Media development in Africa reflects her position in the international flow of information, her status as a prime media target, and, of course, the desire of new nations to express themselves to their own people.

The flow of information around the world is determined by the existing patterns of distribution, ownership and control of mass media facilities. It varies according to standards of living and the general inequalities of political status and power among nations. The facilities for mass communication are not distributed equally among the world's peoples. Most of the world's mass media instruments are concentrated in the Western nations. Half the radio receivers are in the U.S.A. alone, while in tropical Africa there is less than one radio per 100 persons. In the United Kingdom, the world's "most newspaper reading" country, there is a paper for every two persons compared to one for every 100 persons in Africa.

"Who receives what kinds of messages?" is determined by the prevailing pattern of collection and distribution. The world's news is sent internationally by six agencies: Reuters (U.K.), Agence Presse (France), Tass (U.S.S.R.), and Associated Press, United Press International and International News Service (U.S.A.). Many African nations must rely on these world agencies for all domestic as well as international news.

The flow of information across international boundaries is also determined by the cost of transmission. Press rates vary depending on the direction of the message. For example, it costs twice as much to send a Press message from the Republic of the Congo to the United Kingdom as it does to send it in the opposite direction. The general effect is that the volume and variety of news to world communication centres from Africa and under-developed countries is limited. On the contrary, messages from the richer countries have easier access at a cheaper price to the populations of African countries.

THE POLITICS OF COMMUNICATION

The African emergence is one of the most important political economic facts of the twentieth century. As a result, Africa is a world media target and there is a battle on for the "mind of the African". Governments, industries and international agencies seeking to direct or control public opinion increasingly rely on radio as a means of conveying their information and propaganda. External broadcasting to Africa is "big business" and millions of dollars are spent on the export of words, impressions and ideas which affect the attitudes and behaviours of African peoples.

Twenty-two major world external broadcasting stations produce 7,183 hours per week. Of this number Russia, China and the socialist European nations account for 3,197, the non-colonial industrial nations 1,875, the colonial powers 1,403 and the Afro-Asian nations 708.

TABLE 13. WORLD EXTERNAL BROADCASTING RANKED
BY ESTIMATED TOTAL HOURS PER WEEK, 1963*

Socialist nations	*3,197*
Russia and European socialist nations	2,389
China (People's Republic)	808
Non-colonial industrial nations	*1,875*
United States of America (Voice of America)	816
West Germany	522
Japan	238
Italy	209
Israel	90
Ex-colonial powers	*1,132*
United Kingdom (B.B.C.)	603
France	320
Spain	295
Portugal	185
Afro-Asian nations	*708*
Egypt	448
Ghana	100
India	160
TOTAL	7,183

* Source: Based on tables published in the *B.B.C. Handbook 1964*, p. 105. Reproduced by permission of the British Broadcasting Corporation.

Africa's response to these manifold challenges has been to encourage the growth of national media and information services. A selection of objectives for the mass media taken from the publications of ministries of education and information reveals a belief that the mass media are a fundamental part of the development process. They declare that the media should provide cheap means of communication to widely-separated populations and provide a well-planned system emphasizing the interpretation of events and the transmission of political and aesthetic values. Governments use the media as a means of mass mobilization to:

1 integrate diverse populations and encourage them to new efforts,
2 disseminate information which will help to raise living standards,
3 campaign for social justice and elicit support,
4 provide an incentive and aid education, and
5 guide and harness social forces.

FACILITIES FOR MASS COMMUNICATION

Economics and politics thrust Africa into the twentieth century, but it is only now that the consciousness of a place in history is spreading to the majority of the population. Part of the credit is due, undoubtedly, to the expansion of mass communication; newspapers, telecommunications, radio, cinema and television. The broad outlines of media expansion have been established in a number of recent studies and UNO reports.

Newspapers

Africa's 221 daily newspapers have a total circulation of 2·9 million; most of the 835 non-dailies and 1,382 periodicals are concentrated in nine nations. In each country ownership is diffused between the government and a wide variety of political, religious, business and ethnic groups. Most papers were initially European-owned but have gradually given way to African enterprise. Liberia, Tanzania and Ivory Coast are three illustrations of the variety of existing newspaper enterprises.

In Liberia, the Thomson Organization has contracted to produce a daily morning newspaper, *The Liberian Star*, and to operate the Republic's Press in Monrovia on behalf of the government. The paper is edited by the Ministry of Information and its editorial policy controlled by a government-owned corporation.

In Tanzania the expatriate-controlled English language *Daily Tanganyika Standard* has a circulation of 9,000, mainly in Dar es Salaam; in addition there are two dailies, *Mwafrika* and

Ngurumo, published in Swahili. Weeklies include *Uhuru*, journal of the Tanganyika African National Union, and several Asian papers printed in Gujerati and English. Most of these papers are printed and distributed in the capital city. In rural areas people depend on newsheets issued by district officers, missionaries and the Department of Education. The African village "town hall", called the *baraza*, is also an important medium for the transmission of news.

The Ivory Coast has the distinction of being the first French-speaking African territory to have a newspaper founded and published by Africans, *Eclaireur de la Côte d'Ivoire*, begun in 1935. Today there is also *Abidjan Matin*, a European-owned paper, and the journal of the Democratic Party of the Ivory Coast (P.D.C.I.), *Fraternité*.

Newspapers play an important role in reflecting popular language, aspirations and behaviour, Nigeria's *Daily Times* (Lagos), for example, has a popular cartoon serial of Cyprian Ekwensi's "People of the City", a moving tale of love, crime and pathos in a big city. There is also the "World of Off-beat Sam", the scintillating comments on women, fashions and public morality by Theresa Ogunbiyi, and timely items about Nigerian "firsts" like Tokunboh Akintola, "The First African Boy at Eton".

The newspaper is the most common and widespread form of disseminating information about products, projects and campaigns. It has impact, and is the potential customer's first contact with "what a product looks like". Furthermore, the reader can take what he sees home with him, pin it on his wall, dream about it and plan his next shopping expedition.

Millions of people, however, have never seen a newspaper and there are thousands of literates tucked away in the smaller towns and villages who are not reached by a National Press. To meet their needs and expand newspaper facilities, African nations are moving towards the solution of five basic problems:

1 distribution: poor surface transport and costly airmail;
2 production: lack of power, chemicals and newsprint mills;

3 readership: low literacy and low purchasing power;
4 capital: dearth of development capital, insufficiency of advertising support due largely to lack of major industries, heavy taxation on newspaper operations and high import duties on machinery.
5 technological innovation: electronics and automation, e.g., rotary offset, photo-composition, better inking and etching methods.

In spite of these difficulties there are many possibilities for the development of a flourishing and useful African Press. Trust funds can set up newspapers in rural areas for new literates. Expansion can be encouraged by support and assistance from foreign firms and governments through advertising and printing orders. The exposure of workers in factories and plantations to newspapers can be aided by "factory newspapers", posted broadsheets and rural *animateurs*.

News agencies and tele-communications

Most of the external and internal news disseminated in African countries is produced by six world agencies; thus Africa must rely on external agencies for domestic as well as international news. To alleviate this pattern of dependence, 13 nations have already begun national news agencies. Others are in the process of establishing national information services, training qualified personnel, improving facilities and establishing inter-African transmission services. Ghana, for example, has just opened a new international Telex system, the ninth on the Continent, which links her with Britain and seven key African States.

Many new innovations are on the horizon as a result of modern scientific inventions. The facsimile transmission of ideographs through tele-communications will enable the simultaneous publication of newspaper editions in cities hundreds of miles apart. Television owners of the future will be able to dial a telephone number and have the front-page of their paper appear on the television screen, remaining there until a button is pressed and the next page then makes its appearance. The existence of communication satellites will make it possible to by-pass earth-bound systems and relay dispatches by telephone and teleprinter across the Continent. Thus, the Africa of the future may have instantaneous "global" newspapers bringing the world into the home at the flick of a switch.

Radio broadcasting

Radio broadcasting has doubled its output each year and has advanced more rapidly than the Press. The total number of radio receivers exceeds the available copies of newspapers throughout the Continent. Radio transmission is generally owned, operated or controlled by governments. There are about 300 transmitters and 6–7 millon receivers, most of which are concentrated in nine countries.

A glance at the Somali Republic provides an illustration of radio broadcasting in East Africa. There are two radio stations in Somalia. Radio Mogadishu, constructed with Russian aid, broadcasts in Somali, Amharic and Galla to Ethiopia and the British-built 10 kw Radio Hargeisha broadcasts relays from Mogadishu. Across in French Somaliland, Radio Djibouti broadcasts in Somali, Arabic, French and Apar, the language of the Danakil people.

Somalia's importance to foreign governments and agencies far outstrips its small size. The Republic is the target of programmes beamed from Kenya, Moscow, Rome, Cairo, B.B.C., West Germany, Peking, Voice of America, Israel, Ethiopia, and the Lutheran World Federation station, "Radio Voice of the Free Gospel", in Addis Ababa.

Group listening is quite popular and in Hargeisha with its population of 50–60,000 large crowds gather to listen to evening broadcasts. Out in the desert it is not uncommon to see caravans settling down for the night, transistors out and aerials up, listening to Radio Somali from Cairo. The Somali people are avid radio listeners; to them "radio is the voice of the man who comes to tell us about the world outside".

The expansion of African broadcasting and reception is subject to solving the limitations of finance, personnel and the heavy import duties on equipment which raise the cost of a receiver by 30–50 per cent. Short-wave transmission, used for the sake of economy, has not been entirely successful because it is affected by solar interference between October and April.

Wired sets are a partial aid to widening radio audiences. A wired receiver is essentially a loudspeaker that receives broadcasts distributed over a network of wired speakers called a radio-diffusion exchange. They are to be found in public places as well as homes and make radio listening a collective experience. In many nations communal listening is encouraged as a means of expanding the audience to radio broadcasts. Low-cost transistor radios, easily available to the general public, also serve the same function.

Sierra Leone, where the first wired service in Africa was inaugurated in 1934, was the first to substitute transistors for wired services. In March, 1964, the service, which in 30 years had developed from 350 to 5,000 subscribers, was replaced by the Transistor Radio Service. Subscribers can obtain reliable sets through the government and pay for them by instalments. This is the first large-scale hire-purchase scheme in West Africa and was received enthusiastically; in the first few months of the service 2,900 sets were purchased.

These innovations are all the more important because for many years to come it will be radio, not newspapers, which will bring the majority of Africans new ideas and product information.

Within the Continent a dozen states now have external services, most of them addressing other states, though in a few cases they speak to Europe. Radio Ghana, for example, broadcasts in English, French, Portuguese, Hausa, Arabic and Swahili. Radio Cairo, the "Voice of the Arabs" and the "Voice of Islam", broadcast to Ethiopia and Eritrea in Amharic, to East Africa in Swahili and Swaziland in Swazi. They also transmit to West Africa in Hausa, English and French, to North Africa in English and French, to the Sudan in various Sudanese languages and to all Muslim areas in Arabic.

Television

In 1950 there were no television stations in Africa, today television is the newest media phenomenon in Africa. There are almost 500,000 receivers and regular services in thirteen nations: Algeria, Congo (Brazzaville), Gabon, Ivory Coast, Kenya, Liberia, Morocco, Nigeria, Sierra Leone, Sudan, Uganda, UAR and Upper Volta. At least five nations, Ghana, Mauritius, Niger, Senegal and Tunisia, plan to introduce television in the near future.

Like radio and telecommunications, television services tend to be owned, operated and financed, often on a commercial basis, by governments. Significant variations do occur however in the matter of financing. Kenya, Morocco, Ghana and Sudan depend on governmental funds. In Nigeria, Sierra Leone and Uganda television stations rely on advertising revenues and government subsidies. In 1962–63 the Nigerian Federal Television Service established a record for air-time and production services for African television stations with over £5,000 worth of contracts. Senegal's television station is financed by the government, France, UNESCO and other agencies of international and bi-lateral assistance.

The former colonial powers tend to be the main suppliers of technical assistance and programme material. The French-speaking areas depend on the *Office de Co-operation Radiophonique en Afrique* (OCORA); Nigerian stations rely heavily on British and American television organizations.

Drama, music and light entertainment make up the largest proportion of broadcasting time. Western Nigeria TV at Ibadan has the highest percentage of educational broadcasts. Sudan and Uganda lead in time given to news talks and public affairs and Eastern Nigeria TV allots the most time to children's programmes. The average number of broadcasting hours per week is about thirty hours, but this varies by station from the UAR'S 159 hours to 3 hours for the Ivory Coast.

As in the field of radio, many African television stations broadcast in African languages. Swahili is used in East Africa, Luganda in Uganda, Hausa in Northern Nigeria, Mossi in Upper Volta, and Krio, Mende and Temne in Sierra Leone.

The number of television receivers per nation varies considerably. Egypt's 150,000 sets in the main urban and rural areas cover more than 70 per cent of her population; it is, perhaps, the most effective nation-wide coverage in all of Africa. Liberia has 2,000 sets within a 75-mile radius of Monrovia; Sierra Leone has 500 sets in a 10-mile radius of Freetown, and there are 8,000 sets in the vicinity of Nairobi, Kenya, mainly owned by Europeans. Algeria has 60,000 sets, Gabon 300 sets and there are 2,500 sets in the Khartoum–Omdurman urban areas of Sudan.

The main challenges to the expansion of television in Africa are the cost of providing electricity and transmitters in regions of low-purchasing power. There is a vast potential for television as a means of social evolution and some interesting new developments will occur in Pan–African communication when African nations establish an exchange of programmes through an Africa-Vision Service.

Films

In 1960 only two African nations were producing films regularly, the United Arab Republic and Tunisia. Today, newsreels are produced by government agencies in Ghana, Morocco, Tunisia and the United Arab Republic. Documentaries are produced in Algeria, Congo (Leopoldville), Ghana, Morocco, Nigeria, Zambia, Southern Rhodesia, Sudan, Swaziland, Tunisia, Uganda, South Africa, and the United Arab Republic. In addition, features and newsreels from America, Europe and India circulate widely. Out of the world's total of 212,000 cinemas Africa has 2,400 cinemas with a total of 1,300,000 seats. Only four nations have more than two seats per 100 persons.

Some of the difficulties involved in the expansion of cinema and film services in Africa include:

1 lack of production facilities,
2 the dearth of development capital and trained personnel,

TABLE 14. THE GROWTH OF MASS COMMUNICATION IN AFRICA :
RADIO AND TELEVISION RECEIVERS, 1955 AND 1962*

| | Population 1962 (millions) | Sound radio set ownership | | | | Wired broadcasting Number of receivers 1962 | Television Number of receivers 1962 |
		Number of sound radio receiving sets (millions) 1955	1962	Percentage increase 1955–1962	Number of sets per 1,000 population 1962		
North Africa (including Middle-East)	116·0	2·2	7·850	257	67	3,300	450,000
Tropical Africa	175·0	0·360	2·60	622	15	141,000	50,000
South Africa	16·5	0·875	1·30	48	79	11,000	—

* Source: Based on tables published in the *B.B.C. Handbook 1964*, p. 106. Reproduced by permission of the British Broadcasting Corporation.

3 the high cost of importing raw film and equipment,
4 difficulties of organizing film distribution.

Recent advances in film technology can however, create new audiences. Solar-powered battery projectors can be used to screen film-strips in remote non-electrified areas.

COMMUNICATIONS AND URBAN SOCIETY

Beneath these statistics recorded by U.N.E.S.C.O. and the aspirations expressed by administrators there are some basic social facts which are pertinent to our discussion. Mass media are urban phenomena and their availability and use are related to participation in the modern sector of the economy.

In changing Africa, participation in the urban industrial sector provides the literacy and income necessary to purchase mass media. Urbanization-industrialization is correlated with a sharp increase in the demand for the media, and the higher the income the greater the use of mass media.

At the same time, the media are urbanizing factors themselves, pulling rural folk and unskilled labourers into the vortex of national and world affairs. Radio and cinema take on great importance as means of mass communication, largely because they do not require literacy. Radio listening stimulates the quest for learning and the desire to read. What is needed then is not merely a count of media facilities but an understanding of how they relate to other aspects of life. Communicating with people is more than choosing a newspaper or radio station and sending a message, it is a social process.

NIGERIA:
PROFILE OF A MASS-
COMMUNICATIONS NETWORK

NIGERIA, AFRICA'S most populous nation, is experiencing a rapid expansion of mass-media facilities. In this vast land, where 100 languages are spoken by 56 million people, a plethora of services is developing to meet the challenges of development. This brief survey of Nigeria's communications facilities indicates the variety of sources through which people are confronted with change-images.

There are a total of 65 major publications: 23 dailies, 22 weeklies, 10 monthlies and 10 quarterly and occasional journals. The daily newspapers are printed mainly in the English language; they are concentrated in Metropolitan Lagos and the Eastern Region. Northern Region daily papers, by contrast, are all printed in both English and an African language, Hausa.

Weeklies are owned by a variety of interest groups, religious, political, ethnic and governmental. Furthermore, in contrast to the dailies, African languages compete with English as a written medium; of 22 weeklies, five are in Hausa and Yoruba, four in both an African language and English and 13 are printed solely in English. The monthlies and quarterlies are printed in English and published in Lagos. The price of publications ranges from 1d. – 3d. for dailies to 6s. for learned journals published in Ibadan, one of the intellectual centres of Nigeria.

Lagos is the publishing capital of Nigeria; almost half the publications are printed there. The largest paper is the expatriate-owned *Daily Times* with a circulation of 100,000. In addition there are two blocs of daily papers owned by political parties and politicians; each has an estimated circulation of 10,000. The *Daily Morning Post* and the *Sunday Post* are government-owned papers.

A variety of literature in African languages for adult education and literacy programmes is printed by government printing houses.

Radio and television communication, like the Press, has rapidly developed in the past 10 years. In 1959 Nigeria became the first country in Africa south of the Sahara to introduce television. Broadcasting systems are owned and operated by the Federal and Regional Governments; each has a radio and television system. Broadcasting is in English and African languages for 17 hours a day on radio and 5–6 hours a day on television. From a quarter to a half of all advertisements are in one or more Nigerian languages. The Nigerian Broadcasting Company also operates a radio diffusion exchange with transmitters in Lagos and principal cities. Its daily schedule features school programmes, B.B.C. relays and transcriptions, and news and music in the main regional languages.

Recently a film made in Nigeria won an international prize and this may stimulate the growth of a film industry. The film-going public can see British, American, Egyptian and the popular Indian films in theatres throughout the nation. Every major town has a cinema and there are more than 100 privately-owned cinema houses. Cinemas exhibit 500 films a year; they have seven showings a week, a total seating capacity of 50,000 and an annual attendance of seven millions. Film units from Federal and Regional Government ministries provide free showings of educational films in urban and rural centres.

Telecommunications are also centred in Lagos. An automatic telephone system and a multi-channel v.h.f. link the capital with major towns and cities. There are 50,000 telephones and 31 million local trunk calls were made in 1961–63. Access to the outside world is accomplished through several tele-communication devices. There is a telephonic cable connection to the Commonwealth cable system via Accra, and with Dahomey. A multi-channel radio system ties up with London and Europe for radio-Telex, radio telephone and telegraph services. Finally there are direct radio links with Ghana, Sierra Leone, Gambia, Fernando Poo and ships at sea.

K

TABLE 15. 23 NIGERIAN DAILY NEWSPAPERS BY REGION, NAME, PLACE OF PUBLICATION, LANGUAGE OF PUBLICATION, PUBLISHER AND PRICE, 1964

Region	Name	Place of publication	Language of publication	Publisher	Price
I Metropolitan Lagos	Daily Express	Lagos	English	Amalgamated Press	3d.
	Daily Service	Lagos	English	Allied Press of Nigeria	2d.
	Daily Telegraph	Yaba–Lagos	English	United Nigeria Press	1d.
	Daily Times	Lagos	English	Nigerian Printing and Publishing Company Limited	3d.
	Morning Post	Lagos–Apapa	English	Nigerian National Press Limited (a Federal Government Corporation)	2d.
	West African Pilot	Lagos–Yaba	English	Associated Newspapers of Nigeria	2d.
II Western (a)	Mid-West Champion	Sapele	English	Chief F. S. Okotie—Eboh	1d.
	Mid-West Echo	Benin City	English	Allied Newspapers of Nigeria	2d.
	Nigerian Tribune	Ibadan	English	Allied Press	2d.
	Southern Nigeria Defender	Ibadan	English	Associated Newspapers of Nigeria	1d.

III Eastern				
C.O.R. Advocate	Uyo	Efik	Allied Newspapers Limited	2d.
Eastern Nigeria Guardian	Port Harcourt	English	Associated Newspapers of Nigeria	1d.
Eastern Sentinel	Enugu	English	Associated Newspapers of Nigeria Limited	
Eastern Observer	Onitsha	English and Ibo	Allied Newspapers	2d.
New Africa	Onitsha	English	Renascent Africa Press	—
Nigerian Daily Standard	Calabar	English	Old Calabar Press	1d.
Nigerian Monitor	Uyo	English	Associated Newspapers of Nigeria	1d.
Nigerian Outlook	Enugu	English	Eastern Regional Government	2d.
Nigerian Spokesman	Onitsha	English	Associated Newspapers of Nigeria	1d.
IV Northern				
Daily Comet	Kano	English–Hausa	Associated Newspapers of Nigeria	2d.
Daily Mail (b)	Kano	Hausa–English	Northern Peoples' Congress	2d.
Northern Star (b)	Kano	Hausa–English	Allied Newspapers	2d.
Middle Belt Herald	Jos	Hausa–English	Allied Newspapers	2d.

(a) The creation of the Mid-West Region in 1964 alters the regional citation given here for the *Champion* and *Echo*.
(b) Suspended publication in 1964.

TABLE 16. 22 WEEKLY NIGERIAN PUBLICATIONS BY REGION, NAME, PLACE OF PUBLICATION, LANGUAGE OF PUBLICATION, PUBLISHER AND PRICE, 1964

Region	Name	Place of publication	Language of publication	Publisher	Price
I Metropolitan Lagos	Akede Eko	Lagos	English and Yoruba	—	2d.
	Eleti Ofe	Lagos	Yoruba and English	Union Printing and Publishing	2d.
	Egbaland Echo	Lagos	English	Chief Ayo Ajalu	—
	Irohin Imole	Lagos	Yoruba	—	1d.
	Irohin Yoruba	Lagos	Yoruba	Allied Newspapers Limited	2d.
	Nigerian Catholic Herald	Lagos	English	St Paul's Press, Catholic Mission	2d.
	Nigerian Radio Times	Lagos	English	Nigerian Broadcasting Corporation	4d.
	Nigerian Statesman Service	Lagos	English	Statesman Publications	3d.
		Lagos	English	Allied Newspapers Limited	4d.
	Sporting Record	Lagos	English	Nigerian Printing and Publishing Company	4d.

	Title	Place	Language	Publisher	Price
	Sunday Express	Lagos	English	Amalgamated Press of Nigeria Limited	2d.
	Sunday Post	Lagos	English	Nigerian National Press Limited (a Federal Government Corporation)	2d.
	Sunday Times	Lagos	English	Nigerian Printing and Publishing Company	3d.
	Truth	Lagos	English	Ahmadiya Mission (Muslim)	1d.
II Western	Nigerian Guide	Oshogbo	English	Ikemisi Company	2d.
	West African Vanguard	Ilesha	English	—	—
III Eastern	Chronicle	Opobo	English	Western Nigeria Information Service	2d.
	Nigerian Observer	Port Harcourt	English	Enitonna Educational Stores	2d.
IV Northern	Bornu People	Maidugari	Hausa and Kanuri	Allied Newspapers Limited	2d.
	Gaskiya Ta Fi Kwabo	Zaria	Hausa	Gaskiya Corporation for the Government of Northern Nigeria	3d.
	Nigerian Citizen	Zaria	English	Gaskiya Corporation for the Government of Northern Nigeria	3d.
	Sodangi	Kano	Hausa	Kano Native Authority	2d.

TABLE 17. 10 MONTHLY NIGERIAN PUBLICATIONS BY REGION, NAME, PLACE OF PUBLICATION, LANGUAGE OF PUBLICATION, PUBLISHER AND PRICE, 1964

Region	Name	Place of publication	Language of publication	Publisher	Price
I Metropolitan Lagos	African Challenge	Lagos	English	Sudan Interior Mission (Protestant)	6d.
	Drum	Lagos	English	Drum Publications (Nigeria) Limited, Mr. J. R.A. Bailey, Chairman	1s.
	Federal Nigeria	Lagos	English	Federal Information Service	Free
	Children's Own Paper	Lagos	English	Federal Ministry of Information	Free
	Spear	Lagos	English	Nigerian Printing and Publishing Company	1s.
	The War Cry	Lagos	English	Salvation Army (Protestant)	4d.
II Western	In Leisure Hours	Ibadan	English and Yoruba	The Supra-Diocesan Board, Immanuel College, Ibadan	5d.
	Teachers' Monthly	Ibadan	English	Western Region Ministry of Education	4d.
III Eastern	Nigerian Outlook	Enugu	English	Eastern Nigerian Information Service	2d.
IV Northern	Jakadiya	Zaria,	Hausa	Gaskiya Corporation for Ministry of Infor-	—

TABLE 18. 10 QUARTERLY AND OCCASIONAL PUBLICATIONS BY REGION, NAME, PLACE OF PUBLICATION, LANGUAGE OF PUBLICATION, PUBLISHER AND PRICE, 1964

Region	Name	Place of publication	Language of publication	Publisher	Price
I Metropolitan Lagos	Commerce in Nigeria	Lagos	English	Lagos Chamber of Commerce (occasional)	—
	Nigeria	Lagos	English	Federal Government of Nigeria (quarterly)	2s.
	Nigerian Trade Journal	Lagos	English	Federal Ministry of Information (quarterly)	2s. 6d.
	Yoruba Challenge	Lagos	English	Sudan Interior Mission (alternate months)	6d.
II Western	Black Orpheus	Ibadan	English	Mbari Club (quarterly)	—
	Ibadan	Ibadan	English and Yoruba	University of Ibadan (quarterly)	2s. 6d.
	Nigerian Journal of Economic and Social Studies	Ibadan	English	University of Ibadan (occasional)	6s.
	West African Journal of Education	Ibadan	English	University of Ibadan (occasional)	2s.
	West African Medical Journal	Ibadan	English	University of Ibadan (occasional)	6s.
III Eastern	Eastern Nigeria Development	Enugu	English	Eastern Nigeria Development Corporation (quarterly)	2s. 3d.

TABLE 19. 65 NIGERIAN PUBLICATIONS BY REGION AND LANGUAGE, 1964*

Type of publication and language	Lagos	Western (e)	Eastern	Northern	Total
1 Daily					
African	—	—	1(a)	—	1
English	6	4	7	—	17
Both	—	—	1(b)	4(c)	5
TOTAL	6	4	9	4	23
2 Weekly					
African	(2d)	—	—	3	5
English	10	2	—	1	13
Both	2(d)	—	2	—	4
TOTAL	14	2	2	4	22
3 Monthly					
African	—	—	—	1	1
English	6	1	1	—	8
Both	—	1(d)	—	1	1
TOTAL	6	2	1	1	10
4 Quarterly–Occasional					
African	—	—	1	—	—
English	4	4	1	—	9
Both	—	1(d)	—	—	1
TOTAL	4	5	1	—	10
GRAND TOTAL	30	13	13	9	65

* Source: *Nigeria Yearbook 1964*; Helen Kitchen (ed.) *The Press in Africa*, Washington, D.C.: Ruth Sloane Associates, 1956, James Coleman, *Nigeria: Background to Nationalism*, Berkeley: University of California Press, 1958.

(a) Efik. (b) Ibo and English. (c) Hausa. (d) Yoruba, or Yoruba and English.

TABLE 20. THE MODERN COMMUNICATIONS SYSTEM: RADIO AND TELEVISION

BROADCASTING IN NIGERIA, 1964

Name/City	Owner/Operator*	Broadcasting in English	Broadcasting in African languages	Broadcasting hours daily	Networks and coverage	Advertisements
RADIO						
Radio Nigeria Ikoyi	Government owned operated by Nigerian Broadcasting Corporation	Yes	13 languages	17 hours	4 networks covering the nation, transmitters at Ibadan, Kaduna, Enugu and provincial stations	Yes, in English and Hausa in one quarter of programmes
Western Nigeria Broadcasting Service W.N.B.S. Ibadan	Western Region Government	Yes	Yes, Yoruba	17 hours	Regional	Yes, half advertisements in Yoruba and local languages
Eastern Nigeria Broadcasting Service E.N.B.S., Enugu	Eastern Region Government	Yes	Yes, Ibo	17 hours	Regional	Yes, half advertisements in Ibo and local languages
Northern Region Radio & Television Kaduna	Northern Region Government and British Consortium	Yes	Yes, Hausa	17 hours	Regional	Yes, English and Hausa

(continued overleaf)

TABLE 20. THE MODERN COMMUNICATIONS SYSTEM: *continued*

Name/City	Owner/Operator*	Broadcasting in English	Broadcasting in African languages	Broadcasting hours daily	Network and coverage	Advertisements
WIRED DIFFUSION						
Rediffusion (Nigeria) Ltd., Lagos	Subsidiary of Rediffusion Group, London	They operate a single-programme wired-broadcasting system, relaying programmes of Radio Nigeria, and have wired networks in Ibadan, Lagos and 103 other towns and villages in the Western Region with an estimated 80,500 receivers.				
Nigerian Broadcasting Corporation	Federal Government Nigerian Broadcasting Corporation	Yes	Yes	17 hours	Operated in North and East	Yes, in English and in local languages
TELEVISION						
Nigerian Television, Service Lagos	Federal Government Nigerian Broadcasting Corporation	Yes	Yes	5–6 hours	Metropolitan Lagos	Yes, in English and in local languages
Western Nigeria T.V., (W.N.T.V.) at Ibadan and Abafon	Western Region Government	Yes	Yes	5–6 hours	Lagos and Ibadan and Abeokuta in Western Region	,,
Eastern Nigeria T.V. (E.N.T.V.) at Aba and Enugu	Eastern Region Government	Yes	Yes	5–6 hours	Enugu and environs	,,
Northern Region Radio and T.V. Kaduna	Northern Region Government and British Consortium	Yes	Yes	5–6 hours	Kaduna, Zaria and Kano	,,

* Agreements are usually signed between the government, a government corporation and one or more foreign firms responsible for operation and

CHAPTER NINE

COMMUNICATING WITH PEOPLE

MASS COMMUNICATION is a patterned social activity which involves the transmission of meanings, intentions, wishes, feelings, knowledge and experience by mass media. Mass media, the widely-diffused popular Press, magazines, records, motion pictures, radio and television, are ways of transmitting identical messages simultaneously to large heterogeneous and unseen audiences.

The unique character of mass communication lies, however, not in its technical instruments but in its process; not in mere numbers, but in the relationships of mass media to the changing structure of social life.

THE MASS COMMUNICATION PROCESS

The modern media enter Africa with the development of factories and cities. New centres of employment place large numbers of individuals in close proximity to each other, exposing them to media information, new people and differing points of view. New roads bring contact between distant localities; lorry drivers, tradesmen and migrants serve as disseminators of information. Thus, mass communications systems in developing nations are part of a wider range of social interaction which increases the diffusion of information and activates the pace of change.

The mass communications process assumes a distinct set of operating conditions which may be set down as:

1 a complex bureaucratic *structure of control*;
2 a *communicator* who creates the message;

3 a *medium* which serves as a vehicle by which the message is transmitted;

4 a *message* which is public, rapid and intended to be consumed immediately;

5 a relatively *large audience* of a heterogeneous nature;

6 a *response* which may be belief, acceptance, or action on the part of the audience, or apathy and rejection.

THE STRUCTURE OF CONTROLS

Patterns of ownership and control of mass communication media vary throughout Africa. Each nation, however, places emphasis on the value of mass communication as a means of achieving information, education and propaganda objectives.

Radio and television stations are expensive and require huge capital outlays; they are regarded as a proper sphere for government ownership and are generally operated as public corporations. The operation of broadcasting facilities is "big business". Governments are involved in a vast telecommunications organization of capital investment, buildings, recording, broadcasting, training and research.

Newspaper publication, by contrast, is generally in private hands. Expatriates, religious missions, political parties and politicians, governments and business are all involved in the presentation of the printed word. Foreign-owned papers have the most modern equipment, resources, advertising and widespread readership; but the number of African-owned papers is increasing. Two noticeable trends are an increase in concentration of ownership of dailies and the establishment of chain dailies.

Outside the main stream of the commercial Press there are thousands of publications by religious, ethnic and trade union organizations, radical and *avant-garde* groups. These organs often express differing interpretations of social life from the daily Press. They also serve to draw attention to many social problems, inequalities and maladjustments that occur in the process of change.

THE COMMUNICATOR

The development of communications industries has created a new occupational group: communications experts, public-relations men, market researchers, human engineers, pollsters, journalists and broadcasters. They are specialists in the communications arts and in techniques of advertising and persuasion. Their vocabulary centres around such terms as "product", "message", "impact", and "audience". Press releases from their offices are the morning's "news" and their ideas and pictures sell millions of pounds' worth of products annually.

This new social strata serves as a liaison between persons who have something to sell and those to whom something is to be sold. Its members are recruited from many fields within African life, especially teaching and clerical work, though in recent years college-trained men and women have been increasingly attracted to this profession. In the offices and cubicles of major cities communicators create the psychology of consumption, the new jingles and slogans that motivate more people to buy soap powder, toilet articles, clothing and cars. Furthermore their "packaging" of such "products" as "the politician everybody loves", or "the soap of beautiful women" profoundly affects the popular images of who and what is worth while, fashionable, "good for you" and modern.

New nations are fast realizing the crucial importance of the communicator in the dissemination of information. Seminars and institutes have been set up in Cairo, Accra, Kampala and Ibadan; at Dakar there is a special institute for the scientific study of journalism. The major world communications centres have established centres for technical radio training, and in Scotland, the Thomson Organization has inaugurated a training institute for television production especially geared to the needs of developing areas.

THE MEDIA MESSAGE

Most media messages are designed to affect choices, tastes and preferences. Advertising messages are wrapped in glittering generalities, endorsed by famous persons and supported by appeals to loyalty and patriotism in order to increase effectiveness. Some messages have "snob-appeal"; others are presented in the popular colloquialisms of uneducated adult conversation to lend credibility to the ideas communicated.

Advertisements reach out to aspiring wage-earners and stress modernity, success, education, new styles and *élite* occupations. An advertisement showing white-frocked technicians in a laboratory reads, "People in top jobs, the people who have made a success of life, use Parker Super Quink — the wonder ink".

A cigarette advertisement in colour shows three smiling professionals, a doctor, a lawyer and a begowned university lecturer, and assures the reader "Men with a quick brain in a clear head relax with Varsity, the mentholated, king-size cigarette".

"PROVE YOU MEAN TO SUCCEED by taking a Wolsey Hall correspondence course", exhorts a serious-looking white-collar worker with pencil in hand and a telephone to his ear, and across the page a smiling boy, sitting on a huge pile of completed school notebooks, waves his ball-point pen and says, "BICO writes for a long time".

Being neat, handsome, happy and "with it" are all expressed by the clerk who says "The Modern African chooses Persavon" and the flight officer who reminds the reader that "The Modern Man Uses Gillette". And the winsome smiling girl in a bikini who says: "You too can be Savlon sweet" sets fashion on beaches across the Continent.

Pep pills, hair straighteners, wigs and perfume, hair shampoos and skin fresheners are common features of all magazines in English- and French-speaking Africa. Skin cream adverts utilize the selling ideas of the American Negro magazine *Ebony*: "Have lighter and lovelier skin today — the American way."

Sometimes the slant of a message leads to a "boomerang effect".

This is particularly true with advertisements that stress "status aspirations". In Moslem areas of Northern Nigeria, cigarette advertisements, which associate traditional nobility with smoking, jar the sensibilities of many persons and make others laugh at the queer notions of Westerners about social behaviour. Beer and whisky advertisements which link new *élites* to drinking inadvertently present a picture of "high-living" among the privileged classes.

Some advertisements appear offensive in their portrayal of the physical and social characteristics of Africans. For example, the petrol advertisement showing "big-time Africans" smoking huge cigars, riding in massive American cars with little barefoot "piccaninnies" trailing behind, appears as an attempt to belittle African aspirations the Western products.

Advertisers and consumers in changing African societies have differing cultural images of "what is" and "what ought to be" and hence there are many potential areas of conflict. A wide range of accepted Western modes are called into question: sex appeal, religion, politics and human relations, dress, customs, food, colour choices and emotional behaviour. How useful are such ideas as "keeping up with the Joneses" in a society which wishes to control conspicuous spending? Do pictures showing Europeans telling Africans what to do cause hostility? What is the meaning of such slogans and stereotypes as "the well-dressed man with his Swiss watch", "the proud owner of a Fiat", "the girl who wins admiring glances", "the successful man who shaves with Gillette" and "go lighter the American way — with Artra"?

LANGUAGE AND MASS COMMUNICATION

To communicate with people you must speak to them in their own language. But how can this be done, efficiently and effectively, in a Continent of a thousand languages?

Mass communication, education and adult literacy programmes are conducted through European and African languages; within all nations there is a variety of forms and uses of language. Some governments rely on a *lingua franca* to facilitate communication between groups having different mother tongues. The most common African and European *lingua franca* are Hausa, Swahili, Arabic, Mandinga, English and French. In regions within states, the most dominant languages may serve the same purpose, but more often they become vehicles of provincialism turned inward away from the outside world.

In many countries there is mixed use of European and African languages. In the nominally English-speaking nations more than 91 African languages are used for teaching. In the French-influenced tropical areas, French is normally the language of instruction, but African languages are used specifically in adult education. By contrast the French-speaking Arab areas use Arabic along with French in national school systems. Ethiopia uses Amharic as the official language as well as English, which is taught in schools. In Liberia, English is the official language but most school-children are taught in more than six African languages.

Finally, in many English-speaking areas a popular language called "pidgin-English" has emerged from many years of culture contact and in a few cases has been formalized in printed form. For example, the *Nigerian Sketch*, a new English-language Lagos newspaper, has a special commentary in "pidgin-English" called "Na So A See Am O".

The languages of communication are in the process of change and in future years both advertising copy and government appeals may be expressed quite differently from those of today. The purposive and simultaneous communication of ideas to mass audiences will not be the same in 1984 as they are at present. Communication in the future will be affected by the realities of today: multilingualism, political language choices, the growth of cultural nationalism and linguistic studies.

Within nation states the high rate of mobility pushes workers into new "foreign" language areas. Cities are a buzzing *mélange* of different tongues and the migrant countryman seeks protection among his kinsmen who, if not among the advancing segments of the community, drag him into the traditional despond. And, where the worker crosses into the modern sector, the languages of the factory and administration challenge his ability to adjust and succeed in a new situation.

In every community there are sizeable segments of the working population who must learn another language in order to gain their daily bread, to understand mass communication, to raise their standard of living and to participate responsibly in national life. When a man speaks three languages, as many Africans do, in which ones is he most receptive to new ideas — his mother tongue, the *patois* of a second African language learned in the market-place, or the national European language?

The variety of possible types of communication languages in one community is astounding; linguistic experts have classified 10 major language definitions which illustrate this point:

1 *the indigenous language* — the language of the people con-sidered to be the original inhabitants of an area;

2 *lingua franca* — a language which is used habitually by people whose mother tongues are different, in order to facilitate communication between them;

3 *mother or native tongue* — the language which a person acquires in early years, and this normally becomes his natural instrument of thought and communication;

4 *national language* — the language of a political, social and cultural entity;

5 *official language* — used in the business of government, legislative, executive and judicial branches;

6 *pidgin* — which arises as the result of contact between peoples of different language and is usually formed from a mixing of the languages;

7 *regional language* — used as a medium of communication between peoples living within a certain area who have different mother tongues;

8 *second language* — the language acquired by a person in addition to his mother tongue;

9 *vernacular language* — the mother tongue of a group which is socially or politically dominated by another group speaking a different language;

10 *world language* — a language used over wide areas of the world.

It is apparent that under these circumstances the optimum use of language in media messages requires elementary knowledge of the language situation of a given market or audience. All media research should include a general inquiry into the language situation.

How many languages are spoken in local areas?
How many persons speak each language and which ones are most important in various social situations?
How strong is a person's attachment to his language?
Do people feel there is an economic advantage gained through knowing a language other than their own?
Are there written forms of local languages and can they be easily printed and taught?
Do certain languages acquire new words easily?
How adequate is the vocabulary of a language for expressing technical and product ideas?

The choices that governments make concerning national and official languages also affect the language of mass communication. How does the government of a multilingual African state choose a national language? The solutions vary; Tanganyika chose Swahili; in Nigeria English is the official language, though in the Northern region the spread of Hausa is encouraged by the local authorities. Compromises are often made in mass communication; in most states radio and television broadcasting is conducted in from 3 to 15 languages in order to reach all segments of the population.

What is the future role of European languages in independent African nations? The use of European languages poses a paradoxical problem of choice. These languages are cords that bind Africa with world culture and technology, yet they are an ever-present reminder of Africa's earlier dependence upon European States.

TABLE 21. USES OF LANGUAGE IN AFRICA: IN EDUCA-
TION, ADULT LITERACY AND MEDIA BROADCASTING*

I *African states making exclusive use of the official language*

(a) French:
    Cameroon
    Central African Republic
    Gabon
    Guinea
    Ivory Coast

(b) Amharic:
    Ethiopia

(c) Arabic:
    Sudan
    Tunisia
    United Arab Republic

II *French or English for literacy programmes and a number of African languages for other educational programmes, particularly radio broadcasts*

(a) Liberia: English for literacy
    and
    Loma
    Kpelle
    Vai
    Grebo
    Gissi
    Gola

(b) Mali: French and
    Bambara
    Peul
    Sarakolle
    Sonrai

(c) Niger: French and
    Hausa
    Djerma

    Peul
    Tamashek
    Kanuri

(d) Senegal: French and
    Drola
    Mandingo
    Toucouleur
    Wolof

(e) Togo: French and
    Bassouri
    Ewe
    Guin
    Moba
    Hausa
    Kotokoli
    Kabre

III *Official language plus a* lingua franca *or several of them*

(a) Congo (Brazzaville)
    French for literacy and
    Lingala   ⎫ for mass
    Monokutuba ⎭ education

(b) Tanganyika: English
    Swahili for both literacy
    and mass education

(c) *Ghana: English*
     Akan (Ashanti, Fanti and
     Twi)
     Dagbani
     Ewe
     Fra-Fra
     Ga
     Gonja
     Nzima

(d) *Nigeria: English*
     Edo
     Efik
     Hausa
     Ibo
     Nupe
     Tiv
     Yoruba

* Source: Final report: *Conference of African States on the Development of Education in Africa, Addis Ababa, 15–25 May,* 1961. UNESCO.

It is possible that, in the future, greater use will be made of African languages in education, literacy and media communication. A recent conference on multilingualism called for the exploration of the utility of African languages in science and the arts. Recent experiments in teaching mathematics among the Wolof of Senegal tend to support the view that no language is intrinsically better than another for the communication of knowledge. African languages can serve as vehicles for teaching modern concepts in physics, geometry and chemistry. And, when dealing with rural people, they are indispensable means of communicating new ideas orally and recording their hopes and aspirations.

The test of the utility of major African languages for communicating contemporary ideas from the external world will occur when more linguistic scholars, orthographies, dictionaries, grammars and texts are produced. Until these are created and widely diffused, European languages will continue to function as the languages for communicating new ideas in most African states south of the Sahara.

THE MEDIUM

The medium by which information and advertising is transmitted is an important factor in mass communication. In Africa there are two essentially different networks for communication:

1 the traditional, through which ideas are transmitted orally by persons of prestige, interwoven with ethical principles and reinforced by contact with kinsmen;

2 the modern, through which mechanical, literate and costly symbols are transmitted by agents of change.

TABLE 22 PROFILE OF TWO NETWORKS OF COMMUNICATION: MODERN AND TRADITIONAL

Modern media system	Oral traditional system
Means: media, simultaneous reception	oral, face to face
Audience: mass, heterogeneous unknown to communicator	primary-homogeneous and known to the communicator
Communicator: skilled professional	status-person: friend, neighbour, relative, fellow worker, elder
Content: descriptive	proscriptive
Source: unknown complex bureaucracy	known persons of superior status
Interaction: impersonal, one-way to audience	two-way with clusters of interactive comment in process of diffusion
Cost: must be bought	free, a part of living
Speed: instantaneous	leisurely at the pace of the individual capacity to understand

The media system is characterized by a flow of information from a distant unknown source, by professional communicators skilled in producing descriptive messages (news, advertisements, etc.) for simultaneous transmission through impersonal media (print, film, radio, TV) to distant multilingual and multi-ethnic mass audiences.

In the oral traditional system messages come from sources whose status authorizes them to speak and initiate ideas; messages are proscriptive, i.e., geared towards regulating audience behaviour, and directed to one's fellows in natural primary groups of kinship, work and play. And within this pattern each person who has heard "the word" is a deputy and serves to relay information to others along the continuum of social life.

Most developing countries are in a stage of transition from one model type to the other and in any one community you can find both types jostling for the minds of men. Each has its own characteristics, advantages and consequences for the process of transmitting ideas and product information. Some of the major characteristics of the media and oral traditional systems are illustrated in the following discussion.

The power of the media

Film, radio, newspapers and television do not have equal power to attract and hold audiences, nor do they equally convey information, or share the same prestige. My own research suggests the following generalizations:

1 there is higher retention of simple material when it is presented orally rather than visually;
2 a combination of two media is better than either alone;
3 oral communication is more effective with less-educated audiences;
4 there is greater learning and retention of material when the individual sets his own pace for absorbing the material and when he participates and is involved in the process of learning;
5 oral presentation is more effective than printed matter in changing opinion;
6 the use of one medium stimulates the use of another; e.g., the use of radio appears to promote newspaper reading;
7 the prestige of a mass medium varies according to its perceived credibility.
8 face-to-face communication, which allows for greater interaction and flexibility of appeal, is more effective than radio and newspapers under certain conditions.

The choice of a mass medium for communication also depends

on its availability and accessibility to people. In Africa, one can expect personal ownership or use of radios, television, and books to be found among those classes of people who are literate and receive cash wages. In general, the more urban, educated, economically secure, and "cosmopolitan" the individual, the greater his use of mass media.

Restricted access to media often stimulates the development of alternative methods of exposure to news, information, and ideas. In many communities factory workers are exposed to media information through collective radio listening and oral newspaper reading in market-places or in the homes of kin and fellow workers. Local *entrepreneurs* place public address systems above their shops to broadcast commercial advertisements, music, and news reports at certain hours of the day.

Personal influence

Most of what is communicated between men, however, is not transmitted directly through mass media, but orally in face-to-face social situations. Face-to-face communication is of crucial importance in affecting marketing, fashions, and media programme selections. Personal communication influences people not only through what is said, but also through the dynamics of inter-personal conversation. This factor becomes for many people more important than the content of the message itself.

There are four advantageous characteristics of face-to-face communication. First, personal contacts are more casual, and more difficult to avoid than mass communications. Many people are highly selective of mass communications, avoiding matters that do not interest them or that conflict with their personal opinions. In addition, people are less likely to anticipate or to take steps to avoid the content of personal communication. Second, face-to-face communication permits greater flexibility in the presentation of the message. If the communicator meets resistance or avoidance he can change his line of argument. Third, in the direct personal face-to-face relationship he can evaluate and reward the acceptance of the message or argument.

Fourth, people tend to put their trust in the judgement of persons whom they know.

These observations suggest that personal oral communication creates a more intimate selling situation than mass media — you can't ask a wooden box questions, nor can the screen anticipate every facet of the consumer's intentions. This fact has relevance for the expansion of the tertiary sector of the modern economy, service and marketing, and the employment of African shops, "tally-men", distributors and salesmen as marketing outlets.

THE FLOW OF INFLUENCE

People acquire much of their information and many of their ideas through personal contact with information-bearers in their own social groups. Media information reaches people through a "two-step flow" and, in the process, intersects with the oral traditional system. The communication goes from the mass media direct to persons high in the social hierarchy and from them to others via face-to-face situations. The persons who exercise control over the exposure of others may be called "influentials", "gate-keepers" or "opinion leaders".

Leaders in every walk of life tend to read more books and magazines, and attend movies more often than non-leaders. Leaders are also more selective in their exposure to mass media and read magazines which deal with their speciality. These specialized choices of media are made because they serve a specific function for the opinion leader. Opinion leaders are not necessarily social and political leaders, although they may be. Sometimes opinion leaders look to other people for information and advice and some of these "second-level" influentials may depend upon the mass media, while others turn to still a third circle of opinion leaders for advice. Elders, teachers, ministers, shop-owners and educated relatives are often of crucial importance in shaping the individual's final decision.

In Africa personal influence is quite important in all areas of social choices, whether it be in fashions, fads, public issues, or in the choice of radio programmes. Definite social characteristics differentiate influentials from non-influentials. Influence flows from the older to the younger, from those in the higher statuses to those in lower ones, from the boss to the worker, from the powerful to the humble. Persons having greatest access and exposure to mass media control the exposure of other persons and influence the acceptance of the information transmitted.

THE AUDIENCE, RECEPTION AND RESPONSE

Every communication is conditioned by the fact that it is received. The message is sifted through a screen of social taste, attitudes and pre-dispositions. This process has been expressed by Eric Barnouw[1] as follows:

> "In a particular state of feeling and *expectation* certain incoming signals ignite our *attention* then tap our hidden power lines of *emotion* stepping up the voltage of related *information* and impelling us to the formation of an *idea* thereby driving us towards *action*."

It has been discovered, however, that this type of formula over-simplifies the process of response; in addition, its extension to the analysis of communication in Africa is fraught with many dangers. There is no simple cause-and-effect relationship between the intent of a message and the individual's response.

Information exposure is a social and cultural phenomenon. It is related to the structure of human relationships; who talks to whom, how often, on what subjects and with what influences are all aspects of the social structure. The way a person is exposed, when and how frequently, is determined by his social position in the community. In all communities there are well-developed systems of social relationships which influence the exposure of individuals. There are socially approved media and channels of exposure and, as a result, shared selections.

Information exposure occurs as an aspect of the daily life of the individual and is affected by the general pattern of his activities in the society. Members of an audience belong to distinct social groups differing in origin, socio-cultural background, styles of life and their relationships to the means of production and distribution. Thus, the audience to new information is not made up of "individuals" but members of social groups.

In changing African societies, where urbanization–industrialization thrusts traditional folk into the modern world, three basic types of audiences result: the traditional "folk", "transitionals" and "moderns".

The traditional folk:
1 oral interpersonal information exposure;
2 exposure to new information infrequent;
3 persons in this type are rural or illiterate workers having low standards of living;
4 they are "folk people"; that is to say they are traditionally orientated and psychologically unemancipated.

The transitionals:
1 Both oral and direct exposure to information are characteristic; oral exposure supports direct exposure;
2 exposure to media is more frequent than among the traditionals;
3 the members of this type are urban, semi-literate factory workers with a higher standard of living than traditionals;
4 they are an emergent social class, transitional between old and new social patterns.

The moderns:
1 direct use of the media;
2 exposure to media as a daily occurrence;
3 members who are urban literate office workers and professionals with a higher standard of living than either traditionals or transitionals;
4 they are orientated towards urban world culture and European customs, values and norms.

Once a message or product is perceived, there are a number of basic social factors which speed the information through a community. For example, social visits, "town hall" meetings, migration and travelling, and the market-place.

In rural areas, information exposure and diffusion occur through frequent clan and village "town meetings". At these meetings a wide variety of topics is discussed and often it is group consensus that decides the course of individual behaviour. The *baraza*, among the Chagga cash-crop peasants of East Africa, draws together chiefs, councillors and kinsmen into discussions about land, farm equipment, co-operatives, roads, education and politics. The family "get-togethers" common in West Africa provide a means of sharing news, information and products.

The widespread custom of social visiting between relatives diffuses information among kinsmen of all classes. In Central Lagos, where many workers live in close proximity to relatives, frequent visiting takes place; 54–74 per cent of the adult population studied by Marris saw their mother, father, brother and sister within a day or a week, and half saw at least three relatives every day. The mother's residence is the central point of an interlocking system of frequent contact. Periodically large family meetings are held. In Lagos, Marris found that 44 per cent of the weekly meetings involved 11–20 persons, 56 per cent of the monthly meetings comprised 21–30 persons, and half the annual meetings included more than 30 persons.

The exposure of people in small intimate collectives, village groups, factories, families, youth organizations, women's guilds and farms, has certain basic advantages over the large anonymous groupings typical of urban audiences. In the natural groups of kinship, work and play, people know each other, and ideas are more easily assimilated. Some techniques of expanding exposure in small group situations are village cinema showings, mobile film units, and "wall newspapers". The utility of this small-group approach is greatly enhanced when information materials are specially created with the participation of the group and under their own direction.

THE MEANING OF MEDIA EXPOSURE

Window on the world

The mass media provide a window on the world. As wage-earners are exposed to mass communication they develop new images of themselves in relation to the world around them. The sociologists David Reisman and Daniel Lerner[2] have used the term "mobile sensibility" to describe the mechanism by which individuals acquire new information and ideas, and create adaptive personalities. This concept can best be illustrated by quoting from a letter sent to the Lusaka broadcasting station shortly after the introduction of the "Saucepan Special", wired home-reception of radio broadcasts. Scrawled painfully in one of the many vernaculars of the land it read: "We are no longer isolated . . . I feel proud when I switch on my Saucepan Special and have the whole world in my hut."

In the short span of 20 years the wireless spread throughout Central Africa. The "Saucepan", which cost $17.50, was received enthusiastically by workers. Over the thatched huts of villages and the concrete houses of urban compounds, aerials started to rise. African women and men came to broadcasting stations to talk about their problems. Over the years the "Saucepan Special" provided an impetus to community development and self-help.

Desire for social mobility

In Africa, exposure to mass media results in increased desire for social mobility, literacy, new experiences and a more satisfactory life. Exposure serves to motivate persons towards greater knowledge of the world around them. In other words, being exposed increasingly to mass communication also means acquiring the desire to move more freely from one's former position in the social hierarchy to a newer one. A revolution of rising expectations is occurring; there are new aspirations for the "better things of life", and predispositions towards newer forms of social organization.

Listeners write

Radio listening stimulates people to express their feelings in writing. Every day, thousands of town-dwellers and worker-peasants set down their requests to broadcasting stations. They ask for more information about products, news about relatives, and answers to problems. Overseas stations are listened to avidly; one of the B.B.C.'s external programmes to Somalia receives more than 1,000 letters a year. A brief review of these letters provides an illustration of the pulling power of radio among African audiences.

Letters reveal many interesting facets of the unseen audience. The language of written response is not necessarily the same as the language by which a person received the broadcast. In Somalia, where there is no official written Somali language, listeners express their views in English, Arabic, Italian and French.

The geographical coverage of broadcasts is often wider than is assumed by the communicator. Somali broadcasts are listened to in the Horn of Africa, East Africa, Aden, the Arabian Gulf, Madagascar, Congo and ships at sea. Each person identifies with a programme in some way. Letters from Somalia expatriates and seamen say "Your broadcast makes me think of home" and "If you want us to listen in, the programmes should be adapted to suit our tastes".

Letters express a wide variety of requests and social tastes, "Please play Cliff Richard and Ray Charles", "Please explain how the divide-and-rule principle works", "Send my greetings to Uncle Hassan in New York, U.S.A.". Students seek information, "I am wishing you to tell me about a disease called T.B., where it comes from and what causes it, and what will be the result of cigarettes if you smoke." And many wish to know about race relations, "What is the white man's attitude towards the black man's revolt in the U.S.?"

"How others see us"

As more Africans read, listen and view mass-media messages from foreign sources they become aware of "how others see us".

Many of the media messages beamed to Africans are thought of as flattering and praiseworthy and are rewarded by confidence and co-operation. Most externally-created messages to Africa, however, fit the preconceptions of the sender and not the needs of the receiver and strike a discordant note in the dialogue of progress.

Stereotypes about Africa have persisted for centuries after the facts contradicting them have become easily available to all. Few external communicators question the arguments that support their convictions. Psychologists say that most people would like to continue to believe that which is familiar and which has always been accepted as true. We resent it when doubt is cast upon any of our assumptions, and find excuses for clinging to our beliefs. The result is that most of our "reasoning" consists in finding arguments for going on believing as we already do. We rely on short-cuts, simple explanations and "pictures in our heads" obtained from others around us.

Externally-created mass-media messages directed to Africa serve, therefore, as vehicles of mis-information as well as information, of stereotypes as well as product concepts. This is evident in many advertisements, cartoons, newsreels, films and schoolbooks. As a result, stereotypes perceived as unfavourable by Africans block the communication process. On the one hand, the communicator of product information and ideas wrapped in fragile myths becomes a prisoner of his own beliefs. On the other hand, much of what is heard or seen is received with laughter, rancour or distrust. *The Journal of the Lagos Chamber of Commerce*,[3] which speaks for a large segment of Nigeria's businessmen, had this to say editorially about the international Press:

> "We read remarkable articles in the World Press which seem to emphasize our shortcomings. . . . To those visiting writers whose jaded audiences apparently require news that is exotic, we are pleased to display our colourful tribal ceremonies and romantic folk-lore. It is right that these fast-disappearing evidences of our ancient culture should be preserved before we too are translated into the grey mechanized organizational world of the latter twentieth century. But not all Englishmen live in stone

floored thatched cottages and not all Nigerians live in darkest
Africa."

Dr. Nnamdi Azikiwe,[4] writing as Governor-General of the
Federation of Nigeria, sent a vigorous reply to *The Guardian*
concerning a leading article entitled "Nigeria's Struggle":

". . . It is my duty to admonish you and your colleagues of the
Anglo-Saxon Press generally, that you are dabbling too much in
Nigerian problems about which you are fundamentally ignorant
and on which you are least qualified to pontificate.

It is the height of arrogance, if not folly, for an editor of your
standing to encourage regular tendentious references to African
political leaders. This is becoming one fashionable feature of Anglo-
Saxon journalism, on both sides of the Atlantic, and the simple
reason is their congenital snobbery.

I stand to be corrected when I say that neither *Pravda*, *Izvestia* nor
other sections of the Press in u.s.s.r. had been insolent or had encouraged their correspondents and editors to be boorish in writing
about African political leaders as the Anglo-Saxon Press has been
doing from time immemorial.

If you should check on the morgues of *The Times*, *The Econo-
mist*, *Observer*, *Sunday Times*, *Sunday Telegraph*, *Daily Express*,
Daily Mail, *Daily Telegraph and Morning Post*, *New York Times*,
New York Herald-Tribune, *Washington Post*, *Time*, *Newsweek*, to
name a few, you would see how insolently Anglo-Saxon journ-
alists have been writing about Nasser, Tubman, Houphouet
Boigny, Bourguiba, Azikiwe, Nkrumah, Kenyatta, Kaunda,
Banda, Nkomo, and other African Nationalist leaders.

We of the older generation in Nigeria have done our best to
hold on to our British connection and our inflexible faith in liberal
democracy, in spite of regular doses of insults and gibes from the
Anglo-Saxon Press; but I cannot guarantee that our children will
stomach your continued irreverent attitude towards Africans and
their political leaders."

MEDIA, ADVERTISING AND DEVELOPMENT

African governments are increasingly concerned with utilizing
the technical skill and know-how of Western marketing and sales

research to the fullest possible extent; they wish to incorporate these skills into their plans for raising the standards of living of their people. The media are to them mechanisms of change and indispensable aids to social mobilization and progress.

In light of the significant role which the mass media have to play in pre-investment, it has been suggested that the development of the media be treated as a part of national programmes for economic expansion. Media development stands in reciprocal relationship to economic development; media can stimulate the capacity to create further national wealth by enlisting the populace more directly in economic development. This widespread concern of leaders regarding the future of mass media in their nations will, of course, have its effect on advertising.

Many are concerned and alarmed by the potential power of the mass media over the minds of the young and women, and over the choices made by consumers. Leaders who wish to regulate the in-flow of imported goods deplore the "Keep up with the Joneses" type of media presentation. The emphasis on the acquisitive life produces "false standards and illusory ideas of wealth in an economy which has not yet got off to a real start on the road of reconstruction and development", says Ghana's President Nkrumah in his book *Africa must Unite*.

There is considerable concern, especially among educational administrators and social workers, about the deterioration of decorum and taste before the advance of "popular culture". Many sponsored programmes like the racy, wise-cracking "Sergeant Bilko" and "I Love Lucy" shows, are lacking in immediate relevance to the humour, pathos and ethos of Africans.

In the relatively unexplored field of mass marketing through sponsored-media programmes there is considerable room for research. In Africa, as in the Western countries, we do not as yet really know "what the public wants" and what the relationship is between the use of media and brand buying.

In summary, the whole question of formulating and projecting media advertising messages to African audiences needs to be thoroughly reviewed. Despite the expenditure of more than £1m. a year on media advertising, little is known about advertising effectiveness in African cities. It is highly probable that advertising does not "make markets" and that an increase in sales is not the crucial indicator of effectiveness. A growing number of overseas market researchers are laying greater emphasis on the context in which product information is received and on the behavioural impulsions that grow out of the daily lives of people and their development needs.

Advertising, in the years to come, will be a part of the educational process and involve producers and consumers in a learning situation. Improving overall attitudes, awareness and knowledge about a brand will require knowing the goals of consumers as well as the objectives of manufacturers. Looked at from this point of view, the continuous achievement of advertising aims is as much a function of social factors as it is of the worthiness of a product, or how many times it is announced in the media.

M

PROFILE OF A
COMMUNICATIONS NETWORK IN
MUSLIM WEST AFRICA

MUSLIM WEST AFRICAN cities have been crucial links between the Arab lands of the prophet Mohammed and the kingdoms of Black Africa for over 1,000 years. They are cross-roads of Africa shimmering on the edge of the Sahara, stations of the camel *caravanserai*, fingers stretching out to the shores of the Atlantic, the Gulf of Guinea and down to Congo and Angola. Today 30,000,000 West Africans are Muslims and half of them are Nigerians, living in remnants of ancient kingdoms and city-states, like Kano, Nigeria, poised on the brink of industrialization, balancing in dynamic equilibrium the traditional and modern, the sacred and secular.

The whirlpool of contemporary ideas in Kano has three tributaries: the well-springs of the historic African past, the steady flow of Arab Islamic culture warmed by centuries of intimate acquaintance, and the quick impersonal currents emanating from the modern Western world. They meet in Kano and, passing over cataracts of contact, surge turbulently amidst mud, houses mosques and factories. Thrusting changes collide with landmarks of a thousand years, cells of culture which sift alien ideas through a screen of beliefs and sentiments.

Industrialization, a thin line of modern influence, moves across Kano enclosing its different populations in a crucible of change where mass media are employed to convey information, advertisements and propaganda to modify opinion and behaviour. Radio signals from all the world fill the air and radio audiences are sought as clients and political allies. The B.B.C. and the Nigerian broadcasting stations vie for listeners with Voice of America, Radio Moscow, Peking, Congo, Ghana, Mali and Israel. Owning a radio is a mark of distinction and listening is enjoyed because there are a variety of stations, political views and languages to choose from and many new channels to the world.

Radio stimulates conversation and its sounds punctuate the rhythm of life in the *zaure* and in front of the tradesmen's shops. Less than 5 per cent of the people own radios but group listening is widespread and the transistor radio provides a mobile means of transmitting thousands of word images an hour to ever-widening audiences. More people talk about things outside their personal experiences than ever before, especially local politics and parliamentary activities of "our own sons" — the universally-admired Sir Ahmadu Bello, the Regional Governor, Sir Kashim Ibrahim, and the Prime Minister of the Federation, Sir Abubakar Tafawa Balewa. Popular tastes are simple; religious broadcasts guide the faithful, adult literacy programmes instruct the seeker after knowledge and Hausa *goge* music provides mass entertainment.

Going to the cinema is an increasingly important leisure-time activity mainly for adult males. For most Kanawa, the people of the city, stepping outside the ancient walls is an exciting venture, more so than attending the solitary cinema within, where social *mores* discourage smoking and attendance of women. The Plaza, one of five cinemas, owes its popularity to its strategic position near the city gates and is the largest public place frequented by all ethnic groups and classes — Europeans, Ibos, Yorubas, Levantines and the Kanawa. To accommodate varying tastes there are special nights for European films and for Indian films.

Indian films, introduced in 1957 by a Levantine *entrepreneur*, are popular because they are adventurous, romantic and full of action. In a country where no African commercial films are made or shown, Indian films enable Africans to identify themselves with people and situations not too far removed from their own. A night at the Plaza is a journey into a world of fantasy, genii and magic lanterns, horsemen, sword-fights and beautiful maidens in distress — all reminiscent of ancient African kingdoms. Unlike British and American productions, Indian films are not disturbing to the elders, they do not show smoking or drinking, and in the end the bad man is punished and the principle of social integrity triumph's.

More than seven Nigerian daily papers, as well as world newspapers, provide for every reading choice. Readers vividly reflect the city's cosmopolitan character. Ibos are partial to the National Convention of Nigerian Citizens N.C.N.C. paper, *West African Pilot*, and Yorubas like the *Ibadan Tribune* or the Kano *Northern Star*, representing the Action group. Literate Kanawa buy the Northern Peoples' Congress paper, the *Daily Mail*, edited by the stalwart Rasak Aremu, and a minority rely on the *Daily Comet*, the Northern Elements Progressive Union paper founded by Alhaji Aminu Kano. Civil servants read the *Nigerian Citizen*, sponsored by the regional government, and African Christians purchase the Sudan Interior Mission monthly, *African Challenge*. The national Lagos-based newspapers, the *Daily Times*, and the *Nigerian Morning Post*, have, however, the widest reading audience, albeit among English-speaking persons.

Kanawa are very knowledgeable about many issues close to them, such as education, housing and employment, increasing opportunities in the civil service, and the need for regional unity. They are familiar with their leaders' names, to a greater extent locally perhaps than nationally, and support them without great debate.

Political awareness and public debate of major inter-regional federal and international issues are increasing, though to a greater extent among the southerners than among the Kanawa and among N.E.P.U. supporters rather than among N.P.C. cadres. Few Kanawa know about the Lake Chad Development Scheme or discuss the national census, the Coker Commission Report on the Treason Trial or the Morgan Commission Report on wages. But their attendance at classes opened during the "War against Ignorance" campaign indicates a developing interest in community and national affairs. Additional thousands are targets for the literacy campaigns of the Kano Public Enlightenment Office and the illustrated literature and mobile cinemas of the Regional Information Service.

The Kanawa are not without social leadership in their progress towards wider diffusion of information and knowledge. Educated youths applaud the regional government and the Native Authority and urge them to continue their educational efforts. As Mahmud Abubakar, President of the Kano Secondary School Old Students' Association, said in an annual address:

> "There are still thousands of our brothers roaming our streets without an education. This waste of talent must be checked. Educational progress alone is not enough, it must go hand in hand with economic progress so that hundreds of potential school-leavers can obtain jobs."

Mass media are, for most people in Kano, appendages of an alien world. Most media messages are never received directly because exposure is limited by social, economic and cultural factors. Few persons within the walled city own radios or telephones, or purchase newspapers or attend the cinema. Personal ownership of instruments of communication occurs most frequently among traders, the educated, the wealthy and the noble, the wage worker and the city-born. Leaders in all walks of life tend to read more books and newspapers in Hausa, Arabic or English, and listen to the radio more often than non-readers.

New information is transmitted orally in face-to-face situations, through a network of social interaction. Information reaches the ordinary man indirectly, through a "two-step flow"; from the media to persons high in the social hierarchy and, from them, in an ever-widening circuit to others by word of mouth.

Traditional information networks are still the veins of this emerging society and remain the key means of moulding public opinion and engineering consent. Information and ideas are diffused and absorbed through personal allegiance and contacts with social groupings. _Malams_, magistrates, Koranic scholars, nobles and traders are "influentials", "gate-keepers" and "opinion leaders"; they monitor the exposure of others and influence the acceptance or rejection of new ideas. Ideas travel down the social scale and loyalty is more revered than innovation. Social and personal influence, more than mass-media persuasion, assumes importance in fashions, fads, public issues and consumer products.

Information exposure in Moslem Africa is not confined to

modern mass media or Western ideologies. The traditional system is for most people the main vehicle for the reception of new ideas, opinions and information. More important, perhaps, it is the vehicle for the ferment of thought and action emanating from the modernizing Islamic nations of the world.

In Kano, the "Muslim way" stands apart from the "Christian way" and the reception and diffusion of Western communications compete with feelings and sentiments transmitted from the Islamic African world, North Africa, Egypt and the Sudan, from the Middle East, Pakistan and India. Through Islam the bridge across the desert sea, the wisdom of past ages, the wonders of Allah, the sayings of the prophet Mohammed and the hopes of a common future are chronicled by respected individuals and social classes. Traders, militant religious brotherhoods, *Malams* and intellectuals, and the thousands of honoured pilgrims, *alhajiyya*, returning each year from Mecca, are a trans-continental network more powerful than a thousand wavelengths.

Every Muslim is enjoined to make a pilgrimage to Mecca (*Hajj*) at least once in his lifetime. This Islamic institution gives Muslims from all parts of the world the opportunity to congregate every year and fraternize. African Muslims have made pilgrimages for more than eight centuries and there are permanent communities of Northern Nigerians in Mecca. Each year thousands of pilgrims journey overland to Mecca, along well-established routes via Agadez, Ghat, Tripoli and Ghadames or east through Chad and the Sudan to the Red Sea; 8,000 pilgrims annually pass through Sudanic communities and there are as many as 500,000 pilgrims who are on their way to or from Mecca at any given period; for the poor, the journey often takes seven years or more.

The pilgrimage gives Muslim Africans a view of Islam as a world religion, one in which he shares a common inheritance. Passing through Muslim countries gives the impression that Islam is the religion of Africa and through contacts with pilgrims from other communities Africans gain some idea of current political issues in the Muslim world. Back at home his influence is widespread especially when the pilgrim is also wealthy, powerful or learned. Many of the important positions in Hausa-Fulani society are held by *alhaji*; for example, in 1964 the major regional administrative positions in Northern Nigeria were occupied by persons who had made the pilgrimage to Mecca.

Malams are a class of learned religious specialists and through them the presence of Islam is felt in African Muslim communities. They are interpreters of all spiritual and secular life. The *malam* is name-giver, teacher, scribe, family physician, adviser, judge and Allah's agent among the people. It is the *malam*, therefore, in the midst of his fellows, who stands at the doorway of learning and exercises a fundamental control over information exposure.

Islam moves from place to place, from mouth to ear, as traders like the intrepid Hausa, religious militants and intellectuals wend their way from Arabia and North Africa to Dahomey, Nigeria and the Congo lands. Muslim African traders are a supranational influence with widespread links; through travel and settlement they mediate the exchange of ideas within Muslim African communities and between them and the outside Muslim world. The militant *Tijaniyya, Qadiriyya,* and *Ahmadiyya* religious brotherhoods are focal points of Islamic revivalism. Armed with the "sword of Islam" they create bulwarks against the relaxation of religious values through the influence of Christianity and Europeanization, and channel attitudes and initiate action in their own image.

Reciprocal relations among intellectuals over many centuries provide fertile ground for the interchange of ideas. Arab scholars have taught and studied at centres of learning in the ancient West African civilizations of Ghana, Mali, Kano, Kanem and Timbuktu and are doing so today in Kano and Sokoto at modern schools of Arabic studies. Kanem sent students to North Africa as early as the ninth century and today 100 Muslim African youths a year undertake studies at El-azhar, Cairo and Karaouyan, Tunisia.

New political ideas enter quiescent Muslim West African communities from renascent independent and Arab nations. Political leaders and modern youth discuss Arab unity, Arab socialism, the role of Israel in West Africa, the Algerian Revolution and political events affecting Muslims in Africa. Charismatic leaders dream of the unity of Muslim states, of a vast modern Islamic culture reaching from the Mediterranean in the north to Mauritania on the Atlantic across the Continent to the Sudan and Egypt on the Red Sea.

Within the changing Kanawa community the traditional and the modern, the sacred and the secular, exist in a vibrating equilibrium. A student returning from London or Cairo brings new outlooks on traditional teaching methods, the role of women and traditional agricultural methods. The skilled teacher from Pakistan dressed in Western clothes may appear strange to his fellow worshippers in the central mosque, but his labour to teach their children and assist in solving their problems does not go unacknowledged.

In Kano, then, two worlds exist: the Muslim African traditional and the modern Western world of "strangers". The modern Western world brought European contact, wage labour, rapid development and participation with other citizens in a nation-state. Yet Muslim West Africans also share a common pool of culture with the international Islamic community; it is another window on the panorama of recent history and another source of modernizing ideas.

These two worlds exist side by side; both touch across the counter, in the market-place, at the post office, in the Kingsway shop, but part in the church, the home and the school. Agents of change, whether governments, industry or social therapists, are faced with many challenges in this situation. How can one fashion changed behaviour out of the whole cloth of inherited cultural values? How can media nurture a healthy collective image, establish new goals for peasants and workers, consumers and citizens, but strengthen social integrity and cohesion?

Within the framework of these forces a synthesis is taking place; social development gestates in a new form. The statesmen and administrators of Muslim African nations and communities are unanimous in their desire for rapid social and economic development. Alhaji Sir Ahmadu Bello, the secular and spiritual leader of 30 million Northern Nigerians, expresses this belief in his book *My Life*.[5] Political leaders affirm that modernization, like the history of medicine, numbers and the alphabet, is not synonymous with Europeanization. They believe that there is an important place for Islam in Africa and hope to create resurgent technologically-advanced societies which will play a progressive role in African and international affairs.

REFERENCES

1 BARNOUW, ERIC, *Mass Communication,* Rinehart and Co., New York, 1956.

2 REISMAN, DAVID and LERNER, DANIEL, "Self and Society", *Explorations,* No. 5, June, 1955.

3 *Commerce in Nigeria,* Journal of the Lagos Chamber of Commerce, Nigeria, **4,** No. 1, 1962.

4 AZIKIWE, DR. NNAMDI, on the Anglo-Saxon Press, *The Guardian,* 10 August, 1962.

PROFILE

5 BELLO, ALHAJI, SIR AHMADU, *My Life,* Cambridge University Press, London, 1962.

CHAPTER TEN

THE SOCIAL UTILITY OF
INDUSTRY IN HOUSING

AFRICA'S Century of Development presents many unique challenges to industries and marketing companies. As more firms transfer their operations to Africa they will be drawn by the needs and demands of development into co-operation with governments, and the people themselves. They will see new responsibilities and new opportunities to solve short- and long-term problems — business and social problems — ranging from technical training and personnel management to housing, urban development and human relations.

In this chapter the question of housing for workers will be discussed, and the ways in which industry, architects and government can produce a healthier environment for millions of future African worker-consumers.

THE DYNAMICS OF THE PROBLEM

The migration of peasants to cities and centres of employment is the greatest population movement in the world. All over the globe peasants are migrating towards jobs and what they hope will be a better way of life. Many find, however, that their vital energies are sapped by their new environment and trickle away, ill-housed, in little enclaves of despair.

The *caboclos* of the Brazilian backlands trek to the bleak *favelas* of Rio de Janeiro. West Indians forsake their islands in the sun for the grey mid-Victorian working-class boroughs of England. In North America, Mexicans become *los descamisados*, the shirtless ragged "angels" of Los Angeles, and Puerto Ricans see snow for the first time through grimy tenement windows in Spanish Harlem.

In Africa, as well, migration is an effect of economic development and creates new problems for industry and society. The expansion of employment centres and cities creates a back-lash of powerful social and economic forces. One factory or plantation whistle shatters the web of village culture 100 miles away. One industrial estate or large-scale development project changes the whole life pattern of a region. The siting of industries opens up inaccessible areas and right behind come shanties, one-class suburbs and company towns. The industrial thirst for water is quenched in shallow reservoirs and as the level of water supply drops the rate of mud-house building in the city declines. How can the social consequences of industrialization and urbanization be successfully foreseen and resolved? This is industry's number one social challenge in Africa's Century of Development.

Adequate housing is not within the economic reach of the mass of employed workers. Studies in Ethiopia, Guinea, Nigeria, Somalia and the Sudan indicate that most workers cannot afford better housing. In Somalia, where the average annual income of an unskilled labourer is £S90 and the skilled labourer gets £S180, the cost of an adequate modern house is £S800.

Most workers live miles away from their places of employment, and must spend tiring hours and precious wages on commuting. In Lagos, 100,000 people commute daily from the crowded mainland and island communities. For many, it is a two-hour daily trek; for others the cost of transport snatches 15 per cent of meagre family budgets. In Khartoum, Sudan, thousands of worker-pedestrians cause traffic jams at the two local bridges. Workers come from as far as 15 km. away; many spend 1½ hours a day travelling to and from their jobs. The monthly cost of travel reaches £S2 or a quarter of a worker's monthly salary. In Lusaka, Zambia, according to one researcher, "Most people live so far from a bus line that they might just as well walk all the way to the city centre or to their place of work."

The interminable search for better accommodation closer to work results in a high rate of residential mobility. Pat Uriesi,[1] writing in the Daily Times around the time of Nigeria's general strike in the spring of 1964, said "Workers . . . can't get to work on time. The situation is so disgusting at Apapa that many people have given out their houses on cheap rent while they look for houses elsewhere."

Long journeys to work, poor housing, debilitating environments and social tensions all affect the successful management and operation of private and governmental enterprises. The rapid solution of housing and urban problems can have immediate and long-term benefits in all spheres of social and economic activity. Good housing relieves the grimness of impoverished migrancy and stimulates residential stability and a stable work force. Good housing assists the formation of responsible consumer-citizens. Good housing contributes to nation-building by reducing the numbers of persons who merely transfer a subsistence way of life from the countryside to the city.

How can economic development, labour migration and housing be successfully planned and controlled? How can workers be adequately employed, housed and transported within the framework of present and future needs and resources?

INDUSTRY, HOUSING AND SOCIETY IN KANO

Kano has an unusual opportunity to encourage and achieve a stable, orderly and prosperous urban community, unique in Nigeria and perhaps in Africa. In Kano, as in many African cities, modern urban growth has been closely related to development of agro-industrial enterprises, growing and processing of cash crops, trading and commerce. Now there are more than 100 light industries and scores of firms and government offices employing thousands of workers. But the smooth introduction of capital development industries and improvement of existing capital resources necessitate the solution of a number of vital problems — rural depopulation, labour supply, housing, local administration, town planning and human relations.

In this land of variable soils and rainfall, peasants farm two acres of widely scattered holdings, using the traditional hoe. In the past, farm yields have been adequate to feed rural families and supply city populations. With each year, however, more people become dependent on the land. Deaths have been reduced by modern health practices without a corresponding decline in birth rates. Traditional skills and crafts are displaced by manufactured goods. Rural conditions deteriorate and villages become places of unemployment and poverty. Villagers start the long trek to Kano, placing a heavier burden on food supplies, housing and social services. Now within a 30-mile periphery of Kano there are more than $1\frac{1}{2}$ million people; it is one of the most densely-populated areas in Africa.

Dynamic changes in this ancient city create new needs and bring recognition of new problems and solutions. New social institutions sprout like buds of green-blue grass in the red laterite clay after the rains. In the fields of education, social service and housing, many people are engaged in examining and augmenting traditional customs and proposing new paths of progress.

The solution of housing problems presents greater difficulties. Local authorities are ill-equipped to meet the influx of migrants. Overcrowded and sub-standard enclaves exist in low-income districts and market areas, the Syrian quarter, Sabon Gari and fringe communities like Gwargwargwa. Housing densities vary considerably from 15–30 persons per compound in these areas, to three in the "senior-service" and European residential areas in the suburban green belt.

The city's labour market suffers from over-abundance of unskilled and highly mobile labour. Less than one-tenth of the workers in Birnin Kano are engaged in crafts, clerical or administrative positions, and few hold jobs in the modern sector of the economy. Higher-level jobs in the traditional and modern sectors are held by the city-born, and middle-level occupations by older migrants. Newer migrants comprise the low-paid fringe of the labour market. The majority of unskilled workers do not move up the job hierarchy but rather from one unskilled job to another. Thus urban society develops radical disparities in income, housing, social status, education and social origin.

In the next ten years a quarter of a million people will need new housing. The provision of housing for workers by government and industries could go a long way to relieve the housing problem. I discussed this question with over 30 urban authorities from Kano and other parts of the northern region at a seven-day seminar at the Institute of Administration, Zaria, held under the direction of Dr. Richardson and Mr. M. J. Campbell.

The consensus of the group was that the encouragement of new industries was desirable because it brought wealth and housing to the local community. The negative social consequences of industrialization and urban growth were discussed. In conclusion I asked, "If this is the price you also have to pay — new migrants, social tension, breakdown of the family, etc., — would you still want industrial growth?" Around the table each man, from the elders swathed in brightly coloured robes to the young men in Western dress, said, "Yes, yes, yes; it must come, as rapidly as possible, and we will plan to meet these difficulties."

Without assistance new workers will not be able to build homes. As a young textile worker said to me one day: "You can't build and earn at the same time." Furthermore, Kano's income structure, local revenue and traditional *entrepreneurs* are not able to finance local housing. Who should finance urban housing? New industries alone, or in combination with government agencies? Should workers obtain homes on the public market and receive a housing allowance? Or, if houses are built for them, should the cost be deducted from wages in the form of rent? Is it desirable to build factory estates which become "workers' quarters", distinct and apart from the community? Should loans be made to local government for rehabilitating urban housing? These are some of the urgent questions facing Kano and all urban areas in Nigeria and Africa.

Further, if individual houses are built should they be designed to meet traditional cultural patterns, for example, separate female and children's areas? Is it possible to encourage subsidized "do-it-yourself" housing where the worker builds a standard house with a *zaure*, sleeping-room and parlour? Does the community wish to encourage home-ownership or renting? Will home-ownership discourage mobility of workers seeking to take advantage of better labour markets in other towns? The answers to such questions will be vital in determining the urban social environment of future generations.

Home-building and population distribution in Kano are also affected by the supply of water. The present supply of three million gallons per day is not sufficient to meet consumption and building needs, and the expansion of the water-works is handicapped by lack of local finance. Water is the key ingredient in house-building and the increasing shortage of water affects both the rate and the place where new homes are built or old ones repaired. Industrialization places heavier demands on water supply; as more industries and workers come into the city, less water will be available and housing problems will grow more acute.

Industrialization also causes stresses and strains in the machinery of local government. As industrialization proceeds a larger proportion of total fixed capital invested in Kano is introduced through the public sector. New government responsibilities arise and require adjustment in the administrative mechanisms of traditional Native Authority councils.

As in many areas in newly independent countries, there are problems of creating viable forms of local government. How can new political institutions gain the loyalty of citizens? What factors retard progress towards a unified local government incorporating equally Muslims and strangers in Greater Kano? What administrative actions might facilitate peaceful adoption of new predispositions, identifications and allegiances among immigrant workers? If Kano is to build a single unified community it will be necessary to develop facilities for social interaction and to create new social all-community institutions which will bridge the gap of insecurity between Muslims and strangers.

The trend of administrative thinking is in the direction of creating a central agency which will deal with housing and urban problems within the framework of overall economic development plans. One encouraging step towards the "Kano of tomorrow" is the newly-formed Kano Development Corporation. Secondly, there is an expressed desire to form a unified and representative form of local government to supersede the four existing, separate and conflicting systems of authority which hinder uniform industrial-urban growth. Proposals have been made to create one urban council with a full portfolio of responsibilities, trained technical staffs and representation of traditional interests to ensure cultural continuity. The hope is that with the aid of industry a re-designed economic and physical pattern will enable all Kano's citizens, new and old alike, to live, work and contribute to the growth of Northern Nigeria and the nation as a whole.

FINANCING AND BUILDING OF HOUSING

Most African governments recognize the need for a national housing programme based on six principles:

1 housing for all workers and their families;
2 modernization of existing housing;
3 a central agency to assess needs and formulate a programme of housing, slum clearance, and the re-housing of displaced persons;
4 housing should be co-ordinated with economic development;
5 creation of a housing industry;
6 co-operation between industry and government.

However, African governments are not able alone to finance the housing of millions of urban industrial, mining and plantation workers. On the local level, the income structure, revenue and scanty capital possessed by traditional *entrepreneurs* are not sufficient to meet housing needs. Provincial revenues do not grow at the same rate as new demands for social services.

On the national level, it has been estimated that 10 per cent or more of the gross national income should be spent annually on housing and related costs; twice this amount should be spent on gross fixed capital formation in the housing sector. But the attainment and disbursement of these huge sums is hardly possible in the face of other urgent demands on scarce resources. As a result,

3.
Social problems:
a challenge

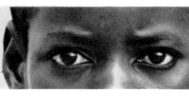

housing receives a small share of national budgets. Less than a quarter of all foreign investment capital goes into housing as compared with 70 per cent put into manufacturing, agriculture and public works.

The house-building situation

Along the continuum of housing needs, from the back-lands to the big city, there are five major target areas: large urban centres, agro-industrial towns, mining centres, plantations, villages and marginal peasant and nomadic settlements. In most nations, the housing of productive workers in the industrial and government sectors of the economy has taken precedence over rural housing. What is the present situation in regard to house-building by and for workers in Africa?

Jobbing builders

Most new urban housing is produced by the people themselves with the co-operation of friends and relatives. As Africa becomes more industrialized and urbanized, however, more people will live in homes they do not build themselves. New trends in traditional and modern housing have already been established by African jobbers, contractors and *entrepreneurs* on the one hand, and industry and government on the other hand.

A large share of new housing in African cities is produced by local jobbing builders. Local builders use traditional techniques and short-life materials such as mud, wattle and daub and sun-dried or kilned mud brick. Building in local materials has several advantages and makes a definite contribution to national housing programmes. A single-storey detached traditional house is half as dear as one made of more durable material. Such houses are built within the local economy and do not compete with large-scale building programmes for finance and materials. They are closer to the means of wage-earning workers and do not require the initial outlay of large sums of capital.

Houses built of traditional short-life materials are capable of

N

continuous improvement with modern materials and techniques. As workers become more secure in the urban environment they improve their homes, "slow-slow". Corrugated metal sheets replace thatched roofs; sawn timber frames doors and windows; concrete takes the place of clay floors; and sockets and wall-points introduce electric lighting. The use of cement is expanding with the growth of cement production. Increasingly, houses built in local materials are being improved with concrete-plastered walls and floors. In future, concrete will be the main material for mass building in many places.

In urban areas and among the fully employed the role of jobbing builders and local *entrepreneurs* is of primary importance for the simple reason that new workers cannot build houses for themselves and work at the same time. Furthermore, the replacement of obsolete housing requires the skills of a specialized cadre of workers devoted to that task. More study is needed of jobbing builders, their economy and techniques. They have the advantage of low overheads and the continuous participation of the house-owner in the building process. The expansion of their activities means an increase in local wealth as well as a market for manufactured materials.

The improvement of local building takes many differing forms in varying parts of the Continent. In some cases, technical assistance is given to improve local techniques. In others, jobbing builders are taught modern techniques, simple business and costing methods and how to design economical and convenient dwellings. In general the direction is towards the creation of a professional house-building industry on the local level which will meet the the needs of local people.

Self-help housing

In rural areas and among the seasonally unemployed, self-help housing rather than the jobbing builder has certain advantages. House-building among plantation workers, cash-crop farmers and agricultural villages can be improved as governments subsidize the mass-production of house parts, and make them available to rural people. The roof is the most important part of the house and in Ghana a roof-loan scheme has been tried which may apply to other parts of Africa. Under the roof-loan scheme the government says, "If you build the walls of the house we will give you a loan in kind for the roof." The worker is given a "chit" with which he can buy house-building supplies at the local trading store. When he has built the walls he gets a further loan for the construction of a safe and adequate roof. The total cost is paid back in instalments.

Under this plan the formation of village housing societies is encouraged. They make house-building part of the collective psyche and also serve as a means of guaranteeing the security of loans. Village societies are composed of elders and capitalized for a certain sum of money. Each society is allowed to propose five persons a year for loans and the society is held responsible by the government for the repayment of loans if bad debts occur. If the loans are not repaid the society is deprived of further participation in the loan scheme. In the few years of its operation there have been few instances of default and village housing societies have spread throughout interior regions.

Employee housing

Modern mass housing for employees is a result of the growth of foreign enterprises and large-scale government administrative and public works agencies. The siting of industry and government agencies in inaccessible areas or new locations requires the provision of housing for workers. In fact many nations encourage decentralization as a means of opening up under-developed regions. In time the worker communities begun around cement factories, government installations and huge dam projects become nuclei for the formation of new urban areas. Some examples are Cité de Fria, Guinea, and the Volta River project. In the plantation and industrialized areas of east, central and southern Africa, "township" housing has been common for half a century.

Mass housing for African employees began with compounds for migrant workers, lines of dreary over-crowded barracks, with communal sanitation and kitchen. These remnants of former times are still all too common in independent states, nevertheless the concept of providing adequate housing for workers is now an accepted part of national policies and has increasingly penetrated the thinking of forward-looking industrial management. Today many government establishments provide housing for all grades of workers, from field hands to senior executives. Industry has begun to provide housing for middle-level African employees, as it does for Europeans, and is slowly introducing better mass housing for lower-grade workers.

The trend in mass housing for company workers is towards two–three-room dwellings with self-contained sanitation and cooking facilities. The designs are simplified versions of European minimum-standard dwellings in area and house plans. One of the most popular plans is the one-storey "four-square" plan.

The one-storey house is called "four-square" because it consists of four rooms: two front and a back bedroom and kitchen. Its advantage is that it can be built detached or in terraces. In addition, one of the bedrooms can be planned with external access so that it can be let to a lodger; furthermore, by adding a walled courtyard more living space is provided. The four-square plan can be adapted for two-storey flats when greater density is required.

Employee housing is mass housing and the major technical problem is to build a large number of dwellings on the same site to an economic design. Pre-fabrication and mechanization are two techniques that have been introduced to meet these demands. Pre-fabricated houses are used for workers on the Volta River dam. In Dakar, concrete shells and steel moulds are used to cast a whole house. In Kenya, large pre-cast units of light-weight pumice concrete are used.

Experience in various parts of the Continent indicates that a combination of conventional methods, brick and concrete, with traditional local materials gives improved economy. Furthermore it has the advantage of providing training for local workers in better building methods which can be immediately applied in the

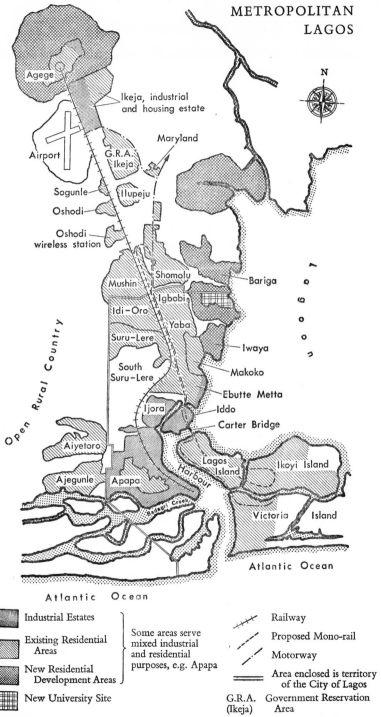

METROPOLITAN LAGOS

N

Agege

Ikeja, industrial
and housing estate

Maryland

Airport

G.R.A.
Ikeja

Sogunle

Ilupeju

Oshodi

Oshodi
wireless station

Mushin

Shomolu

Bariga

Igbobi

Idi-Oro

Yaba

Suru-Lere

Iwaya

South
Suru-Lere

Makoko

Ebutte Metta

Ijora

Iddo

Carter Bridge

Aiyetoro

Lagos
Island

Ikoyi Island

Ajegunle

Apapa

Harbour

Badagri Creek

Victoria   Island

Lagos   Lagoon

Open Rural Country

Atlantic Ocean

Atlantic   Ocean

	Industrial Estates	⎫		⊹⊹⊹	Railway
	Existing Residential Areas	Some areas serve mixed industrial and residential purposes, e.g. Apapa			Proposed Mono-rail
	New Residential Development Areas	⎭			Motorway
	New University Site				Area enclosed is territory of the City of Lagos

G.R.A.   Government Reservation
(Ikeja)   Area

Lagos Island is the urban centre of the City of Lagos, and it is the Federal District and
capital of the Federal Republic of Nigeria.

local community; it also stimulates the creation of a local housing industry and cash wages.

INDUSTRY AND HOUSING

Housing and re-housing people are not easy processes in any part of the world, and certainly not in the newly-developing countries of the *tiers monde*. Housing and community development are major political and economic issues in African nations, aggravated by problems peculiar to their recent history and political economy. Nevertheless, the people and leaders of new nations are searching for new ways to solve or control their problems, many of which like slum housing still plague the industrial nations. And, together with industry, they are beginning to plan for the changing housing needs of workers.

Lagos, Nigeria

The twin forces of industrialization and urbanization in Lagos have strung a chain of settlements north to south along a highway and railway line. Lagos is a linear conurbation consisting of Lagos Island and a series of island colonies and villages stretching on to the mainland amidst harbours, lagoons, creeks and swamps. Employment is concentrated at the southern end of the chain in the business centre of Lagos Island and the port-industrial zone of Apapa. At the opposite end, 20 miles into the interior of the mainland, are the Ikeja industrial estate and the village of Agege.

Lagos, with its population of almost half a million, is at the same time the Federal District of the Republic of Nigeria; officially it includes Lagos Island (the most densely populated area), Ikoyi and Victoria Islands, Apapa, Yaba, Ebute Metta and Suru Lere. Lagos is surrounded by an urbanized area of more than 275,000 people — Igbobi, Mushin, Shomolu, Oshodi and Agege, for example — under the jurisdiction of the Western Region Government.

This total area has doubled in the period 1952–62 at an average annual rate of 14 per cent. The rate of growth in the Western Region urban area far outstrips that of Lagos City. In a few years the urbanites who live outside the Federal Territory will be in the majority.

The inhabitants of Lagos have been the subject of several government inquiries in the last few years and it is possible to formulate a general picture of the population and its housing problems. Like other African cities, Lagos is a man's town and there are more males than females. Four and a half per cent of the adult males are unemployed, 25 per cent are self-employed or work for small firms and 5½ per cent are students. One third of the persons employed in large firms live outside Lagos City.

The cost of land is the initial barrier to private house-building. It ranges from 10 per cent of construction costs in the outskirts to 200 per cent in desirable central neighbourhoods. Land prices vary from £35 per acre of unused land in outlying districts to £4,000–£5,000 per acre in the central areas.

Housing materials range from mud to cement, depending on the wealth of the owner. The cheapest houses have mud walls, corrugated-iron roofs supported by rough timbers and, with the price of mud-wall building being about £9 per room, may cost as little as 3s. or 4s. per sq. ft. If not maintained properly, however, this type of house collapses in a few years. In houses made of unrendered cement blocks, the cost rises to 7s. per sq. ft., but the blocks are not very strong and are suitable for one-storey buildings only. The "best" houses have insulated ceilings, glazed windows, two-storey construction made of hollow concrete blocks, cement or terrasso floors, cement-asbestos roofs and ceiling supports in the form of hardwood trusses and purlins. This type of house may cost as much as 15s. to 20s. per square foot. Clearly, in this situation it is impossible for a worker who earns £8–£12 a month to finance a new home for his family.

A powerful impetus for urban development in Lagos is the desire to have a favourable urban image. Lagos, like other capital cities, is viewed by its residents as the "gateway to the nation". "With the approach of independence, the people of Nigeria began to look more critically at their Federal Capital, and saw in its congested lanes and ramshackle houses a poor reflection of their aspirations" observes Peter Marris. Industry agreed also that adequate housing for Lagosian workers was a necessary part of economic development. So, a start was made on slum clearance, and residents of one quarter were re-housed in the model suburban community of Suru Lere.

In 1963,[2] the Ministry of Lagos Affairs of the Federal Government of Nigeria invited a United Nations research team to make a comprehensive survey of Lagos. The team consisted of experts in urban land policies, transport, social science, public health, engineering and physical planning. Their terms of reference were: (a) to make recommendations on the expansion of the city, (b) to propose solutions to problems of slums, over-crowded housing, transport, rising land values and community facilities, and (c) to suggest solutions to the administrative problems of an expanding city.

The research team made a number of specific recommendations for organizing the future industrial and urban growth of the city. At present, plants and factories are sited to the detriment of the balanced needs of the city as a whole. Land space for industry, government and people in Lagos could be obtained by drainage and reclamation of swamps and the development of mainland settlements towards the north and west.

The long daily trek to work is partly due to an imperfect relationship between employment and residential areas. The lagging development of public transport is a major problem requiring solution; during the mid-summer general strike in 1964, transport was a basic grievance felt by workers. A unified transport system could speed workers and shoppers safely and efficiently to their destinations. Some recommended innovations are:

1 mono-rail passenger service between Apapa, Mushin and Agege;
2 water-bus service on the harbour and lagoon to Lagos Island and Apapa;
3 cheap transfer tickets between bus, train, mono-rail and launch services.

The shortage of housing requires a target of 6,000 new homes per year. And a housing agency is needed to secure land for low-cost housing, to aid house-building by co-operative societies, and to advise on home loans and improvement of design standards and by-laws.

The growth of slums can be curtailed by aided rehabilitation schemes which offset the necessity of moving large numbers of people at once. Existing dwellings can be improved by re-roofing, bigger windows, paint, landscaping, air and sanitary improvements. This technique of aided rehabilitation requires a community development approach with the assistance of skilled social workers.

The expansion of water-works and water supply is required to meet future needs. The revision and standardization of water rates can bring cheap water supply to the poorer areas of the city. Control over industrial waste and sewage disposal is a prime necessity. At present, 400 workers collect 13,000 pails of night soil each evening; these are dumped into the lagoon near Carter Bridge where industrial wastes are disposed of in a similar way.

Lagos, its suburbs and rural periphery, should be looked at as one metropolitan region. The research team suggested the formation of a Metropolitan Development Agency which would co-ordinate the interests of the Federal, Western Regional and local administrations. This agency would be responsible for the planning of water supply, waste removal, land use and house-building to keep pace with accelerating population growth.

The planned decentralization of business and government establishments also plays an essential part in relieving urban congestion and avoiding urban sprawl. The planned development of "satellite" towns at outlying villages, for example Agege, can meet future industrial and urban needs. Agege is a fast-growing marketing, warehousing and small industrial centre. In the last ten years it has doubled its population to 32,000 and because it adjoins the vast Ikeja estate and is the farthest metropolitan terminus of the rail line it may become a booming satellite worker-community in the next few years.

By 1984, the population of Agege will be pushing towards 450,000. Workers in the new Agege city will be employed in local plants, the airport and Ikeja estate. Others will commute to factories and government establishments in Lagos-Apapa. Commuters will need daily bus and rail transport, motorists will require improved highways. Housewives will shop in an expanded modern shopping centre and well-planned local markets. Agege will also be a centre for large office blocks, small service industries and government offices.

A new Agege could become an example of a modern well-functioning satellite city. The United Nations team made several recommendations to ensure that this happens. They envisage Agege as a pedestrian city, small enough for people to walk to the rail station and cycle to the Ikeja estate. The bulk of the 3,000 units built per year would be owner-occupied and built by individual private investors. Recognizing the difficulties associated with slum clearance the team has suggested that the removal of existing houses and the dislocating of present populations should be kept at a minimum. In sum, they foresee a balanced community of all income and age groups including some "high-income" housing for senior executives.

From my own participation in the experimental formulation of the plan for Agege, it is apparent that Agege can become the technical training centre of this 20-mile-long industrializing urban region. If the city draws on the resources of the Yaba Technical Institute, Ibadan University and the Ikeja estates it is possible to create an important scientific technical complex. Such a centre would be instrumental in linking new technological ideas with job-training programmes. It would also provide a symbol of civic pride and identification for Agege and the whole metropolitan area.

The Copper Belt, Zambia

Zambia is one of Africa's newest nations; like many other East and Central African countries, it inherits a social, racial and economic structure skewed by the colonial situation. Mass modern housing for workers in outlying African townships separate from central city amenities and European communities is a common feature today; what shall it be tomorrow? In independent Zambia certain established industrial housing practices and responsibilities will devolve on government or will be co-operatively dealt with by both government and industry. What should be modified and why? Let us look at the present status of housing for workers and the future possibilities for the development of the six Copper Belt communities and Lusaka, the nation's capital.

Zambia's famed Copper Belt is a string of rich mineral pearls 20 miles wide and stretching for 80 miles. The provision of housing for workers in the mining areas of Zambia is unique in all independent Africa. As a carry-over from the past, all the inhabitants of urban areas who are in fixed employment are by law entitled to housing in government- or employer-financed dwellings.

Workers earning up to £15 a month are entitled to a dwelling at the expense of the employer. Companies pay rent to the local authority and this rent is not considered part of the worker's salary. Government and senior executives are provided with housing under a similar system, but few pay the full economic rent for their quarters. Housing built by local authorities is financed by loans from the national government. Under this system, housing is tied to employment. Housing is available when needed and the company has only to notify the local authority of a new influx of workers and is assured that the requisite number of dwellings will be available.

The Copper Belt housing system was reviewed on the eve of independence by Dr. Otto Koenigsbergerat the request of Mr. Kenneth Kaunda, Prime Minister of Zambia and Sir Ronald Prain, a director of the Rhodesian Selection Trust. His study had four objectives:

1 to review the housing and planning situation with particular reference to Lusaka and the Copper Belt;
2 to identify general policy questions which require top-level decisions as prerequisites for a programme of action;

3 to point out problems of particular urgency;
4 to suggest sources of technical assistance, advice and help.

Dr. Koenigsberger noted that the Zambia system has several advantages. It is the only source of modern housing available to workers; it is an extra benefit which attracts workers.

"The orderliness of the procedure and the clean and orderly state of the low-income suburbs are one of the most striking features of the system. One appreciates these advantages particularly on comparing them with experiences in other parts of the tropical world where attempts to make industrialists build houses for their own labourers have met with very little success."

Some of the disadvantages of the system are the segregation of workers' communities, the lack of amenities in these "one-class suburbs" and the long journeys that employees must make to work. The patronizing atmosphere which tinges European–African contact does not aid the creation of a responsible consumer-citizenry. In addition, the houses do not meet the climatic and social needs of people.

"One-class suburbs are monotonous and ugly. Poor and wealthy citizens depend on each other economically. Their lives are enriched by proximity. The separation of social groups, which looks so neat on paper and is so dear to the heart of the land speculator, is economically inefficient and a poor basis for the emergence of a healthy urban community."

The transference of the town administration from industry to government is another knotty problem related to company towns. Copper Belt townships have been controlled by local industrial authorities; the company is house-builder, landlord and town administrator. The transference of powers from company management Boards to new local public authorities should have top priority. How swiftly this is accomplished may depend on the viability of the community. Some, like Ndola and Kitwe, have in the last 20 years grown from dependence on local mines to viable centres of secondary industries and could survive on their own. Others, like Luanshya, Chambisi and Bancroft, will need assistance through economic planning. What is important is that government and industry recognize that now is the time to sit down with trade unions and representative citizens' groups and hammer out a workable policy.

Lusaka, the manufacturing and transport centre, is the capital of Zambia and has many problems similar to the company towns. Laid out on the lines of a "garden city", Lusaka has many pleasant open spaces and amenities. But the poorer sections are located on the fringe of an urban area as large as Liverpool; thus Lusaka's workers have a long, tedious journey to work.

The residential segregation of economic and racial groups is not without its deleterious effects on the total life of the city, observes Dr. Koenigsberger.[3]

> "The Lusaka of the past suffered not only from racial but also social segregation. Any plan, whether for moderate or low density development, should contain measures to improve the character of the town in this respect. To achieve desegregation, it is not enough not to segregate. Positive steps are necessary to convert Lusaka into a healthy community without physically segregated social and economic groups."

Now, what is being done? First of all there has been a recognition of these problems by government and industry. Secondly the preliminary survey recommended that urgent attention be given to six important requirements for a forward-looking housing programme:

1 the need for demographic studies and population forecasts;
2 a comprehensive housing policy;
3 planned desegregation;
4 local-authority tax reforms;
5 the reorganization of the present "African Housing Board" as a National Housing Board for all citizens;
6 the establishment of a research and development group for urban housing.

If these recommendations are implemented on the Copper Belt, it will become the first urban industrial area in Africa to experiment and benefit from this approach. The solution to three basic questions facing Zambia will, of course, have relevance in other parts of Africa:

1 Should urban housing be provided as a social service or should private initiative and investment in housing be encouraged or both?

2 Should loosely scattered suburbs be left as they are, connected by subsidized public transport, or can they be made economically self-sufficient?

3 How fast and in what ways can the present patterns of social segregation be scrapped, and the democratization of urban life be accomplished?

What has been recognized in Zambia is that an independent nation should have a well-planned housing policy and a programme of public action that will not only be economic but will also ensure a maximum of social justice.

THE CONTRIBUTION OF ARCHITECTURE

In the process of planning for adequate worker housing and urban development the role of architects and planners takes on crucial importance. Architects and building engineers retained by companies and governments are responsible for most of the new housing in emerging Africa. Their buildings will shape the personalities and aesthetic tastes of future citizens; they can either be cultural coffins or life-generating stations along the path to healthy urban industrial societies.

How can Africa avoid urban sprawl and squalor?
How can architects, both African and European, evolve a style and approach that reflects tradition but has a functional modern utility?

What shall be the face of African cities in the future?
Is enough time and money being spent on training the men
who will build the new Africa? And, who shall plan for the
planners?

Overcoming the past

The resolution of new problems requires some drastic changes
in our theories, concepts and techniques. Much of the building of
the past sixty years, and of the present, is a response not to Africa's
problems but to those of the Western metropolis. For example, the
lay-out of many cities in Africa, like Lusaka, dates from the
1930's when British planners were enamoured with "garden
cities". Garden cities in England were a reaction to the depressing
ugliness of industrial cities; apparently it did not occur to the
founders of Lusaka that Africa had not had an Industrial Revolution.

Building to meet the needs of families and employers in a
rapidly-changing continent is handicapped by the transference
of outmoded assumptions into the African context. Housing plans
and designs have too often been predicated on an assumption of
slow gradual change in a *laissez-faire* society concerned with
preservation of the past. Africa, enmeshed in the forward thrust
of change, defies these three assumptions. Administrators are
experimenting with alternative economic systems, as we have seen,
and few persons glorify the 400 years of the immediate past.

Facilities and resources

The climate of opinion in architecture is changing through the
activities of a growing number of European and African institutions. Their experiments in planning worker housing and urban
development offer many possibilities for resolving employee
housing problems.

Britain. One of Britain's most important institutions providing
training and expertise for building in Africa is the Department of
Tropical Studies of the Architectural Association School of

Architecture, London. The Department, the first of its kind in the world, owes its origins to the initiative of a young African student. Ten years ago, while reading architecture, a Nigerian student discovered that his professional education had little relevance to the problems facing him upon his return home. His discussions with British architects led to a unanimous resolution to establish the Department of Tropical Studies in 1954.

The Department's refresher and experimental courses attract architects from many parts of the world. Each year some 35 professionals, almost a quarter of them African, spend six to nine months in study and research. The Department is a centre of innovation and involvement in the building problems of tropical areas. In 1963–4, with the support of the Ministry of Education and the Department of Technical Co-operation, a six-month course in educational building was inaugurated. During the same session two groups of European, African and Asian student-architects dealt with problems of urban development and worker dwellings in Wad Medani, Sudan and Lagos-Agege, Nigeria. The work of the Department has helped to establish some important basic principles of designing and planning for the tropics. It also provides an opportunity for young African architects to develop their professional competence.

Members of the Department have been directly involved in the practical tasks of building in tropical areas, particularly in Nigeria, Zambia and Ghana, where they have an institutional relationship with the Faculty of Architecture at Kumasi. Faculty members readily agree that the challenge of working in the African context has sharpened their awareness of new possibilities of resolving housing problems.

Many u.k. organizations conducting research on the housing problems of changing British society are gradually developing a fund of knowledge which might be tested and applied in Africa. Architectural research and development teams are at work in the Ministry of Education, the Building Research Station and the universities. The London County Council and the Ministry of Housing and Local Government are engaged in research on new towns, traffic and the redevelopment of slum areas. Among the

4.
The changing woman consumer

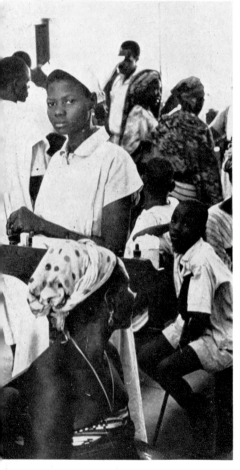

universities, there are housing research units at the Division of Architecture, University College of London, and at Edinburgh and Liverpool. Social scientists at the Centre of Urban Studies, University of London, are conducting a large-scale London survey and their techniques may have relevance for urban surveys in Africa.

France. French architects, working under co-operative agreements between French and African governments, are also involved in housing development and urban and regional planning. One outstanding group is the *Société pour l'Etude d'Aménagements Planifiés* (s.e.t.a.p.), a private independent firm of technical consultants. One of s.e.t.a.p.'s most ambitious industrial building projects is related to bauxite mining and aluminium production in the Republic of Guinea by the Société Bauxites du Midi. Their buildings for workers, industrial processing and administration are located at three interrelated sites: Landgarejda (the bauxite mine, Boké (the aluminium site) and Port Kakande (the exportation centre).

Three of the long-term objectives of s.e.t.a.p. are: to aid the evolution of healthful dwelling-places, to synthesize industrial and local construction techniques and to create a viable building industry. s.e.t.a.p. believes that aluminium is well suited for housing development in the wet tropical belt of Africa. It proposes to use Guinean aluminium and local materials in building workers' homes and resolving ventilation problems. In Port Kakande, houses partly made of aluminium stripping will soon rise among the storage depots and rice plantations.

s.e.t.a.p. is also engaged in industrial building projects in other parts of Africa. At Port Etienne, Mauritania, it is erecting port installations, residential zones and dwellings for the *Société des Mines de Fer de Mauritania*. In Abidjan, Ivory Coast, a city of 200,000 people, it is planning an extension to accommodate an expected doubling of the population in a few years; in addition, they are surveying the development of six regional centres. At Tivaouane, Senegal, s.e.t.a.p. is building an industrial site and housing for skilled workers and administration for the *Compagnie Sénégalaise des Phosphates de Taiba*.

o

Another important organization is the *Secrétariat des Missions d'Urbanisme et d'Habitat* (S.M.U.H.) created in July 1960 by the French Ministry of Co-operation. S.M.U.H. is an association of 50 organizations, mainly governmental, taking part in technical assistance programmes. It is an "instrument of co-operation" to co-ordinate the work of architects and town planners.

The directors of S.M.U.H. believe that "the strength and speed of economic and social change in our time demand immediate and constant action". Their tasks begin with a request from a developing country or governmental agency; then a mission is sent out for a short duration, two weeks to two months in length. Twenty-eight missions have visited 12 countries and overseas departments in the last three years.

One notable achievement is a territorial improvement survey in the Niari Valley of Congo (Brazzaville) where five towns — Dolisie, Loudima, Jacob, Madingou and Mindouli — lie chaotically within a few dozen kilometres of each other. They have also surveyed the housing and town-planning needs of Tananarive, and the provincial capitals of Malagache, Majunga, Tuléar, Tamatave, Diego-Suarez and Fianarantsoa.

After the initial survey, S.M.U.H. architect-planners suggest a framework for action. Later, the detailed surveys and execution of plans are carried out by parties nominated by the assisted states. At its Paris secretariat S.M.U.H. offers training courses and facilities for the exchange of research information. African students from the two-year Institut d'Urbanisme attend lectures and participate in the association's activities.

Three of the most important contributions of French architect-planners to the kinds of problems of industry, housing and economic development that we are concerned with are:

1 the creation of *"un pole de développement"* in provincial areas, for example Dabou and Korhogo in Ivory Coast, to halt migration to the capital city,

2 slum clearance and urban redevelopment, for example, Ambodin Isotry, Malagache and Fort Lamy, Chad;

3 employee housing, the notable example being Fria, Guinea.

The most outstanding examples of French attempts at worker housing are given in the table following.

TABLE 23

City	Country	Company	Product
Fria	Guinea	Société Pechiney	Aluminium
Ede'a	Cameroon	Société Pechiney	Aluminium
Moanda	Gabon	Comilog	—
Port Gentil	Gabon	Société des Petroles d'A.E.F.	Petrol
Idjil	Mauritania	Miferma	Mining
Port Etienne	Mauritania	Miferma	Mining
Port Kakande and Boké	Guinea	Société Bauxites du Midi	Bauxite
Tivouane	Senegal	Compagnie Sénégalaise des Phosphates	Phosphates

Africa. In the development of housing programmes, industry and government will also have available the services of an increasing number of African architects. Much of the future of mass house-building in Africa will depend on young African architect-planners who are beginning their work now. The Nigerian Oluwole Olusegun Olumunyiwa, who studied at Manchester and is a member of R.I.B.A., has his own agency in Lagos and is co-director of Africa's first architectural review, *The West African Builder and Architect.* H. Iseanyi Ekwuene, who studied in America, and Hameed Balogun are also practising in Nigeria. In Kenya there is a Ugandan, Kersey D. Moddie, and in Dahomey, Max Niran Faladé. Morocco has Jean-François Zevaco and Elie Azagoury, and in Cameroon there is some interesting work being done by Jacques Nsagne Akwa and a Haitian, Raymond Charlier.

Graduates from universities, students from the Department of Tropical Studies and the Paris *Beaux Arts* School, represent a growing cadre of specialized professionals. One of the Paris

Beaux Arts school students, Sidibé Bâhna, has written a penetrating analysis of architecture and man in Africa in the journal *Présence Africaine.*[4] The influence of the Association of Arab Architects and Town Planners is growing in Islamic areas; some of their work is reviewed in the book *The New Metropolis in the Arab World.*[5] Finally, of course, there are the schools of architecture in Africa itself; they include faculties at Kumasi, Ahmadu Bello University, Zaria, Nigeria, Algiers and Khartoum.

SOME NEW APPROACHES

In the future, industry and governments will want to undertake systematic research before embarking on costly housing and building programmes. Just as in African factories there will be research on climate, lighting and noise and their effects on comfort, acuity and skilled work, so there should be environmental and social research on problems of housing.

More research knowledge is needed concerning the ways in which people use, modify and adapt to physical structures. This is the only way in which employers can learn how to provide sufficient living space for families and to create healthy communities with convenient access to social amenities.

Role of sociologists

Architects will be increasingly drawn into participation with sociologists in order to formulate efficient research designs. This is inevitable because working in Africa is a radical variation on the traditional relationship between the architect and a single owner-client. In Africa he deals with mass, rather than individual, housing; he designs multiple buildings for occupants whose culture he knows little about. At the outset it is necessary for the architect to discover the "sociological correlates" of architectural decision-making, i.e. the things about people that he has to know in order to formulate and realize technical decisions. And in this task, the social scientist is a necessary member of the planning team.

Sociologists can also contribute in terms of studies of existing new towns, worker housing estates and redeveloped areas. If the errors of Suru Lere, Lusaka and other cities are not to harden into custom it is necessary to conduct continuous research and implement the findings in new settlements. Some questions for investigation include:

1 What are the special problems of communities with unbalanced age structures?

2 What are the attitudes of residents towards their houses and amenities?

3 What are the emerging patterns of social associations and small-group interaction?

4 What is the distribution of social problems: psychopathology, suicide, crime and delinquency, and how does it compare with older residential areas?

5 What are the patterns of residential mobility?

6 How does living in a modern area affect the purchase of furniture, motorcars and other manufactured items?

7 What are the effects of re-housing on income and cost of living of families?

8 How do people get along with their neighbours, what are the social class relationships?

9 What are the positive and negative factors involved in "one-class" suburbs?

10 How do people use communal facilities: laundries, green spaces, garages and playgrounds?

Research information on these questions has utility for industry, marketing and society at large. It can be of use in a number of practical ways:

1 developing new housing designs to meet the needs of changing families;

2 developing better usages of materials in house construction;

3 helping families to furnish and equip their homes for healthy living;

4 educating families for better use of modern household equipment and the facilities of urban life;

5 planning neighbourhood units and provision of facilities which enhance collective life.

Development group work

Modern architects and planners have formulated a number of concepts to guide private initiative and public action. One of them, called development group work, can be of great utility in providing housing for workers and their families.

Development group work is a method of applied inter-disciplinary research and design. It involves a team of specialists, including social scientists, in the total process of building, from the first proposals to the final tenant. Its primary objectives are to improve housing standards and reduce costs. Four stages are involved and they are implemented in a continuous series:

1 designing new houses;

2 building groups of prototype houses to test new designs;

3 monitoring the process of construction and occupation of these houses;

4 feeding-back observations and experiences into improved designs to the end that substantial savings and improvements are obtained.

This approach to housing encompasses the whole building process: the design and construction of houses, area layouts, roads and utilities, material production, methods of finance, forms of contracts, transport of men and materials, operations at the building site and the selection of tenants. The utility of this method is that it places specific building programmes within a broader context. It is a way of looking at housing within the urban and regional framework. It predicates the co-ordination of urban life with industrial growth.

Development group work is a means of organizing the urban environment as a desirable place in which to work and live. It is broad enough to include investment in social services, reception centres for migrants, expansion of primary schools, girls' and workers' education, measures to balance urban and rural development, and transport.

In conclusion, social needs and industrial purposes can be effectively integrated to raise not only incomes but also living standards. The evidence from housing research in Africa indicates that industrialization can be socially useful. Comprehensive planning can modify the flow and direction of rural migration and adjust urban growth to employment opportunities. It can create pleasant surroundings and assist the development of new social patterns compatible with industrial labour.

The time is not far off when there will be a kind of continuous market research in the field of housing which will monitor the needs of working populations and translate findings into efficient low-cost dwellings.

REFERENCES

1 URIESI, PAT, *Daily Times*, Lagos, Nigeria, Spring, 1964.

2 ABRAMS, CHARLES, KOENIGSBERGER, DR. OTTO, *et al.*, "Report on Metropolitan Lagos", United Nations, April, 1963.

3 KOENIGSBERGER, DR. OTTO, *Housing and Planning in Northern Rhodesia: A Reconnaissance Survey*, Architectural Association, London, April, 1964.

4 BAHNA, SIDIBE, "L'Architecture et les hommes", *Présence Africaine*, No. 49, 1964.

5 BERGER, MORROE (ed.) *The New Metropolis in the Arab World*. Allied Publishers Limited for the Office of Asian Affairs, Congress of Cultural Freedom, 1963.

CHAPTER ELEVEN

AFRICA'S CHALLENGE TO MARKET RESEARCH

IN THE MIDST of development and change a reconstructed science of market research has a definite priority. Market research is the key to appraising the market. It provides a firm basis for development and a means of monitoring the growth of communities and nations. Market research is an instrument for helping people to achieve their stated goals. Market research is the tie that binds Africa and the exterior forces of development into a dialogue of progress.

DEFINITIONS

Market research grew "like Topsy" out of the widespread development of consumer markets in Western countries in the early years of this century. For many market researchers their functions were directly related to the "performance of business activities that direct the flow of goods and services from producer to consumer".

In two decades definitions of market research have greatly changed in emphasis; they have become more scientific, comparative and socially responsible. Examples from three highly-respected sources illustrate this trend.

Mr. K. Dyce-Sharp defines market research as "the investigations made by firms, or by research organizations on behalf of firms, to find out how well a certain product was selling compared to its competitors and what sort of person is buying it, and why."[1] He further adds that market research is a tool of management and of good government.

John Downham and his colleagues[2] stress the "provision of information — designed to help in the formulation and solution

204

of business problems" and the analysis of consumer demand and product distribution. They add that market research has a social function to "reduce waste of economic resources caused by inadequate information".

Max Adler[3] says it is a "branch of social science. It uses the methods of scientific inquiry for the purpose of discovering human behaviour and opinions. The scientific methods used are particular to market research. Its most powerful tool is a branch of statistics applied to well-defined phenomena".

CONTRIBUTIONS OF SCIENCE

Market research has developed through selective borrowing of methods, concepts and findings from the natural and social sciences. A brief review of a few of the scientific disciplines will serve to indicate the degree of cross-fertilization which has taken place.

Statistics

Statistical sampling theory and techniques have released market researchers from dependence on large, costly surveys and censuses; they provide a method of obtaining accurate information gathered from selected samples within clearly specified and calculable limits.

Statistical theories and techniques also assist in formulating efficient research designs and examining research data. Some commonly used computations involve tests of significance, association and variation, probability and causality. A whole new vocabulary has entered the field, Chi-square, standard deviation, non-parametric, analysis of variance and factorial analysis.

Economics

Three specialized fields of economics have proved useful to market researchers. Descriptive economics aids in describing and forecasting the structure of economies and industries. Theoretical economics extrapolates models of consumer choice and market behaviour. Macro-economics constructs a picture of the market through such techniques as demand analysis and multiple regression analysis of time series. In addition there is experimental work being done in decision-making and consumer choice in risk-taking situations.

Psychology

Psychology has had the greatest impact on market research. Every researcher knows that he must take into account human desires and fears in questionnaire design and in the interview situation. "Personality", "subliminal" and "motivation" are examples of psychological concepts which have entered the popular idiom. Market research utilizes attitude scaling, depth interviews and projective tests to establish patterns of psychological behaviour. Researchers try to answer such questions as "How do different personality groups react to advertising appeals? What is the range of emotional responses to the taste, touch and sight of products and packs? What is the optimum number of exposures to an advertisement necessary to produce a recall 10 days later?" On the horizon is continuing research into human needs and desires, decision-making and concept formation.

Sociology and anthropology

Descriptive sociological studies have enriched our awareness of the human group; they have helped us to understand the social factors affecting consumer behaviour. There is a large body of useful concepts in the specialized studies of population, demography, group dynamics, and public opinion. Anthropology and its related branches have increased our knowledge about national cultures and the range of similarities and differences which mark the family of man.

Natural sciences

From the natural sciences, market research has taken the classical scientific method and the formation and testing of hypotheses in controlled experiments. Mathematics has contributed the construction of quantitative models of consumer behaviour and responses to advertising. Models devised in the laboratory are tested for closeness to reality, solved *in vitro*, and applied to the real world. Mathematics also has applications in computer programming, a vital innovation in modern large-scale research analysis.

Finally, market research draws upon the arts, humanities and linguistics especially in dealing with the formulation of media messages, questionnaires, interviewing techniques and content analysis.

THE RESEARCH SPONSOR

Who sponsors market research in Africa? There are three categories of research sponsors:

1 the market research divisions of manufacturing and distributing firms, advertising agencies, public corporations and international concerns — their major products include tobacco, food and consumer durables, paraffin and petrol, pharmaceuticals, newspapers, spirits and beer;

2 international private, public and social welfare organizations like B.B.C. Overseas Audience Research, U.N.E.S.C.O., I.L.O., and Political and Economic Planning;

3 governments, both African and foreign, who are concerned with a variety of topics from public opinion to trade statistics.

Not every U.K. company with products selling in Africa conducts market research. A general rule of thumb for judging the potentiality of companies for research is provided by answers to the following questions. Do they market or sell products in Africa, or have subsidiary companies in Africa? Are they engaged in manufacturing consumer products? Is their market considered to be a Continent-wide mass-market? To what extent are they involved with African customers or clients? Finally, where is the company's head office? A company with a head office in London, e.g., British–American Tobacco Company, will have a greater research interest in Africa than those which are subsidiaries or associates of a non-U.K. company.

THE RESEARCH AGENCY

In modern Africa a significant and growing proportion of research investigations are carried out by marketing and opinion research agencies who sell their services to clients. These agencies may be of three types: locally-based independent groups like Marco Surveys Limited of East Africa, subsidiaries of U.K. market research agencies like Market Research Africa (South Africa) associated with the London Press Exchange, or branches of U.K. agencies like Benson's International in East and West Africa. In some cases international companies like Colgate–Palmolive or Unilever have local affiliated advertising and research associates.

The organization of market research in Africa has progressively developed towards the formation of locally-based African-staffed research units. In the earliest days there was little interest in researching the African market. Local agents and distributors monitored the sale of particular products. Occasionally a company representative would fly out to Africa for particular product campaigns and gather as much information as possible in a short stay. The common practice today is to create the research design in the metropolitan headquarters and send a research director to the field. He recruits local interviewers, completes the search and returns home to tabulate the results. The trend for the future is towards more permanent independent or affiliated research units, locally based, doing continuous market research.

South Africa

It is in South Africa that wage-earning consumer markets have attracted extensive research. There are three large market-research firms including the newest agency, Market Research, Africa, and the oldest, S. H. Franklins. In addition there are subsidiaries of U.K. research agencies and the market research divisions of international concerns, for example, Lever Brothers and Colgate–Palmolive.

The four-year-old Market Research Africa is the youngest research organization and has done the most work among urban African populations. M.R.A. has an internal staff of 40, a team of permanent African and European interviewers and facilities for computerized data processing. M.R.A. recently completed the first full-scale "all-races" readership survey in South Africa. Under the direction of Walter Langeschmidt, M.R.A. has sponsored a survey of a portion of the Johannesburg African market, entitled *An African Day*.

East Africa

"Before independence the colonial officers supposedly knew all because they asked their houseboys. That was the survey system then," says Dr. Gordon M. Wilson, head of the Kenya-based research agency, Marco Surveys Limited. In a few years, this Canadian-born social anthropologist has created a staff of full-time Swahili-speaking interviewers and a modernized data-processing office.

Dr. Wilson, who had formerly worked for the Kenya Government, made a number of candid observations about the East African consumer in an article in *Newsweek*.[4] He says the African "wants something to show for his independence. He wants such things as a wrist-watch, bicycle, radio, better clothing". Called the "bwana mkubwa" or "big man" of East African pollsters, Dr. Wilson is hopeful about the future of market research and is planning to expand his activities.

West Africa

In West Africa, where there are the most universities, research institutes and overseas companies selling consumer goods there has been a considerable variety of research done. Shell and B.P. Limited, British-American Tobacco Company, United Africa Company, Lever Brothers, B.B.C. Overseas Audience Research, Guinness, Overseas Newspapers Limited and many others are among the sponsors of market research. West Africans are the most "researched" population in Tropical Africa and increasing amounts are being spent each year to reach this expanding market. One of the prominent research agencies is Research Bureau Limited (West Africa) located in Lagos.

THE COSTS OF RESEARCH

The costs of research in Africa are as high as in the U.K. and vary according to the type and size of the project. Using the U.K. as a model, a typical piece of *ad hoc* consumer research with 4,000 interviews would cost £2 a head for interviewing time (or £8,000) and £1 a head for executive time (or £4,000). In general, costs are roughly distributed as follows, field operations 50–65 per cent, tabulation 20 per cent and executive time 25 per cent. Costs of training a researcher, in a group, average £20 a person.

In Africa, executive time remains relatively the same because the formulation and tabulation of questionnaires are all done in the U.K. Executive salary costs remain the same or increase because of the practice of sending or maintaining a European research executive in the field. Costs also rise for two additional reasons: (*a*) research teams must traverse great distances, and (*b*) the research period is often extended because of failure to take into account African national holidays, festivals, holy days, the rainy season, and other climatic conditions.

FINANCING MARKET RESEARCH

The expansion of market research is not keeping pace with the expanding African market. There is greater need for research than the relatively few current projects would indicate. By far the most serious barrier to the expansion of research is that of money. It is not the lack of money but the criterion by which it is, in effect, withheld from financing productive research. In general the criterion which determines whether or not a given company commissions research depends on its absolute volume of sales, the absolute operating margin and its total expenditure on advertising in Africa. The companies having a large volume of sales in Africa tend to spend the most money on advertising and the most on market research. None, however, spends more than 1 per cent of their sales turnover on research.

The annual expenditures on advertising in Africa are a negligible part of the world total of $19,000m. Whereas the larger international companies, many of them with subsidiaries in Africa, spend as much as $150–$300m. a year on world advertising, it is rare to find an advertising budget of $150,000 in Africa.

Why are advertising budgets so small in Africa? From the point of view of the company it is a question of a low sales volume. Markets are small, resulting in a high cost per unit in both manufacturing, transport and selling. Furthermore, money for advertising is withheld because of the lack of media, widespread illiteracy and the absence of competitive conditions which usually give the urge to create advertising which will have more impact.

The company is not the sole decision-maker in regard to advertising and market research. Allocation for research in Africa is affected by a triangular relationship between companies, advertising and market research agencies. Of all billings held by u.k. advertising agencies 95 per cent are for work in the u.k. market. From the advertising agency point of view, the proportion of a company's budget available for advertising in Africa may not be enough to entice it to seek the account. A company selling in Africa may wish to have some research done but is not prepared to spend more than a pittance and the market research agency may not want to undertake the research. Marketing divisions of companies may propose a series of projects and have them turned down by the company Board. In general, it is the top companies, those having a large or profitable volume of sales and those which deal with the African mass consumer market, that spend the most money on advertising and on market research.

In the Western countries product development and related consumer research are powerful stimulants for financing research; a businessman researches the market to find out what people might want to buy. In Africa, however, the great bulk of products sold are made in the West and are already researched. In some cases, a few adaptations are made and this is thought to be enough. It is only now that companies are really becoming interested in finding out the special characteristics and tastes of the African market.

It is highly probable that, in the future, research, like good personnel relations and worker housing, will be looked at as a form of capital investment with long-term positive effects. Where individual companies are unable to finance basic research, consortia will develop to do the task. Co-operation between industry, government, universities and social institutions will become vitally important.

GATHERING THE BASIC FACTS

Assessing the African market requires knowledge of a wide range of basic facts. Elementary geographic and climatic studies tell us that all of Africa is not "hot swampy jungles". For the millions who live in the highlands and desert areas, blankets and sweaters are welcome additions to the wardrobe. Climate affects the packaging of products; butter sold in grease-packets in Europe must be sold in moisture-proof air-tight cans in Brazzaville.

Knowledge of Africa's abundant resources opens up the possibility of local production of items presently manufactured abroad. A bottle-making plant recently opened on the sandy Nigerian plains will produce 36 million bottles annually, half the present supply shipped from abroad. Companies searching for skilled and educable workers require information on manpower resources, the annual school-leaving population and other demographic factors.

Researching the needs of industries, governments and consumers begins with two basic kinds of questions:

1 How much do we already know? What can we learn from desk research, from the analyses of modern African literature, published data, censuses, directories, sales and trade statistics?

2 How do we go about collecting new information, following up hunches, searching for new consumption indicators, testing products and gaining new insights into consumer behaviour?

More and more it is the market researcher who is called upon to fill in the gaps left by the insufficiently-financed social sciences. As a result, the researcher is called upon to assimilate a large body of knowledge and carry out a project among people about whom he has little personal knowledge. He must begin, therefore, with basic facts.

Demographic factors

What knowledge is basic? Looked at from the broadest possible view, the rate of demand for products in Africa will be correlated with future probable rates of growth in national incomes. In addition to national income statistics there are 10 demographic factors which are also correlated with rising product demand·

1 Annual rate of growth in population;
2 Age-structure and fertility ratios;
3 Population density;
4 Language spoken;
5 Urban and rural population, and geographical mobility;
6 Composition of the labour force: in the modern and

P

traditional sectors and in government and private companies;

7 Female labour: married, unmarried, full-time, part-time,
skilled, unskilled jobs and contributions in trade and
agriculture;

8 Home ownership and home renting;

9 Distribution of standard-of-living indicators : radio, TV,
motorcars, refrigerators, washing machines, holidays,
health, nutrition and disease;

10 Educational levels: school-age population and students/
school-leavers in primary, secondary and university education; also adult literacy.

One elementary technique for introducing the businessman to
the urban African consumer is to present skilfully, visually and
statistically, a quick overall summary of the social status of the
group in which he is interested. Such a presentation might consist
of the following:

1 a map of all residential areas, industries and shopping
centres, rail and bus routes and distances into the central
city;

2 an ethnic map of the city to indicate the variety of groupings in each area and their demographic characteristics.

It is also necessary to put some flesh on the bones of this skeleton
of facts and to place the population into perspective within an
on-going social structure. What are the historical and cultural
characteristics of the population? What is the nature of the socio-
economic order, its systems of organization, values, norms and
ideologies? Where has it come from and where is it going? What
are the effects of social and economic change? What are the
structural tensions, constraints and psychological deprivations?

Family and household composition

Knowledge of the structure of families and households is of
crucial importance in all aspects of market research. As we have

discussed earlier, the composition of families and households is changing towards the self-contained conjugal type common in Western countries. But a variety of types still exists, particularly the three-generation household; and furthermore perhaps a third of urban adults live in the bosom of a kinship community.

An adequate survey of household composition begins with an analysis of at least five fundamental characteristics:

1 household income from all sources;
2 age, occupation and education of household head and members;
3 household size, and stage of the household members in the family life-cycle: young single persons, young marrieds with and without children, elders, relatives;
4 household expenditures, especially the share of money spent in a given classification: food, beverages and tobacco; clothing and accessories; home operation and improvement; home furnishings, equipment and appliances; medical and personal care; bicycle and automotive maintenance and leisure and recreation.
5 total current expenditures and savings.

Basic research is required to establish the utility of Western concepts of "the family" and "the household". What is "the household" in Africa; is it the same as in other developing areas about which we have knowledge? If it is not, can definitions from one part of the world be applied to another?

Some anthropologists have crudely defined a household as "all the persons who eat from the same pot". Peter Marris, in his book *Family and Social Change in an African City*,[5] defined a household as a group of people living under the same roof and who keep house together; he designated the household head as the most senior family member. However, he notes that these definitions had to be modified at several points during the course of his research.

Many British market researchers use home and household appearance as one of several indicators of income or social class status. This technique has limited use in Africa where rising incomes are not yet expressly exhibited in home exteriors or interiors. Only the glistening chrome of a Mercedes parked in a narrow street may distinguish the residence of a £3,000-pound-a-year trader from that of his poorer neighbour.

In addition, without detailed family budgets recorded over several years, it is difficult to ascertain family income by question-naire methods. People simply do not remember all the sources from which their income is derived: trading, garden and cash-crop sales, barter and part-time wage labour. Furthermore what they made last month may be different this month because the relative financial contribution of each of the sources varies from month to month.

Social class

What social class definition should be used? From the foregoing discussion it is apparent that this is another crucial area for basic research. Current definitions have little relevance in African nations where there is a multiplicity of potential status-giving characteristics. Individuals do not simply opt out of the traditional milieu for membership in the modern economy, they more often occupy a position in both. One's "relation to the means of pro-duction and distribution" lacks specificity when 75-85 per cent of the people are subsistence peasants.

Western definitions of social class — those of Weber, Warner, Marx, Centers and others — have not been shown to be universal. As a matter of fact the definitions used by market researchers in different countries vary in several respects. For example, in Great Britain social class is really a "socio-economic group" defined in terms of the occupational status of the head of the household. German and French market researchers tend to concur with this view, while in the U.S.A. social class centres on the income of the individual head of the household or family.

The Working Party on Social Class Definitions of the British Market Research Society is engaged in a continuous programme of re-evaluation of social class definitions and has published a provocative report. Perhaps the overseas research members of M.R.S. might find it worth while to organize a similar "working party" directed towards Africa and the developing countries.

THE EXECUTION OF RESEARCH

The general problems of doing research in Africa are fairly well known. Interviewing is complicated by the multiplicity of languages, low levels of literacy and education and the intricacies of social customs. Geographically Africa is characterized by large, thinly-populated areas which necessitate much travelling and many scattered interviews. In one recent readership survey there were 18 cars on the road simultaneously, each with its own team of interviewers; the total mileage for 21,086 interviews ran close to 152,000 miles — 7 miles per interview. There is a shortage of local interviewers and many expatriates find it difficult to apply their skill in an alien society.

But research must be done, and it is up to the market researcher to devise ways of overcoming as many problems as possible and reduce the area of uncertainty in decision making. Fortunately there is an increasing fund of knowledge available from the social sciences and statistics. Some of the most difficult research problems have to do with sampling and interviewing and I have briefly reviewed them in the following discussion.

Choosing a sample

Most manufactured consumer goods have an urban market, and researchers will be mainly concerned with studying behaviour in these large centres of media and social interaction. The first essential in choosing a sample for field research is knowing and describing the universe of which the sample is a part. Basic information about a sample's universe — e.g., all wage-earners, all readers, or all urban dwellers — is an invaluable research aid. It helps the researcher to formulate a sampling design and to judge its representativeness. He can answer such questions as: "Do we have proportionately as many Yoruba housewives in our sample as there are in the city?" If the residence of significant ethnic groups varies according to the area of the city, he will want to ensure that they are adequately accounted for in the final sample.

The limits of generalization

Aside from assuring the "representativeness" of his sample survey, the researcher must also determine the limits within which he can generalize to wider segments of the community. It is not enough to take a random sample of the women one may contact in a house-to-house survey and assume that they represent all the housewives in that area. Probably these women share particular rather than universal characteristics. They may be only those wives whose husbands are employed at jobs which pay enough money for the wife to stay at home. Or they may have their own sources of trading income in the neighbourhood or at home, in contrast to all the housewives who must engage in daily labour away from home during the day. Finally the women contacted may simply be those who happen to be at home during the survey. It is necessary to know much more about the universe before accepting a "random" sample as representative of anything more than simply "those people whom we have in our sample".

Choosing a sample from lists

Market researchers in Africa tend to rely on the use of lists and registers, a common though not unchallenged practice in Western countries. Where such information exists, its utility depends primarily on determining how accurate it is and clearly specifying the purpose for which it will be utilized in the research. There are few reliable registers of telephones, households, voting and tax payments. Furthermore, these instruments are "status indicators" and using them leads to over-representation of the more affluent sections of the community.

In obtaining such things as lists of car owners it is not wise to rely on residential data, since car owners may not be residents of the particular city. Nor is it adequate to check lists of automobile associations, since not all car owners would be members. In such a situation it might be possible to compile a list from the municipal vehicle tax register.

Availability for interviewing

Patterns of residence, work and social custom determine to a great degree who will be available for interviewing and where. Availability is correlated with occupation. Migrant illiterate workers and traders are less easily available than clerks, petrol-station attendants and company messengers. Persons with higher education are more easily available than illiterates.

In the satellite communities surrounding employment centres males commute to work and hence are not available during the day nor perhaps during the whole week. It is possible in these circumstances to offset this by doing interviews in bus queues, lorry parks and railway stations. In the worker compounds of mines and plantations it is often necessary to interview at focal points of social gatherings: the company store, the near-by *dukka* and market.

Selecting interviewers

Getting the best results from research requires competent and skilled research teams. There are several qualities which are essential to a good interviewer. He must have a good command of the major European language as well as some familiarity with the local regional languages. Personality and dress of the interviewers are also important; if, for example, an interviewer is too "Westernized" he may create hostility in a local area. He must also be able to operate under all sorts of conditions, notably, dealing with the crowds that invariably gather when an interview is taking place. Above all he must undergo a period of training.

The interview situation

The interview situation is normally one of multiple interaction. The two-way communication between interviewer and informant is augmented by the real presence of other persons, household members and crowds that gather in the streets. Such factors as "saving face", "how will others see me?" and "what ought to be my response?" play an important role in the interview situation.

What a respondent will reveal to an investigator depends, therefore, not only on his recall and his ability to express himself in the language of the interview but also on the dynamics of the interview process itself.

Pilot studies are a useful technique for establishing the optimum conditions for:

1 length and scope of the interview,
2 the range of reactions to interviewers and the question-naire,
3 the wording of questions, and
4 the kinds of prompts necessary.

Time is an important factor in the interview situation. First of all, different activities take place at different times of the day. A person may have plenty of leisure time at the market-place and literally no time at all at home. Secondly, the time span of interviews will be longer than expected because it is customary good manners to offer lengthy salutations before and after a visit. There are two problems in this regard, the interviewer is in danger of disrupting the acquisition of information if: (*a*) he does not carry out the appropriate patterns of salutations, and if (*b*) he wears out his welcome by staying too long.

The interviewer must establish confidence and rapport with his respondent. This is especially important when dealing with such questions as product usage. He must be able to validate such questions as "Where did you buy it?" and "Can you show it to me?" without implying that the respondent is not telling the truth about his purchasing habits. The question of gifts should also be considered. Sometimes respondents are given a product which is not being studied at the time and this seems to make them more co-operative. But, on the other hand, such a practice may greatly affect the information given by the respondents.

The interview instruments

The most common instrument for gathering data is the questionnaire. Its purpose is to gather a range of data and responses according to a pre-classified category of questions. The design of questionnaires requires especial precautions in terms of language of inquiry.

In multilingual areas, the choice of language is a grave one and modifications in the data and findings often result from errors of language interview techniques. If, for example, interviews are conducted in only one language in a multilingual area the sample cannot possibly be representative of the whole population. It only "stands for" those persons who speak this particular language. This fact has special significance when using European languages. European languages are used in industry and commerce and they are understood by fairly large numbers of town-dwellers. But for the remainder of the urban population and for virtually the whole of the rural population it is impossible to restrict research to a European language.

Language has social meaning; it is universally true throughout the Continent that a knowledge of a European language indicates that its possessor has already attained some degree of acculturation into "Western society". Interviewers who speak a European language exhibit social status characteristics and attitudes which set them apart from their counterparts. Therefore, the sample and findings may be biased not only in favour of a particular language group but also of a particular social group. If, on the other hand, the researcher's specific objective is to study, say, English-speaking "Westernized" African housewives, to test the hypothesis that they are more receptive to European products, then he must state this particular purpose in his research design.

In most cases, however, the researcher wishes to reach as many and as representative a portion of the total population as possible. Thus arise a number of problems associated with the translation of questionnaires from the original European language into African languages. First, emphasis and meaning change when the question-naire is translated into the language of inquiry. Secondly, in translating and coding back into English the translator is at the disadvantage of not having been in the field, and is liable to make serious errors. One solution in the first case is to create a multilingual staff of interviewers and standardized translations plus pre-testing of all translated questions.

It would be interesting to experiment with the creation and formulation of interview instruments in major African languages by Africans themselves. This might be particularly effective in cases requiring detailed depth interviewing where the logic of European probing clashes with the cosmogony of the African community.

Language is also, of course, significantly related to literacy. Data on literacy is virtually valueless when it simply states that a certain proportion of the sample are literate without giving particulars of the languages in which they are literate. This point is particularly significant in media and advertising research. Although a large proportion of a given population may indeed be literate in some language, newspaper and other visual advertising may be lost to them if it is presented in a language in which they are *not* literate. In questionnaire design, low literacy rates restrict the use of written prompting aids. This can be overcome as more manufacturers identify their brands by symbols which can be used as prompts.

It is possible that simple visual and manipulative devices could be designed which would allow the informant to demonstrate his choice and degree of liking for a product. For example, a magnetic board equipped with magnets and a scale of colours and symbols could be devised. The respondents would be instructed to indicate his rating of Product "A" — high, low or in-between — by placing the magnet on the board and moving it to the appropriate spot.

As market research in Africa progresses new techniques of interviewing and surveying are being devised. One firm has attempted a "bin survey" whereby they provide a sample of urban housewives with a plastic bin and instruct them to deposit in it any used containers for a given range of products. In future it may be possible to use personality testing techniques but at present researchers are hampered by methods which are not "culture-free". Anthropologists have used tests among Africans like the Rorschach Ink Blot test, a projective test of association and psychological processes, but much experimental work remains to be done. The day is not too far off when market researchers will find it necessary to create a standard manual of cross-cultural market research which will provide an easily accessible pool of knowledge and data.

Responsibility to informants

Interviewers have a great responsibility to their informants. This is a point which is often overlooked when dealing with peoples of another culture. Fortunately the British Market Research Society's code[6] provides a moral framework for the interviewing situation:

> "Most market research depends upon the co-operation of informants either in their personal capacity or in their business capacity. In consequence, all practitioners have a direct responsibility towards these informants to ensure that they are in no way embarrassed or in other ways hindered as a result of an interview.
>
> In the conduct and control of interviews, members are required to exercise all reasonable precautions that the informants will be in no way adversely affected as a result of the questions administered or the interviewing process itself. No procedure or technique shall be used in which the informant is put in such a position that he cannot exercise his right to withdraw or refuse to answer *at any stage* in the interview."

TOWARDS A NEW SCIENCE

The market research and marketing definitions of 20 years ago have been rapidly overtaken in developing Africa. Social scientific researchers and theoreticians have had to devise new models of human behaviour in the teeth of change. Not because "they" (the Africans) are different, but because with more cases to be studied we learn more; with new circumstances, new theories arise and enrich science. As a result, the implicit underlying assumptions of the sciences which are hosts to market research are being challenged and revised in accordance with new findings.

The "rational, economic man" mode of classical economics is giving way to new formulations. The emphasis is shifting from studying "static" or "primitive" communities to researching modernizing nations and change situations. Social anthropologists now study Nigerians and Kenyans as workers and peasants not as "tribesmen and pagans".

Market research in developing nations requires the joint co-operation of market researchers and social scientists. In fact, commercial market research has a substantial contribution to make towards analysing the social behaviour of developing countries; and by doing so can enrich social science. It may be that market research, with its greater resources and more pressing commercial interests, will be better equipped than the university social scientist to do the kinds of basic research necessary to understand the modern African people.

It should be recognized, however, that any final decisions about "who and what the emerging African is" will have to wait until more African social scientists have been heard. As Professor Dike said to 500 delegates at the First International Congress of Africanist scholars:

> "It is my sincere hope that the formation of this International Congress will end a period in which foreign scholars spoke for us. We do not want to minimize the splendid achievements and extensive knowledge of our foreign colleagues and are fully aware that there were many of them in the past who knew more about our culture than we ourselves. They were, on one hand, in a position to observe this Continent from a distance as a whole, to interconnect events and values from various countries and were able, on the other hand, to reveal our cultural bonds with America and the Caribbean.
>
> "But I hope they will understand when I say that we Africans

now see the time has come to speak for ourselves and take over the responsibility of thoroughly and deeply exploring our past, present and future prospects ourselves. It is time for the world to be given an African interpretation,"

A revived and reconstructed market research approach can provide services to a wide range of clients: business, government, social institutions, municipal councils and national resource agencies. Market research methods of inquiry can be applied to problems of statecraft, public administration and social and economic development.

Market research can be an indispensable aid to progress when applied to:

1 *Agriculture:* agrarian statistics, production, wholesale and consumer prices;

2 *Marketing flow:* the origin and destination of products, production trends, consumer preferences, territorial purchasing power indices, incidence of price increases in the flow of goods from producer to consumer;

3 *Market geography:* establish commercially attractive areas for crops and products, test markets for launching new products;

4 *Public affairs:* analysis of public opinion and voting behaviour, planning for housing, urban re-development and slum clearance and new towns; for health, education and "human-investment" campaigns;

5 *Social inventories:* analysis of the distribution of blood groups, intelligence testing, savings habits and planning for the technical education and formation of skilled cadres.

Marketing and market research in the future will have to be equipped with dynamic concepts big enough to encompass the vast volatile African market. They must have techniques sensitive enough to monitor the accelerating changes of the next decades, and beyond.

Marketing to modern Africans will be more than producing a

good product and letting it sell on its own merits, more than simply finding convenient outlets for surplus goods, more than studying Africans with an inventory of outmoded concepts from Western experience. Good marketing in Africa will be consumer-orientated and development-centred.

Forward-looking industries, governments, advertising and market-research agencies will recognize the inherent changeability of the African market. They will understand that the traits of African consumers are not yet fused together. Africans are not yet a type; there are no ready-made cubby-holes to place them in. There are instead countless variations on the continental theme of development.

While it is a sure bet that Englishmen will still be drinking afternoon tea 50 years from now, Africans may be spending millions on new products, yet to be created. Products which now compete for the merest foothold on the African Continent may flourish, while those which nourish great industries today may wither away.

I have no doubt that a new science of marketing will emerge during Africa's Century of Development. What will be the main characteristics of this new science?

It will be a problem-orientated study of the properties of groups for immediate application to planning and action programmes. It will be a science of collectivities devoted to the study of pre-action, action and re-action. It will be an instrument of social and economic development, monitoring between homogeneous chaos and idiosyncratic organization. It will be comparative, and seek to establish significant cross-cultural generalizations about marketing and the social milieu through the study of the origins, forms, interrelationships and directions of marketing practices in the various cultural settings of mankind.

REFERENCES

1 DYCE-SHARP, K., *Teach Yourself Market Research,* English Universities Press London, 1963.

2 DOWNHAM, JOHN, *et al.,* "Introduction: A Survey of Market Research in Great Britain". *Readings in Market Research,* The British Market Research Bureau, London, 1956.

3 ADLER, MAX, *A Short Course in Market Research,* C. E. Fisher and Co., London, undated.

4 "Africa: Say 'Olympia'", *Newsweek,* 9 March, 1964.

5 MARRIS, PETER, *Family and Social Change in an African City,* Routledge and Kegan Paul, London, 1961.

6 Market Research Society, *Standards in Market Research,* Revised December, 1960.

CHARTER OF THE ORGAN-IZATION OF AFRICAN UNITY, ADDIS ABABA, MAY 1963

We, the Heads of African States and Governments assembled in the City of Addis Ababa, Ethiopa;

CONVINCED that it is the inalienable right of all people to control their own destiny;

CONSCIOUS of the fact that freedom, equality, justice and dignity are essential objectives for the achievement of the legitimate aspirations of the African peoples;

CONSCIOUS of our responsibility to harness the natural and human resources of our continent for the total advancement of our peoples in spheres of human endeavour;

INSPIRED by a common determination to promote understanding among our peoples and co-operation among our States in response to the aspirations of our peoples for brotherhood and solidarity, in a larger unity transcending ethnic and national differences;

CONVINCED that, in order to translate this determination into a dynamic force in the cause of human progress, conditions for peace and security must be established and maintained;

DETERMINED to safeguard and consolidate the hard-won independence as well as the sovereignty and territorial integrity of our States, and to fight against neo-colonialism in all its forms;

DEDICATED to the general progress of Africa;

PERSUADED that the Charter of the United Nations and the Universal Declaration of Human Rights, to the principles of which we reaffirm our adherence, provide a solid foundation for peaceful and positive co-operation among States;

DESIROUS that all African States should henceforth unite so that the welfare and well-being of their peoples can be assured;

RESOLVED to reinforce the links between our states by establishing and strengthening common institutions;

HAVE agreed to the present Charter.

ESTABLISHMENT

Article I

1 The High Contracting Parties do by the present Charter establish an Organization to be known as the ORGANIZATION OF AFRICAN UNITY.
2 The Organization shall include the Continental African States, Madagascar and other Islands surrounding Africa.

PURPOSES

Article II

1 The Organization shall have the following purposes:
    (*a*) to promote the unity and solidarity of the African States;
    (*b*) to co-ordinate and intensify their co-operation and efforts to achieve a better life for the peoples of Africa;
    (*c*) to defend their sovereignty, their territorial integrity and independence;
    (*d*) to eradicate all forms of colonialism from Africa; and
    (*e*) to promote international co-operation, having due regard to the Charter of the United Nations and the Universal Declaration of Human Rights.
2 To these ends, the Member States shall co-ordinate and harmonize their general policies, especially in the following fields:
    (*a*) political and diplomatic co-operation;
    (*b*) economic co-operation, including transport and communications;
    (*c*) educational and cultural co-operation;
    (*d*) health, sanitation, and nutritional co-operation;
    (*e*) scientific and technical co-operation; and
    (*f*) co-operation for defence and security.

PRINCIPLES

Article III

The Member States, in pursuit of the purposes stated in Article II, solemnly affirm and declare their adherence to the following principles:
    1 the sovereign equality of all Member States;
    2 non-interference in the internal affairs of States;

Q

3 respect for the sovereignty and territorial integrity of each State
and for its inalienable right to independent existence;
4 peaceful settlement of disputes by negotiation, mediation, conciliation or arbitration;
5 unreserved condemnation, in all its forms, of political assassina-
tion as well as of subversive activities on the part of neighbouring States or any other State:
6 absolute dedication to the total emancipation of the African
territories which are still dependent;
7 affirmation of a policy of non-alignment with regard to all blocs.

MEMBERSHIP

Article IV

Each independent sovereign African State shall be entitled to become
a Member of the Organization.

RIGHTS AND DUTIES OF MEMBER STATES

Article V

All Member States shall enjoy equal rights and have equal duties.

Article VI

The Member States pledge themselves to observe scrupulously the
principles enumerated in Article III of the present Charter.

INSTITUTIONS

Article VII

The Organization shall accomplish its purposes through the following principal institutions:
1 the Assembly of Heads of State and Government;
2 the Council of Ministers;
3 the General Secretariat;
4 the Commission of Mediation, Conciliation and Arbitration.

THE ASSEMBLY OF HEADS OF STATE AND GOVERNMENT

Article VIII

The Assembly of Heads of State and Government shall be the
supreme organ of the Organization. It shall, subject to the provisions

of this Charter, discuss matters of common concern to Africa with a view to co-ordinating and harmonizing the general policy of the Organization. It may in addition review the structure, functions and acts of all the organs and any specialized agencies which may be created in accordance with the present Charter.

Article IX

The Assembly shall be composed of the Heads of State and Government or their duly accredited representatives and it shall meet at least once a year. At the request of any Member State and on approval by a two-thirds majority of the Member States, the Assembly shall meet in extraordinary session.

Article X

1 Each Member State shall have one vote.
2 All resolutions shall be determined by a two-thirds majority of the Members of the Organization.
3 Questions of procedure shall require a simple majority. Whether or not a question is one of procedure shall be determined by a simple majority of all Member States of the Organization.
4 Two-thirds of the total membership of the Organization shall form a quorum at any meeting of the Assembly.

Article XI

The Assembly shall have the power to determine its own rules of procedure.

THE COUNCIL OF MINISTERS

Article XII

1 The Council of Ministers shall consist of Foreign Ministers or such other Ministers as are designated by the Governments of Member States.
2 The Council of Ministers shall meet at least twice a year. When requested by any Member State and approved by two-thirds of all Member States, it shall meet in extraordinary session.

Article XIII

1 The Council of Ministers shall be responsible to the Assembly of

Heads of State and Government. It shall be entrusted with the responsibility of preparing conferences of the Assembly.

2 It shall take cognisance of any matter referred to it by the Assembly. It shall be entrusted with the implementation of the decision of the Assembly of Heads of State and Government. It shall co-ordinate inter-African co-operation in accordance with the instructions of the Assembly and in conformity with Article II (2) of the present Charter.

Article XIV

1 Each Member State shall have one vote.

2 All resolutions shall be determined by a simple majority of the members of the Council of Ministers.

3 Two-thirds of the total membership of the Council of Ministers shall form a quorum for any meeting of the Council.

Article XV

The Council shall have the power to determine its own rules of procedure.

GENERAL SECRETARIAT

Article XVI

There shall be an Administrative Secretary-General of the Organization, who shall be appointed by the Assembly of Heads of State and Government. The Administrative Secretary-General shall direct the affairs of the Secretariat.

Article XVII

There shall be one or more Assistant Secretaries-General of the Organization, who shall be appointed by the Assembly of Heads of State and Government.

Article XVIII

The functions and conditions of services of the Secretary-General, of the Assistant Secretaries-General and other employees of the Secretariat shall be governed by the provisions of this Charter and the regulations approved by the Assembly of Heads of State and Government.

1 In the performance of their duties the Administrative Secretary-General and the staff shall not seek or receive instructions from any government or from any other authority external to the

Organization. They shall refrain from any action which might reflect on their position as international officials responsible only to the Organization.

2 Each member of the Organization undertakes to respect the exclusive character of the responsibilities of the Administrative Secretary-General and the staff and not to seek to influence them in the discharge of their responsibilities.

COMMISSION OF MEDIATION, CONCILIATION AND ARBITRATION

Article XIX

Member States pledge to settle all disputes among themselves by peaceful means and, to this end decide to establish a Commission of Mediation, Conciliation and Arbitration, the composition of which and conditions of service shall be defined by a separate Protocol to be approved by the Assembly of Heads of State and Government. Said Protocol shall be regarded as forming an integral part of the present Charter.

SPECIALIZED COMMISSIONS

Article XX

The Assembly shall establish such Specialized Commissions as it may deem necessary, including the following:
1 Economic and Social Commission;
2 Educational and Cultural Commission;
3 Health, Sanitation and Nutrition Commission;
4 Defence Commission;
5 Scientific, Technical and Research Commission.

Article XXI

Each Specialized Commission referred to in Article XX shall be composed of the Ministers concerned or other Ministers or Plenipotentiaries designated by the Governments of the Member States.

Article XXII

The functions of the Specialized Commissions shall be carried out in accordance with the provisions of the present Charter and of the regulations approved by the Council of Ministers.

THE BUDGET

Article XXIII

The budget of the Organization prepared by the Administrative Secretary-General shall be approved by the Council of Ministers. The budget shall be provided by contributions from Member States in accordance with the scale of assessment of the United Nations; provided, however, that no Member State shall be assessed an amount exceeding 20 per cent of the yearly regular budget of the Organization. The Member States agree to pay their respective contributions regularly.

SIGNATURE AND RATIFICATION OF CHARTER

Article XXIV

1 This Charter shall be open for signature to all independent sovereign African States and shall be ratified by the signatory States in accordance with their respective constitutional processes.

2 The original instrument, done, if possible in African languages, in English and French, all texts being equally authentic, shall be deposited with the Government of Ethiopia which shall transmit certified copies thereof to all independent sovereign African States.

3 Instruments of ratification shall be deposited with the Government of Ethiopia, which shall notify all signatories of each such deposit.

ENTRY INTO FORCE

Article XXV

This Charter shall enter into force immediately upon receipt by the Government of Ethiopia of the instruments of ratification from two-thirds of the signatory States.

REGISTRATION OF THE CHARTER

Article XXVI

This Charter shall, after due ratification, be registered with the Secretariat of the United Nations through the Government of Ethiopia in conformity with Article 102 of the Charter of the United Nations.

INTERPRETATION OF THE CHARTER

Article XXVII

Any question which may arise concerning the interpretation of this Charter shall be decided by a vote of two-thirds of the Assembly of Heads of State and Government of the Organization.

ADHESION AND ACCESSION

Article XXVIII

1 Any independent sovereign African State may at any time notify the Administrative Secretary-General of its intention to adhere or accede to this Charter.

2 The Administrative Secretary-General shall, on receipt of such notification, communicate a copy of it to all the Member States. Admission shall be decided by a simple majority of the Member States. The decision of each Member State shall be transmitted to the Administrative Secretary-General, who shall, upon receipt of the required number of votes, communicate the decision to the State concerned.

MISCELLANEOUS

Article XXIX

The working languages of the Organization and all its institutions shall be, if possible African languages, English and French.

Article XXX

The Administrative Secretary-General may accept on behalf of the Organization gifts, bequests and other donations made to the Organization, provided that this is approved by the Council of Ministers.

Article XXXI

The Council of Ministers shall decide on the privileges and immunities to be accorded to the personnel of the Secretariat in the respective territories of the Member States.

CESSATION OF MEMBERSHIP

Article XXXII

Any State which desires to renounce its membership shall forward a written notification to the Administrative Secretary-General. At the end of one year from the date of such notification, if not withdrawn, the Charter shall cease to apply with respect to the renouncing State, which shall thereby cease to belong to the Organization.

AMENDMENT OF THE CHARTER

Article XXXIII

This Charter may be amended or revised if any Member State makes a written request to the Administrative Secretary-General to that effect; provided, however, that the proposed amendment is not submitted to the Assembly for consideration until all the Member States have been duly notified of it and a period of one year has elapsed. Such an amendment shall not be effective unless approved by at least two-thirds of all the Member States.

IN FAITH WHEREOF, We, the Heads of African State and Government have signed this Charter.

Done in the City of Addis Ababa, Ethiopia, this 25th day of May, 1963.

ALGERIA	MALI
BURUNDI	MAURITANIA
CAMEROUN	MOROCCO
CENTRAL AFRICAN REPUBLIC	NIGER
CHAD	NIGERIA
CONGO (Brazzaville)	RWANDA
CONGO (Leopoldville)	SENEGAL
DAHOMEY	SIERRA LEONE
ETHIOPIA	SOMALIA
GABON	SUDAN
GHANA	TANGANYIKA
GUINEA	TOGO
IVORY COAST	TUNISIA
LIBERIA	UGANDA
LIBYA	UNITED ARAB REPUBLIC
MADAGASCAR	UPPER VOLTA

RESOLUTIONS ADOPTED BY THE FIRST CONFERENCE OF INDEPENDENT AFRICAN HEADS OF STATE AND GOVERNMENT, ADDIS ABABA, MAY, 1963

A

DECOLONIZATION

The Summit Conference of Independent African States meeting in Addis Ababa, Ethiopia, from 22 May to 25 May, 1963;

Having considered all aspects of the questions of decolonization;

Unanimously convinced of the imperious and urgent necessity of co-ordinating and intensifying their efforts to accelerate the uncondi-tional attainment of national independence by all African territories still under foreign domination;

Reaffirming that it is the duty of all African Independent States to support dependent peoples in Africa in their struggle for freedom and independence;

Noting with deep concern that most of the remaining dependent territories in Africa are dominated by foreign settlers;

Convinced that the colonial powers, by their forcible imposition of the settlers to control the governments and administrations of those territories, are thus establishing colonial bases in the heart of Africa;

Have agreed unanimously to concert and co-ordinate their efforts and actions in this field, and to this end have decided on the following measures:

1 *Declares* that the forcible imposition by the colonial powers of the settlers to control the governments and administrations of the dependent territories is a flagrant violation of the inalienable rights of the legitimate inhabitants of the territories concerned;

2 *Invites* the colonial powers to take the necessary measures for the

immediate application of the Declaration of the Granting of Independence to Colonial Countries and Peoples; and *insists* that their determination to maintain colonies or semi-colonies in Africa constitutes a menace to the peace of the continent;

3 *Invites*, further, the colonial powers, particularly the United Kingdom with regard to Southern Rhodesia, not to transfer the powers and attributes of sovereignty to foreign minority governments imposed on African peoples by the use of force and under cover of racial legislation; and the transfer of power to settler minorities would amount to a violation of the provision of United Nations Resolution 1514 (XV) on Independence;

4 *Reaffirms* its support of African nationalists of Southern Rhodesia and solemnly declares that if power in Southern Rhodesia were to be usurped by a racial white minority government, State Members of the Conference would lend their effective moral and practical support to any legitimate measures which the African nationalist leaders may devise for the purpose of recovering such power and restoring it to the African majority : the Conference also *undertakes* henceforth to concert the efforts of its Members to take such measures as the situation demands against any State according recognition to the minority government;

5 *Reaffirms*, further, that the territory of South-West Africa is an African territory under international mandate and that any attempt by the Republic of South Africa to annex it would be regarded as an act of aggression; *Reaffirms* also its determination to render all necessary support to the second phase of the South-West Africa case before the International Court of Justice; *Reaffirms* still further, the inalienable right of the people of South-West Africa to self-determination and independence;

6 *Intervenes* expressly with the Great Powers so that they cease, without exception, to lend direct or indirect support or assistance to all those colonialist governments which might use such assistance to suppress national liberation movements, particularly the Portuguese Government which is conducting a real war of genocide in Africa; *informs* the allies of colonial powers that they must choose between their friendship for the African peoples and their support of powers that oppress African peoples;

7 *Decides* to send a delegation of Ministers of Foreign Affairs to speak on behalf of all African States in the meetings of the Security Council which will be called to examine the report of the United Nations Committee of 24 on the situation in African territories under Portuguese domination: (The Conference has decided the members of the Delegation to be: Liberia, Tunisia, Madagascar and Sierra Leone);

8 *Decides* further the breaking off of diplomatic and consular relations between all African States and the Governments of Portugal and South Africa so long as they persist in their present attitude towards decolonization;

9 *Asks for an effective boycott* of the foreign trade of Portugal and South Africa by:

(*a*) prohibiting the import of goods from those two countries;
(*b*) closing African ports and airports to their ships and planes;
(*c*) forbidding the planes of those two countries to overfly the territories of all African States.

10 *Earnestly invites* all national liberation movements to co-ordinate their efforts by establishing common action fronts wherever necessary so as to strengthen the effectiveness of their struggle and the rational use of the concerted assistance given them;

11 *Establishes* a Co-ordinating Committee consisting of Algeria, Ethiopia, Guinea, Congo (Leopoldville), Nigeria, Senegal, Tanganyika, United Arab Republic and Uganda, with Headquarters in Dar-es-Salaam, Tanganyika, responsible for harmonizing the assistance from African States and for managing the Special Fund to be set up for that purpose;

12 *Establishes* a Special Fund to be raised by voluntary contribution of Member States for the current year, the deadline for such contribution being 15 July, 1963; *Requests* the Co-ordinating Committee to propose the necessary fund and the apportionment among Member States to the Council of Ministers so as to supply the necessary practical and financial aid to the various African national liberation movements;

13 *Appoints* the day of 25 May as African Liberation Day so as to organize popular demonstrations on that day to disseminate the recommendations of the Summit Conference and to collect sums over and above the national contributions for the Special Fund; (The Conference has decided that this year it will be the opening

day of the 18th Session of the General Assembly of the United Nations);

14 *Decides* to receive on the territories of independent African States, nationalists from liberation movements in order to give them training in all sectors and afford young people all the assistance they need for their education and vocational training;

15 *Decides* further to promote, in each State, the transit of all material aid and the establishment of a body of volunteers in various fields, with a view to providing the various African national liberation movements with the assistance they need in the various sectors.

B

APARTHEID AND RACIAL DISCRIMINATION

The Summit Conference of Independent African States meeting in Addis Ababa, Ethiopia, from 22 May to 25 May 1963;

Having considered all aspects of the questions of apartheid and racial discriminations;

Unanimously convinced of the imperious and urgent necessity of co-ordinating and intensifying their efforts to put an end to the South African Government's criminal policy of apartheid and wipe out racial discrimination in all its forms;

Have agreed unanimously to concert and co-ordinate their efforts and actions in this field, and to this end have decided on the following measures;

(*a*) To grant scholarships, educational facilities and possibilities of employment in African government services to refugees from South Africa;

(*b*) To support the recommendations presented to the Security Council and the General Assembly by the Special Committee of the United Nations on the apartheid policies of the South African Government;

(*c*) To dispatch a delegation of Foreign Ministers to inform the Security Council of the explosive situation existing in South Africa: (The Conference has decided the members of the Delegation to be: Liberia, Tunisia, Madagascar and Sierra Leone);

(*d*) To co-ordinate concerted measures of sanction against the Government of South Africa;

1 *Appeals* to all States, and more particularly to those which have traditional relations and co-operate with the Government of South Africa, to apply strictly UN resolution 1761 (XVII) of 6 November 1962 concerning apartheid;

2 *Appeals* to all governments who still have diplomatic, consular and economic relations with the Government of South Africa to break off those relations and to cease any other form of encouragement for the policy of apartheid;

3 *Stresses* the great responsibility incurred by the colonial authorities administering territories neighbouring South Africa in the pursuit of the policy of apartheid;

4 *Condemns* racial discrimination in all its forms in Africa and all over the world;

5 *Expresses* the deep concern aroused in all African peoples and governments by the measures of racial discrimination taken against communities of African origin living outside the continent and particularly in the United States of America; *Expresses* appreciation for the efforts of the Federal Government of the United States of America to put an end to these intolerable malpractices which are likely seriously to deteriorate relations between the African peoples and governments on the one hand and the people and Government of the United States of America on the other.

C

AFRICA AND THE UNITED NATIONS

The Summit Conference of Independent African States meeting in Addis Ababa, Ethiopia, from 22 May to 25 May, 1963;

Believing that the United Nations is an important instrument for the maintenance of peace and security among nations and for the promotion of the economic and social advancement of all peoples;

Reiterating its desire to strengthen and support the United Nations;

Noting with regret that Africa as a region is not equitably represented in the principal organs of the United Nations;

Convinced of the need for closer co-operation and co-ordination among the African Member States of the United Nations;

1 *Reaffirms* its dedication to the purposes and principles of the United Nations Charter and its acceptance of all obligations contained in the Charter, including financial obligations;

2 *Insists* that Africa as a geographical region should have equitable representation in the principal organs of the United Nations, particularly the Security Council and the Economic and Social Council and its Specialized Agencies;

3 *Invites* African Governments to instruct their representatives in the United Nations to take all possible steps to achieve a more equitable representation of the African region;

4 *Further invites* African Governments to instruct their representatives in the United Nations, without prejudice to their membership in and collaboration with the African-Asian Group, to constitute a more effective African Group with a permanent secretariat so as to bring about closer co-operation and better co-ordination in matters of common concern.

D

GENERAL DISARMAMENT

The Summit Conference of Independent African States meeting in Addis Ababa, Ethiopia, from 22 May to 25 May, 1963;

Having considered all aspects of the questions of general disarmament;

Unanimously convinced of the imperious and urgent necessity of co-ordinating and intensifying their efforts to contribute to the achievement of a realistic disarmament programme through the signing, by all States concerned, of a treaty on general and complete disarmament under strict and effective international control;

Have agreed unanimously to concert and co-ordinate their efforts and actions in this field, and to this end have decided on the following measures:

1 To affirm and respect the principle of declaring Africa a Denuclearized Zone: to oppose all nuclear and thermo-nuclear tests, as well as the manufacture of nuclear weapons; and to promote the peaceful uses of nuclear energy;

2 The destruction of existing nuclear weapons;

3 To undertake to bring about, by means of negotiation, the end

of military occupation of the African continent and the elimination of military bases and nuclear tests, which elimination constitutes a basic element of African Independence and Unity;

4 To appeal to the Great Powers to:
  (a) reduce conventional weapons;
  (b) put an end to the arms race; and
  (c) sign a general and complete disarmament agreement under strict and effective international control;

5 To appeal to the Great Powers, in particular to the Soviet Union and the United States of America, to use their best endeavours to secure the objectives stated above.

E

AREAS OF CO-OPERATION IN ECONOMIC PROBLEMS

The Summit Conference of Independent African States meeting in Addis Ababa, Ethiopia, from 22 May to 25 May, 1963;

Concerned with the active share of the developing countries in world trade and at the persistent deterioration of the terms of trade in their external commercial relationships;

Conscious of the fact that owing to its extreme dependence on the export of primary products, Africa, more than any other developing region, is adversely affected by persistent deteriorations in export earnings;

Convinced of the necessity for concerted action by the African countries in order to ensure a much more remunerative price from the sale of their primary products;

Mindful of the need to eliminate the barriers to trade among the African countries and thereby to strengthen their economies;

Considering that economic development, including the expansion of trade on the basis of fair and remunerative prices, should tend to eliminate the need for external economic aid and that such external economic aid should be unconditional and should not prejudice the independence of African States;

Considering the imperative necessity for African countries to pool their resources and harmonize their activities in the economic field;

Aware of the necessity for the joint utilization of river basin resources, the study of the use of Sahara Zone, the co-ordination of means of transport and communication systems, and the provision of research facilities, all of which serve to stimulate economic growth and expansion of trade, both regionally and inter-regionally;

Convinced that the acceleration of the rate of economic and social development of the various African countries lies in the industrialization of these countries and the diversification of their production;

Considering the serious problems arising from the great shortage of trained and skilled personnel, the lack of qualified staff, scarce capital resources, grossly inadequate infrastructure, limited outlines for industrial products and the far too inadequate participation of Africans in the economic construction of their countries;

Desiring to explore the effects of regional economic groupings on the African economy;

Noting with satisfaction that the Executive Secretary of the Economic Commission for Africa has decided to convene a Conference of African Ministers of Finance, to be held in Khartoum (Sudan) in July 1963, with a view to setting up an African Development Bank;

Resolves to:

1 *Appoint*, pending the establishment of the Economic Commission of the Organization, a preparatory economic committee to study, in collaboration with governments and in consultation with the Economic Commission for Africa, *inter alia*, the following questions and submit their findings to Member States:

(*a*) the possibility of establishing a free trade area between the various African countries;

(*b*) the establishment of a common external tariff to protect the emergent industries and the setting up of a raw material price stabilization fund;

(*c*) the restructuralization of international trade;

(*d*) the means for developing trade among African countries by the organization and participation in African trade fairs and exhibitions and by the granting of transport and transit facilities;

(*e*) the co-ordination of means of transport and the establishment of road, air and maritime companies;

(*f*) the establishment of an African Payments and Clearing Union;

(*g*) a progressive freeing of national currencies from all nontechnical external attachments and the establishment of a Pan-African monetary zone; and

(h) the ways and means of effecting the harmonization of existing and future national development plans.

2 *Invite* ECA to request its Executive Secretary to give the Commission of Experts all the necessary support and assistance which it may require in the fulfilment of its assignment;

3 *Welcome* the forthcoming Conference of African Ministers of Finance and to give the respective Ministers of Finance instructions to take the necessary measures for the rapid establishment of the African Development Bank;

4 *Note* with satisfaction the progress achieved by the Economic Commission for Africa in establishing the Dakar Institute of Economic Development and Planning and to affirm their profound interest in that institute and their intention of giving it appropriate financial and other support;

5 *Welcome* the forthcoming World Conference on Trade and Development which is to examine international trade problems in relation to the economic development of emerging countries;

6 *Urge* all States concerned to conduct negotiations, in concert, with a view to obtaining from the consumer countries real price stabilization and guaranteed outlets on the world market so that the developing countries may derive considerably greater revenue from international trade.

F

AREAS OF CO-OPERATION — THE FUTURE OF THE C.C.T.A.

The Summit Conference of Independent African States meeting in Addis Ababa, Ethiopia, from 22 May to 25 May 1963;

Considering that at the last C.C.T.A. session in Dar-es-Salaam in January to February 1963, the final adoption of the new C.C.T.A. convention was deferred until the Heads of African States had had an opportunity to consider the role and direction of the C.C.T.A. within the overall context of Pan-African Co-operation,

And in view of the fact that Article 23 of this new convention lays down as follows:

R

"Pending the signature and the ratification of this convention as provided in Article 16, the Parties having initialled this convention agree to apply it provisionally as if it had entered into force as from the date of initialling, subject to any decision which may be taken by the Heads of African and Malagasy States at the Conference at Addis Ababa or at any subsequent conference on the role of the C.C.T.A. within the overall context of Pan-African Co-operation."

Decides to maintain C.C.T.A. and to reconsider its role in order to bring it eventually within the scope of the Organization of African States which will have, as one of its arms, an organ for technical, scientific and cultural co-operation.

Supplementary Resolutions adopted by the Summit Conference of the Independent African States on the proposal of the delegation of the Kingdom of Libya and to be presented to the appropriate institutions provided for under Article X of the Charter of the Organization of African Unity.

A

SOCIAL AND LABOUR MATTERS

The Summit Conference of Independent African States meeting in Addis Ababa, Ethiopia, from 22 to 25 May 1963;

Realizing the importance of social standard for the African peoples and the urgent need for raising such standard;

Considering that co-operation amongst the African States in the social and labour fields is vital and will contribute to the realization of a sound solidarity amongst their peoples;

Believing that the coming together of youth from African States will create better understanding and contribute to the realization of the desired African unity;

Believing further that co-operation in the labour field amongst African States is vital for our continent;

DECIDES that a Committee of Experts be called to convene within three months, pending the setting up of the Economic and Social Commission provided for in Article XX of the Charter of the Organization of African Unity, to submit a report to the above Commission:

With regard to social and labour matters:

1 To conduct extensive studies on social and labour problems in the continent;

2 To lay down detailed programmes with a view to raising the social standard and to strengthen inter African co-operation through:

(*a*) The exchange of social and labour legislations;

(*b*) The establishment of African Youth Organization;

(*c*) The organization of African Scouts Union and an annual continental jamboree;

(*d*) The organization of an annual African Sport Games;

(*e*) The organization of vocational training courses in which African workers will participate;

(*f*) The establishment of an African Trade Union.

B

EDUCATION AND CULTURE

The Summit Conference of Independent African States meeting in Addis Ababa, Ethiopia, from 22 to 25 May 1963;

Desirous of strengthening educational and cultural ties amongst the peoples of Africa;

Considering that the educational and cultural co-operation amongst African States will break down linguistic barriers and promote understanding amongst the peoples of the continent;

Believing that once this co-operation in the educational and cultural fields amongst African States has been organized, co-ordinated and harmonized and fully implemented, it will pave the way to the final goal, namely African Unity;

Realizing the lack of information media in various parts of the African continent and the necessity of strengthening exchange of information amongst African States in order to promote better understanding amongst their peoples;

1 DECIDES that a Committee of Experts be called to convene within three months, pending the setting up of the Educational and Cultural Commission provided for in Article XX of the Charter of the Organization of African Unity, to submit a report to the above Commission on educational and cultural matters by taking into account the resolutions which have been adopted by the Conferences of Casablanca and Lagos;

2 PROPOSES: (a) the establishment of an institute of African Studies to be a department of the African University proposed by Ethiopia;

(b) the introduction, as soon as possible, of programmes in the major African languages in the Broadcasting Stations of the various African States and the exchanges of radio and television programmes;

(c) the establishment of an African News Agency.

C

HEALTH, SANITATION AND NUTRITION

The Summit Conference of Independent African States meeting in Addis Ababa, Ethiopia, from 22 to 25 May 1963;

Realizing the importance of health standard for the African peoples and the urgent need for raising such standard and improving sanitation and nutrition amongst the peoples;

Considering that the co-operation amongst the African States in health, sanitation and nutrition fields is vital and will contribute to the realization of stronger solidarity amongst their peoples;

DECIDES that a Committee of Experts be called to convene within three months, pending the setting up of the Commission on Health, Sanitation and Nutrition provided for in Article XX of the Organization of African Unity, to submit a report to the above Commission:

With regard to health:

1 To conduct extensive studies on health problems facing the continent;

2 To lay down detailed programmes with a view to raising health standard among the peoples and to strengthen inter-African co-operation through:

(a) The exchange of information about endemic and epidemic diseases and the means to control them;

(b) The exchange of health legislations;

(c) The exchange of doctors, technicians and nurses;

(d) The reciprocal offer of scholarships for medical students and the establishment of training courses on health, sanitation and nutrition;

3 To conduct research in all African States on sanitation and nutrition and to study ways and means to improve them.

SOME RESOURCES ON AFRICA

Readers will find the publications and organizations listed below a useful introduction to the wealth of resources available to them.

ADVERTISING

Advertiser's Weekly
Advertising Expenditure 1960, prepared by Economist Intelligence Unit
Advertising Association
Incorporated Advertising Managers' Association
Incorporated Sales Managers' Association
Incorporated Society of British Advertising
Institute of Practitioners of Advertising
Journal of Advertising Research
Statistical Review of Advertising Expenditure

ARCHITECTURE AND HOUSING

Afrique
Architectural Association Journal
Architecture D'Aujourdhui
Architectural Design
Architectural Review
The Building Centre, Addis Ababa, Ethiopia
Overseas Building Notes
West African Builder and Architect
Charles Abrams, *Man's Struggle for Shelter in an Urbanizing World,* Massachusetts Institute of Technology Press, 1964
Maxwell Fry & Jane Drew, *Tropical Architecture*, Batsford, London, 1964
Charles Abrams, Otto Koenigsberger *et al., Metropolitan Lagos,* Report prepared for the Ministry of Lagos Affairs of the Federal Government of Nigeria, United Nations, Commissioner for Technical Assistance, Department of Economic & Social Affairs, April 1963
Charles Abrams, V. Bodiansky & Otto Koenigsberger, *Report on Housing in the Gold Coast,* United Nations, New York, 1956
United Nations, Social Commission, 14th Session, *Report of the Ad Hoc Group of Experts on Housing & Urban Development,* New York, March 16, 1962

COMMUNICATIONS

W. Buchanan & H. Cantril, *How Nations See Each Other: A Study in Public Opinion*, University of Illinois Press, 1953

Conference of African States on the Development of Education in Africa, Final Report, UNECA & UNESCO, 1961

L. W. Doob, *Communications in Africa*, Yale University Press, 1961

International Social Science Bulletin, "Opinion Surveys in Developing Countries". **XV**, I, 1963

Leo Lowenthal (ed.), Special Issue on International Communications Research, *Public Opinion Quarterly*, **16**, No. 4, Winter 1952–53

Committee on Inter-African Relations, *The Press in West Africa*, Ibadan, Extra-Mural Studies Dept., 1960

Reports & Papers on Mass Communication, No. 57, "Developing Information Media in Africa: Press, Radio & Television," UNESCO, 1962

UNESCO, *The Problems of Transmitting Press Messages*, UNESCO, Paris, 1956

West African Annual Directory, 1964, Thomas Skinner & Son, London, 1963

Francis Williams, *Transmitting World News*, United Nations, London.

Helen Kitchen (ed.), *The Press in Africa*, Ruth Sloane Associates, Washington, D.C., 1956

West Africa, "Whither African Television", No. 2473, 24 October 1964, p. 1187; and "Television in Africa", No. 2474, 31 October 1964, p. 1229

World Radio and TV Handbook, 1964

Advertiser's Annual, 1963

DEVELOPMENT AND CHANGE

Bert Hoselitz & W. E. Moore (eds.), *Industrialization & Society*, UNESCO, 1963

International Co-operation and programmes of Economic and Social Development, UNESCO, 1961

"Economic Survey of Africa Since 1950". United Nations Department of Economic and Social Affairs, New York, 1959. E/CN. 14/28; Sales No. 59. II. k.1.

"Economic Bulletin for Africa." United Nations Economic Commission for Africa, Addis Ababa, Ethiopia, June 1962, **II**, No. 2; E/CN. 14/71; Sales No. 62. II. k.3.

"Bulletin Général de Statistiques des Associés d'Outre-Mer à la C.E.E." Communauté Économique Européenne. Office Statistique des Communautés Européennes, No. 2, première partie, Bruxelles, Février, 1964

H.R.H. Prince Philip, Duke of Edinburgh, *Oxford Study Conference on the Human Problems of Industrial Communities*. Oxford University Press, 1956

Guy Hunter, *The New Societies of Tropical Africa*, Oxford University Press, London, 1962

Social Implications of Industrialization and Urbanization in Africa. UNESCO. Tensions & Technology Series, 1956

Walter Goldschmidt, *The U.S. and Africa* (Revised). Praeger, N.Y. 1963
Directory of Non-Governmental European Organizations Offering Assistance in the Developing Countries. Centre for Labour & Social Studies. Rome
Ronald Robinson (ed.), *African Development Planning,* Cambridge University Overseas Studies Committee, 1964
J. K. Galbraith, *Economic Development,* Oxford University Press, 1964
U.N. Economic Commission for Africa, *Economic & Social Consequences of Racial Discriminatory Practices,* United Nations, New York, 1963

EUROPE — AFRICA (MARKETING & TRADE INFORMATION)

Associates of Gallup Poll
Bundesstelle fur Assenhandlesinformation, Cologne
Centre National du Commerce Extérieur, Paris
DOXA, Istituto per le Ricerche Statische, e l'Analisi dell' Opinione Publica, Milan
EMNID. K.G., Bielefeld, Germany
Institut Français d'Opinion Publique, L'Institut pour l'Étude des Marchés en France et à l'Étranger (ETMAR), Paris
Istituto Nazionale per il Comercio con l'Estero, Rome
Institut pour l'Étude des Marchés (IEM), Brussels, Office du Commerce Extérieur, Brussels
Deutsche Afrika Gesellschaft, Bonn
Afrika Verein, Hamburg
Hamburgische Welt-Wirtschafts-Archiv, Hamburg
Dynamar, Bazainville, France

JOURNALS AND PERIODIC SURVEYS

The Director, Journal of the Institute of Directors
Optima, Journal of the Anglo-American Company
Progress, The Unilever Quarterly
West Africa Journal
Reports, Bank of London
Economic Surveys, Barclays Bank
General Electric Review
Overseas Economic Surveys, HMSO
Handbook for Exporters, Westminster Bank
The Standard Bank Review

MARKETING

Robert Bartels, *Comparative Marketing: Wholesaling in 15 Countries,* Richard D. Irwin Publishers, Homewood, Illinois, 1963
Max K. Adler, *A Short Course in Market Research,* C. E. Fisher Co., London, undated

Readings in Market Research : A Selection of Papers by British Authors, British Market Research Bureau, London, 1956

Social Class Definition in Market Research : Objectives and Practices, Market Research Society Working Party on Social Class Definition, London, October, 1963

H. G. Wales and R. A. Ferber, *A Basic Bibliography on Marketing Research*, American Marketing Association, Chicago, 1963

Who Owns Whom (U.K. Edition), O. W. Roskill & Co., (Reports) Ltd., 1964

British Institute of Public Opinion

Commentary, Journal of the Market Research Society (U.K.)

Marketing Forum, Journal of the College of Marketing

Institute of Marketing and Sales Management

Journal of Marketing (U.S.A.)

Market Research Services in Great Britain, The Market Research Society

Africa : Sales Frontier for U.S. Business — Supplement to International Commerce. Washington, D.C., U.S. Government Printing Office, U.S. Department of Commerce, March, 1963

Jean et René Charbonneau, *Marchés et Marchands d'Afrique Noire*, La Colombe, Paris, 1961

L. H. Samuel, *African Studies in Income and Wealth*, for the International Association for Research in Income and Wealth, Bowes and Bowes, London, 1963

C. A. O. Van Nieuwen Nuijze (ed.), *Markets and Marketing as Factors of Development in the Mediterranean Basin*, Second Assembly of the Mediterranean Social Sciences Research Council, Mouton and Co., The Hague, 1963

RESOURCE ORGANIZATIONS

Africa Research Bureau

Federation of British Industries

Federation of Chambers of Commerce of the British Empire

Commonwealth Industries Association

East African Railways and Harbours

Joint East and Central Africa Board

National Union of Manufacturers

Central Office of Information

Overseas Development Institute

United Nations, London Office

Institute of Export

Board of Trade

Government Customs and Excise Service, Trade and Navigation Accounts

Export Credits Guarantees Department

The Board of Trade, *The Board of Trade Journal, Export Services Bulletin; Hints to Businessmen*
Economist Intelligence Unit
Cambridge University Overseas Studies Committee
Department of Technical Co-operation
International African Institute, *African Abstracts*
Standing Conference on Library Materials on Africa (SCOLMA), *Directory of Libraries and Special Collections on Africa*, Heffer, Cambridge, 1963; and *Theses on Africa*, Heffer, Cambridge, 1964
The Secretariat, Organization of African Unity, Addis Ababa, Ethiopia
United Nations Economic Commission for Africa, Addis Ababa, Ethiopia
Inter-African Labour Institute, Commission for Technical Co-operation (CCTA), Brazzaville, Congo
Royal Institute of International Affairs

WRITINGS OF AFRICAN AUTHORS

Cyprian Ekwensi, *People of the City*, Heinemann, London, 1963
W. E. Abrahams, *The Mind of Africa*, Weidenfeld & Nicolson, London, 1962
Kwame Nkrumah, *Towards Colonial Freedom*, Heinemann, London, 1962
Tom Mboya, *Freedom and After*, André Deutsch, London, 1963
Kwame Nkrumah, *Consciencism*, Heinemann, London, 1963
H. Passin & K. A. B. Quartey (eds.), *Africa; The Dynamics of Change*, Ibadan University Press, 1963
W. E. B. DuBois, *The Souls of Black Folk*, Blue Heron Press, New York, 1953
Frantz Fanon, *The Damned*, Présence Africaine, Paris, 1964
Jomo Kenyatta, *Facing Mt. Kenya*, Secker and Warburg, London, 1938
Kenneth Kaunda, *Zambia Shall be Free*, Heinemann, London, 1962
Léopold Senghor, *Nation et Voie du Socialisme*, Présence Africaine, Paris, 1961
Julius Nyerere, *Ujumaa'*, Tanganyika Standard Limited, Dar es Salaam, 1962
O. Awolowo, *Path to Nigerian Freedom*, Faber, London, 1947
Nnamdi Azikiwe, *Renascent Africa*, Accra, 1937
Gamal Abdel Nasser, *The Philosophy of the Revolution*, National Publishing House, Cairo, 1954
Mamadou Dia, *The African Nations and World Solidarity*, Thames and Hudson, London, 1962
Nnamdi Azikiwe, *Zik: A Selection from the Speeches of Nnamdi Azikiwe*, Cambridge University Press, 1961
O. Awolowo, *Awo: The Autobiography of Chief Obafemi Awolowo*, Cambridge University Press, 1960
Alhaji Sir Ahmadu Bello, *My Life*, Cambridge University Press, 1960
Alex Quaison-Sackey, *Africa Unbound*, Praeger, New York, 1963
Aimé Césaire, *Discours Sur Le Colonialisme*, Présence Africaine, Paris
Sekou Touré, *La Guinée et l'Emancipation Africaine*, Présence Africaine, Paris, 1962

GLOSSARY OF AFRICAN TERMS*

akaregbe: an alcoholic beverage brewed in a traditional manner (Sierra Leone).

akasa: a basic food dish made from corn starch paste (Dahomey).

akpateshie: an alcoholic beverage brewed in a traditional manner from sugar cane, palm wine or maize; now, when treated and distilled it is used as the base for an alcohol and spirits industry (Ghana).

alhaji (m.); *alhajiyya* (f.): a devout Muslim who has completed a pilgrimage to Mecca.

alkali: a judge in a Muslim court (Northern Nigeria).

attajirai: a social status group of wealthy individuals, e.g., large-scale traders and contractors.

bahin: a type of incense used as a curative (Hausa-Fulani).

baraza: a traditional African council; a meeting of kinsmen or villagers to discuss, plan and resolve matters of common interest (East Africa).

burkutu: a beer made from millet or maize (Hausa-Fulani).

dillali: commission agents or brokers, who act as middlemen between sellers and buyers; they have detailed and extensive knowledge of prices and conditions in specialized markets (Hausa-Fulani).

dukka: a shop selling a wide variety of goods (Swahili, East Africa).

dukkawala: owner or proprietor of a dukka (Swahili, East Africa).

fakirai: a social status group encompassing the indigent, sick and poverty-stricken (Hausa-Fulani).

fatauci: long-distance trading operations involving Kola nuts, silk, hides and cloth, e.g., between Kano and Ibadan, Nigeria, Leopoldville, Congo and Sudanic and trans-Saharan areas (Hausa-Fulani).

* Places or peoples among whom these terms are commonly used appear in parenthesis; "Hausa-Fulani" as used here refers to the Hausa-speaking peoples of the Kano area,

fu-fu: a basic food dish made from yams or cassava (West Africa).

gaat: a plant (Catha edulis) whose leaf when chewed has a stimulant effect; a widely-used stimulant cultivated in Ethiopia and distributed to other areas, e.g. Somalia.

gari: a meal made from manioc root; a basic food dish (West Africa).

goge: a form of music associated with the bowing of a stringed instrument (Hausa-Fulani).

Kanawa: citizens of Kano City, Northern Nigeria.

kenke: a food dish made from maize and eaten with stew (Ghana).

kipande: a 30-day unit of work for which labourers are paid; a work book signed by one's employer; a pay book (East Africa).

kokonte: a food dish made of manioc flour and eaten with stew (Ghana).

malam: Muslim cleric; teacher-scholar in law and religion; term of respect; educated person; "Mr." (Hausa-Fulani).

malamin tsibbu: collective term for malams who specialize in medical knowledge and healing (Hausa-Fulani).

matsakai: a social status group including urban peasant-labourers, house servants, musicians and dyers; "Those who have little strength" (Hausa-Fulani).

omole: a traditional alcoholic beverage (Yoruba and West Africa).

"ospikin": a traditional alcoholic beverage nicknamed after the colloquial expression "house piccin", or "child of the house", a child sent down to the coast for education and household service (Sierra Leone).

panga: a heavy, broad-bladed machete, or hacking knife, used on the farm or plantation (Angola).

pombe: a traditional alcoholic beverage made from bananas (East Africa).

rawaya: a yellow herb used for medicinal purposes (Hausa-Fulani).

sabon gari: "new town", a new extension of a community meant to accommodate strangers; an enclave of Southern Nigerians in Northern region towns (Hausa-Fulani).

saraki: a social status group of rich and noble persons (Hausa-Fulani).

shaah: a tea made by brewing tea leaves, water, sugar and milk (Somali).

shamba: a peasant farm; a small plot of land on which staple foods are grown; a kitchen-garden (East Africa).

talauci: a collective term for the poorer but able-bodied members of the community (Hausa-Fulani).

zaure: a hall or one-roomed building at entrance to courtyard or house used by the male householder for entertaining male guests (Hausa-Fulani).

zongo: a camp, often associated with caravans; a settlement of Hausa or Muslim Sudanic peoples among non-Muslims (Ghana).

INDEX